PARADISE DISLOCATED
Morris, Politics, Art

VICTORIAN LITERATURE AND CULTURE SERIES
Karen Chase, Jerome J. McGann, *and* Herbert Tucker, *General Editors*

———◦∞◦———

DANIEL ALBRIGHT
> Tennyson: *The Muses' Tug-of-War*

DAVID G. RIEDE
> Matthew Arnold and the Betrayal of Language

ANTHONY WINNER
> Culture and Irony: *Studies in Joseph Conrad's Major Novels*

JAMES RICHARDSON
> Vanishing Lives: *Style and Self in Tennyson, D. G. Rossetti, Swinburne, and Yeats*

JEROME J. MCGANN, EDITOR
> Victorian Connections

ANTONY H. HARRISON
> Victorian Poets and Romantic Poems: *Intertextuality and Ideology*

E. WARWICK SLINN
> The Discourse of Self in Victorian Poetry

LINDA K. HUGHES and MICHAEL LUND
> The Victorian Serial

ANNA LEONOWENS
> The Romance of the Harem
> Edited and with an Introduction by Susan Morgan

ALAN FISCHLER
> Modified Rapture: *Comedy in W. S. Gilbert's Savoy Operas*

BARBARA TIMM GATES, EDITOR
> *Journal of Emily Shore,* with a new Introduction by the Editor

RICHARD MAXWELL
> The Mysteries of Paris and London

FELICIA BONAPARTE
> The Gypsy-Bachelor of Manchester: *The Life of Mrs. Gaskell's Demon*

PETER L. SHILLINGSBURG
> Pegasus in Harness: *Victorian Publishing and W. M. Thackeray*

ALLAN C. DOOLEY
> Author and Printer in Victorian England

JEFFREY SKOBLOW
> Paradise Dislocated: *Morris, Politics, Art*

PARADISE DISLOCATED

Morris,
Politics,
Art

Jeffrey Skoblow

UNIVERSITY PRESS OF VIRGINIA
Charlottesville and London

THE UNIVERSITY PRESS OF VIRGINIA
Copyright © 1993 by the Rector and Visitors
of the University of Virginia

First published 1993

Library of Congress Cataloging-in-Publication Data

Skoblow, Jeffrey.
    Paradise dislocated : Morris, politics, art / Jeffrey Skoblow.
        p.   .cm. — (Victorian literature and culture series)
    Includes bibliographical references and index.
    ISBN 0-8139-1439-6
    1. Morris, William, 1834–1896.   Earthly paradise.   2. Morris,
William, 1834–1896—Political and social views.   3. Politics and
literature—England—History—19th century.   4. Art and literature—
England—History—19th century.   5. Morris, William, 1834–1896—
Aesthetics.   6. Paradise in literature. 7. Aesthetics, British.
I. Title.   II. Series.
PR5075.S56   1993
821'.8—dc20   93–2748
                                                                                      CIP

Printed in the United States of America

for my
father mother
sister brother

Contents

The Author to the Reader   xi
Apology   xiii

Intro: Administered World   1
    Body Politic   2
    Aesthetics of Immersion   3
    Art   5
    Extremity/Complicity   6
    Fragment   8
    Idle/Empty   10
    Fears and Hopes   14
    Boredom   17
    Si Je Puis   18
    Illth   21
    Love   23
    Syntax Bound   25

Habundian World I: End of Transcendence   29
    Death of Art of Death   30
    Phantom of Delight   32
    Thing to Mind   36
    Far Otherwise   40

Habundian World II: Still Predominance   53
    Happy Only   54
    Matters Unforgot   61
    Not for Nought   79
    Present Sight   91

Habundian World III: Gratified Despair   105
    News from Nowhere   107
    Glittering Plain   123

Behold the Remnant   139
Living Not / Not Alone   163

Envoi   183

Notes   191
Bibliography   197
Index   203

What then are the situations, from the representation of which, though accurate, no poetical enjoyment can be derived? They are those in which the suffering finds no vent in action; in which a continuous state of mental distress is prolonged, unrelieved by incident, hope, or resistance; in which there is everything to be endured, nothing to be done. In such situations there is inevitably something morbid, in the description of them something monotonous.

—ARNOLD

DROWNED

What is the bottom of the river like?
O! green it is with swinging weeds,
O! yellow with bright gravel,
O! blue with the water overhead,
Through which the pike does travel,
Tenderly poised is the yellow-eyed pike.

I said "the water overhead"
For I lie here a-dying,
The pike looks down on my weedy bed,
How sweet it is to be dying!

—MORRIS

The Author to the Reader

The academic reader is likely to find in the introductory chapter, "Administered World," that the favored mode of discourse does not quite meet conventional scholarly expectations, and that I pursue my argument instead in a fashion rather aggressively disjointed, elliptical, and circular. My intention in doing so is to indicate (and to embody) the point, which is central to my argument, that the relation of *The Earthly Paradise* both to literary history and to the cultural assumptions of critical discourse is one of dislocation: to emphasize the fact that the poem is marginal to any conventional definition of the canon, and further, that the poem challenges the prerogatives of interpretation and scholarship, that it challenges even the very possibility of transmission. My intention is also to situate *The Earthly Paradise* in a critical context defined itself by dislocation, a tradition of criticism similarly marginal and making similar challenges. I invite the reader who finds my procedure here just a bit too much to bear, to note its rationale and to move on to the textual readings that occupy the subsequent chapters of "Habundian World."

But the main body of the book may itself appear little less peculiar than the introductory chapter, little more accommodating of conventional expectations. In a sense the work as a whole seems neither fish nor fowl; it neither embraces nor rejects the assumptions and procedures of standard academic discourse (or both embraces and rejects them), and this is, again, because Morris's poem itself seems to stand in the same precarious relation to the assumptions and procedures of cultural production. My own understanding of that relation is what the introductory chapter gives an account of; should the reader choose to skip ahead to the body of the work, this account, and perhaps this understanding, is what will be missed.

Apology

The peculiar difficulty of dialectical writing lies indeed in its holistic, "totalizing" character: as though you could not say any one thing until you had first said everything; as though with each new idea you were bound to recapitulate the entire system.

—JAMESON

I have tried to write Paradise

    Do not move
        Let the wind speak
            that is paradise.

    Let the Gods forgive what I
        have made
    Let those I love try to forgive
        what I have made.

—POUND

"Thou mayst toil in vain," the narrator of *The Earthly Paradise* says in closing his book, addressing the book itself. What I have been after in my book may be seen as a gloss on those words: on the vain toil of making art (which is to say, in Morris's terms, of making anything at all) in a world pervasively administered, a state of consciousness shaped and managed and sickened, by the profit motive regnant. On the vain toil of Morris's poem itself, and on the vain toil of my own effort to "read aright."

Some facts about *The Earthly Paradise:* it was published in three volumes from 1868 to 1870 and made Morris's reputation as one of the central literary figures on the Victorian scene. It is explicitly concerned with a group of men, the Wanderers, whose toil is vain, who seek and do not find the Earthly Paradise of which they dream. What they find instead is "a nameless city in a distant sea" with whose inhabitants they exchange tales, each of which is itself concerned with utter fruitlessness and wild, unaccountable desire. The Wanderers and their hosts are further the "hollow puppets" of the poem's narrator, one "idle singer of an empty day," whose toil is also vain, failed, a utopian labor begotten by despair upon impossibility: to "Forget six counties overhung with smoke, / Forget the snorting steam and piston stroke, / Forget the spreading of the hideous town" and to "dream of London, small, and white, and clean." The poem is thus arranged like boxes within boxes of futility. It is largely unread nowadays: Morris no less than the idle singer or than his hollow puppets or than the figures in the tales the Wanderers and their hosts tell each other, the hollow puppets' hollow puppets, all toilers in vain, all comrades in Loss, and each reader a recruit to the Cause.

L oss, vain toil, empty day, the spreading of the hideous town: this is our object in approaching *The Earthly Paradise*. As such, the poem participates in a discussion that spans the full reach of Morris's career, from the late Romanticism of his early verse and later prose fantasies to the early Socialism of his essays and lectures. The poem is thus central to any understanding of what William Morris's work as a whole might mean.

At least since the publication of J. W. Mackail's official biography, *The Life of William Morris,* in 1899, and unavoidably since E. P. Thompson's *William Morris: Romantic to Revolutionary* appeared in 1955 (revised 1976), the relationship between Morris's literary and political activities has been the central text, so to speak, of the Morris industry's attention. And though this industry has operated somewhat on the fringes of the mainstream—Morris consigned by the literary industry at large to the major-minor bin, and by Friedrich Engels to the company of "settled, sentimental Socialist[s]"[1]—the questions that Morris's work raises are central to the broader discussion that spans the period of the last two hundred years in what we call the Western world. This is a discussion that we call, variously, Romanticism, Modernism, Socialism, Industrial or Advanced or Late or State Capitalism, a discussion (and enactment) of the direction of European culture "amid these latter days," under dark Satanic mills hurtling through history as bunk. In one way or another, from Morris's perspective as from Wordsworth's or Blake's or Marx's or Pound's or Henry Ford's, the only question is what is to be made of "the spreading of the hideous town," what might yet be possible or only now newly possible in the context of this inexorable advent.

In taking *The Earthly Paradise* as my subject, then, I have been inquiring not only into the relationship between Morris's literary pursuits and his social critique but also into that larger relationship between the modern imagination and the modern world, of which Morris's case is but one example. This inquiry requires, perhaps, some justification: the poem is, after all, all but forgotten, and I wish to argue for it a compelling place in the cultural conversation that excludes it. In any event, if my inquiry is to advance at all, it requires that the *Paradise* be recontextualized, resituated from the verge of oblivion to just this side of the verge. (The act, perhaps, will justify itself.)

The manner in which I have gone about constructing such a new context for the poem seems to me somewhat obsessive, and the obsessiveness itself part of the effort: the received condition of the poem, its status, in Henry James's phrase, as an "[object] of vague and sapient reference," would seem to require extreme means for its recovery.[2] What I have tried to do, simply, is to place *The Earthly Paradise* in the context of twentieth-century dialectical thought, the somewhat subdominant tradition of late theoretical Marxism associated with the Frankfurt School, in particular Adorno, Marcuse, Horkheimer and Benjamin, and a tradition carried forward by other individuals as well, here notably Bataille and Raymond Williams and Unger and Jameson, and groups such as the so-called L = A = N = G = U = A = G = E poets. I have tried as well to place the poem in the context of a nineteenth-century tradition of dialectical thought, namely romanticism, in the work of Shelley, Wordsworth, and Coleridge especially.[3] I have used terms and phrases and references drawn from these sources over and over in endless recombination, repeating myself and others and piling variant upon variant, in an effort to entangle Morris's poem in the strands of the conversation that these sources represent, to reorient our discussion of the poem (which is at once to orient and to disorient that discussion). I have tried as well by these means to suggest more immediately than critical discourse often allows—to embody or at least ape—the formal and stylistic strategies of *The Earthly Paradise* itself,

Morris's dream of a radical reorientation. "If ye will read aright, and pardon me . . ."

Cash is King: I wish first to acknowledge the National Endowment for the Humanities for a Travel to Collections Grant, Southern Illinois University at Edwardsville for both a Fourth Quarter Research Fellowship and a sabbatical period, and the Huntington Library in San Marino, California, for a Dr. and Mrs. James Caillouette Fellowship—all of which enabled me to gain access to manuscripts necessary to my research and provided me time to read them, and to write. I'd like especially to thank the staffs of the British Library and the Huntington Library for their patient help, and in particular the garden staff at the Huntington, in the shade of whose work I began writing this book, for helping to make my work there so delightful.

For hospitality, spiritual and material support, I am grateful to my friends Anthony Cross, Sarah Davies, and Pen Davies in London, and in Los Angeles, my friends Lester Burg and Jay McCaslin. Richard Stack and Jerome McGann have been teachers of mine and have given me years of loving conversation which it is impossible for me to imagine myself without: my deep thanks to them as well, and for reading my work here on Morris too, and bringing to it their critical enthusiasms and eagle eyes. Others who have read portions of the text and offered helpful suggestions, confusions, and support, and to whom I am very grateful as well, are: Lyell Asher, Lynn Casmier-Paz, Susanna Ferlito, Cheryl Giuliano, Victor Ingrassia, Naka Ishii, Ted Leinwand, John Mascaro, Tino Paz, Kevin Ross, Jack Voller, and Angela Vuagniaux. Nancy Ruff, Alex Babione, and Wes Westmaas provided me with valuable computer help on several occasions when I needed it badly, Florence Boos provided me with microfilm of manuscripts at the Fitzwilliam Library in Cambridge, Norman Kelvin encouraged this project (unwittingly, no doubt, to him and me alike) at an early stage in its development: my thanks to all.

And for all of the above, as well as for the couch and pillows and every thing else, my gratitude to my wife, Mary Grose: thank you, love.

PARADISE DISLOCATED
Morris, Politics, Art

Intro:
Administered World

I spend my life in ministering to the swinish luxury
of the rich.
—MORRIS

Body Politic

the only foolscap available, his own body

—JOYCE

In "ZYXT" Ron Silliman writes that "joy of words and syntax" slows us down as we read and that attention to "ideas and referents" speeds us up: two different desires, one to *be with* (the body) and one to *get,* to have, to acquire (a commodity).[1] For Silliman, the erotic body is a form of resistance to the cultural hegemony of capitalism. Desire is the dialectical negation of the Administered World, Theodor Adorno's term for capitalism in full, hideous bloom. Desire, that is, the capacity for joy, for pleasure, is what the Administered World negates. Instead the World manufactures desires, which is to say it manufactures an inner life for each individual, a kind of parody of collective consciousness: in this context, the assertion of desire, the experience of pleasure unadministered, the manifestation of joy, is an act of resistance.[2]

Desire, of course, is also what the Administered World hoists on its flag—emblem and chief raw material of its empire. It is an act of resistance in profound subjection to what manipulates it. Desire, thus self-contradicted, is the organizing principle for a particular tradition in Socialist thought, both pre- and post-Marxist: Fourier, Ruskin, Marx himself, Morris, Benjamin and Adorno and Horkheimer and Marcuse, Bloch, Bataille, Raymond Williams, Jameson, Unger, and Silliman are all preoccupied with the possibilities for desire, the condition of desire at the present time.[3] It is in this context that I wish to place my discussion of *The Earthly Paradise.*

The Earthly Paradise does not work, primarily, in terms of "ideas and referents," does not function as a commodity. (Although in its existence as a Book—not as poem but as book—it has been very much a commodity, a best-seller first and then a discard: and both are part of its meaning for us, that it was capable of nourishing the illusions of a wide and varied audience for a short time and that it has come to assume the status of waste.) It moves slowly, predictably, repetitiously, monotonously—but to speak of it in these terms is not to speak pejoratively. These qualities—monotony, repetition, poverty of vocabulary, equability of pace—are what make the Paradise a body. There are pleasures to be had in them. ("Pleasures to be had"—there's the dialectic right there.) And there is resistance in them to being had—they make the poem a site for the enactment of desire, a site to *be with* rather than (as with Dickens, say) to get to, get through, get, have, want. (A want is not a desire, though we use the words interchangeably—a want is a lack, and if it has an element of desire to it, it is desire oriented toward the past, toward what's wanting: desire proper is a projection toward the future.)

The Paradise also includes the tales, which in spite of the predictability and monotony that characterize the whole poem, do work in narrative terms, as sequences with complication, climax, and resolution (another way of saying getting to, getting through and getting): these tales, however, are embedded in the totality of the poem, which is markedly non-narrative, cyclical, and virtually uniform throughout the cycle. This totality is itself compromised, sharing with the tales the movement of complication, climax, and resolution—the seasons are full of these effects moving from Spring to Winter, and the tales, taken as a whole, display some shifts of emphasis in theme and style as the seasons go by.[4] But the most striking effect—which has indeed been a blinding effect—is the body of the totality: the uniformity of the thing, insusceptible to excerpt but open it anywhere and be enchanted (so say early reviewers). The aesthetics of acquisition, the procession of complication, climax, and resolution, is deployed in such a distended way that its effects are difficult to perceive: if they work on us at all—if they are indeed *effects*—then they work below the level of consciousness. They work on the body, the reading body, where desire lives: Morris appropriates the aesthetics of acquisition and stands it in dialectical relation to an aesthetics of immersion, the uniformity of the thing, its monotony, its long room with a low roof, a Palace of Art. *The Earthly Paradise* is a commodity embodied: a contradiction in terms.

Aesthetics of Immersion

Morris is rigorous in his attention to physical detail, virtually free of introspection—it is a commonplace among his critics, whether they admire him for it or not. The Paradise is full of details but they are always the same ones: *blossom, shoe, hair, kiss, house, blush, hand, flowering white-thorn,* endlessly repeated. This speaks in part of the restricted circumstances of the poem's production: the low ceiling, the shadowy isle, the fleeting thoughts, the idle singer—unadministered and thus, by definition, without much room to move. The extension, therefore, of this meager vocabulary—all that's left of the language of desire—is an act of affirmation, of resistance to extinguishment, to absolute hegemony. An aesthetics of immersion: the repetitive and well-nigh exclusive insistence on physical details (even when there are precious few, and useless ones at that) is the site where the Paradise locates its desire. A fainting gesture toward where desire lives—in bodies. (Shelley's discussion in "A Defence of Poetry" of "the extinction or suspension of the creative faculty in Greece" during the late period of that empire offers a model of the context in which Morris works here. "At the approach of such a period poetry ever addresses itself to those faculties which are the last to be destroyed, and its voice is heard, like the footsteps of Astraea, departing from the world." This is the voice of "the erotic writers," conservationists of "the sensibility to pleasure, passion, and natural scenery," and without whom "the last triumph of evil would have been achieved.")[5]

The aesthetics of immersion stands to the totalitarianism of the Administered World as both reflex and opposition. Immersion is a counterpoint to hegemonic administration, a mockery of it. It assumes the possibility of another, an alternative totality (assumes, that is both pretends and claims) and thus embodies at once both the totality and its negation.

Desire embodied in the immersive body: a matter of being with the thing, becoming hypnotized so that nothing else is *but* the thing, the desired thing, the thing that escapes administration, the object of desire. The hypnotic mode of Morris or Swinburne thus has a different edge to it from the immersion effects of, say, Dickens or Austen, who also create alternative totalities, or Scott—though Scott approaches the hypnotic sometimes. The extension of the details of this totality, the protraction of the voice of the desire, creates a world (both feeble and strong) in which that desire can be embodied: a sanctuary from administration.

The aesthetics of immersion is a function of Morris's profoundly materialist conception of Art; it is part of his effort to transform the Transcendental Imagination of Romanticism into an imagination of habitation, a nontranscendental, sensuous mode of praxis, a collective enterprise. John Reed, *Victorian Conventions* (1975): Morris "resisted the decadent impulse to fashion a world of memory within the imagination, and sought instead to draw the racial memory back from the self to be applied to the world of the present at large."[6] The aesthetics of immersion is an effort at materializing a world in this way, drawn from the body and brought into the world as a body, making its own claims to itself.

(Immersion: as in drawing, minute attention to what you see, patiently deployed attention—this is in part what the Pre-Raphaelite painters were engaged in, and Morris too in *The Defence of Guenevere,* and what "post-literate" commix like *RAW* are up to.[7] Immersion in the sensuous details present to one's perception: the body politic. The aesthetics, the erotics, the politics of immersion are involved in Morris's characteristic methods of revision too: putting aside complete drafts of tales and beginning them from scratch, a matter of attending to the tale as it presents itself to his perception and not as it compares to his first attempt to tell it; being with the body of the tale again, its fresh embodiment in new words, in a fresh assertion of desire. Morris rarely tinkers with isolated words or passages, and when he does it's not to much effect. His only choice would seem to be between totality and nothing.)

Art

Herbert Sussman, *Victorians and the Machine: The Literary Response to Technology* (1968): Morris's "main contribution is the secularization of Ruskin. For Morris saw artistic expression not in the Christian terms of Ruskin, as the expression of delight in the world God had made, but in more 'modern' terms, as the release of instinctive energies repressed by the rigid patterns of mechanized society: 'What is meant by *art* . . . is, I contend, no mere accident to human life, which people can take or leave as they choose, but a positive necessity of life, if we are to live as nature meant us to'. The substitution of 'as nature meant us to' for 'as God meant us to' has far-reaching implications for his social as well as his aesthetic theory." This "necessity of life" Sussman notes is the possibility of "the free play of sensual, particularly sexual, energy."[8]

  Morris writing on the subject of capitalism in 1883 has this to say: "I have been gradually driven to the conclusion that Art has been handcuffed by it and will die out of civilization if the system lasts. That of itself does to me carry with it the condemnation of the whole system, and I admit has been the thing which has drawn my attention to the subject in general."[9] "That of itself does to me carry"—Morris is emphatic, and apologetic too, "I admit" a hint of confession, of grudging embarrassment: the passage carries with it both the marginalization of Morris's position toward capitalism and the germ of his critique. "What is meant by *art*"—"the embodiment of dreams in one form or another," "a joy to the maker, a pleasure to the user," the collective life of people, every individual human transfiguration of Nature, playful work, the solace of labor, the enactment of desire (in the free hand of the Gothic stonecarver, or *A Book of Verse* for Georgiana Burne-Jones): the conception of Art seems diffuse, which contributes to its marginalization, but it remains notably precise nonetheless. In each case it is a function of (and a form of resistance to) the Administered World: Art as a mode of behavior, Art as a body. Its conception as *material* is one defense against administration, its association with desire another— a habitation, a home and a way of being that is self-determining, though not wholly self-determined.

If it is difficult to speak anymore of "instinctive energies" or "nature," it may yet be possible to speak of "free play," even if it is only in terms of its own repression, its dialectical partner, the negation of free play. Art is the negation of the negation. It is also no less a freeway, polluted air, or a planted field than a spoon or an oil painting. Art is the embodiment of Beauty adored and defiled: in Paradise the embodiment of the unad-ministered, the lineaments of gratified desire in opposition to, and defined by, the hegemony of manufactured want.

Resistance in the case of *The Earthly Paradise:* the response of the withered subject to his condition, of "the idle singer" to "the empty day," a response that consists of waste, hope, trance, materiality and faintness, withdrawal, refusal. Free play bound tight and swelling: an aneurism.

Extremity/Complicity

the world has made men speechless

—ADORNO

Capitalism destroys collectivity: it turns it into collection. It destroys the collective to the extent that it destroys free play, the unadministered desire of the body. No collective is possible where there are no free human agents to associate with one another, and human association is possible only to the extent that the hegemony of administration is not absolute, and vice versa.

(Free agency in baseball is a capitalist parody of human desire, the mocking mirror of the Administered World: individuals pay their dues, measured in units of time, and then are free to sell themselves to the highest bidder—it is a profoundly appealing take on what it might mean to say "free agency," and it is bitterly resented for the same reason: all this *money* for all these *guys* who don't do *anything* but *play* a *game,* something seems wrong and terribly glamorous at the same time. This free agency, in fact, means no free play.)

Adorno: "Society is integral even before it undergoes totalitarian rule. Its organization also embraces those at war with it by co-ordinating their consciousness to its own. Even those intellectuals [and this must include Adorno himself] who have all the political arguments against bourgeois ideology at their fingertips, undergo a process of standardization which—despite crassly contrasting content, through readiness on their part to accommodate themselves—approximates them to the prevailing mentality."10 Readiness is a critical term: it suggests preparation more than willingness, or a state of affairs—within integral society, in an Administered World—in which the distinction between preparation and willingness is moot. It is a readiness "to accommodate" oneself to an aggressively invasive condition.

The condition of desire, of Art, of freedom from repression and manipulation, under capitalism is extreme. "It occurs to nobody that there might be services that are not expressible in terms of exchange value": nobody includes philosophers and poets. The World is very bad and we, the collective, are dying, the hegemony of administration more like Circe than Cyclops penetrating the most personal impulses, turning desire into exchange value. "The new human type cannot be properly understood without awareness of what he is continuously exposed to from the world of things about him, even in his most secret innervations."11

From Marx and Morris to Adorno and Bataille to Silliman is a development toward a more complete—more totalized—analysis of this extremity, and toward more marginalized forms of resistance.

Adorno: "Love of stone walls and barred windows is the last resort of someone who sees and has nothing else to love. [It is a case of] ignominious adaptation . . . in order to endure the world's horror."12 The aesthetics of immersion is an effort to create an alternative totality in which might live an object of love other than the prison of contemporary culture, the Administered World of advanced capitalism. At the same time the immersive experience submits to the condition of those walls, those bars: it is a mockery in both senses of the term, a denial and a replication, an embodiment and its negation. Morris must bend his method to such an extreme that in effect the object of his love *is* those walls and bars that force him to do so, that determine the form of the love-object. *The Earthly Paradise* represents the endless extension of constraint: it is a counterargument that takes the form of a surrender.

Adorno: "The more passionately thought denies its conditionality for the sake of the unconditional, the more unconsciously, and so calamitously, it is delivered up to the world. Even its own impossibility it must at least comprehend for the sake of the possible."13 The passage conjures hope ("for the sake of the possible") and despair ("calamitously") in the face of complicity, the dialectical necessity of submission to the hegemony of "the world"—hope and despair both modes of resistance, unconditionally conditional. Complicity: the embrace of those at war, the coordinating of consciousness to bourgeois ideology, the taming of alterity, the approximations of standardization. The fragmentary form of *The Earthly Paradise,* its totalizing effects, the aesthetics of immersion, faintness of voice, interchangeability of parts—all are functions of this standardization, and all function in complicity with its logic, the logic of a ravening monster. Each of these features of the Paradise sustains the bourgeois ideology it despairs of escaping, sustains it by mocking its form, proclaiming and demonstrating its hegemony.

The reception history of the Paradise is bound to this same defeat: from the poem's initial popularity and subsequent, rather precipitous fall in estimation and from print, each stage in the development of this history is bound to the logic of commodity production. The poem's status as waste, perhaps the most appropriate word for its current critical incarnation, is no less so bound.

Fragment

The absolute is utterly eternal.
—SCHELLING

The Earthly Paradise is a series of grouped fragments, arranged so that the relationship between them develops in an "acentric" rather than progressive way. There is a relevant precedent for this structure in the medieval romance. Blue Calhoun: "Defining form and meaning in medieval romance, Eugène Vinaver distinguishes between Aristotelian structure and the '*acentric* composition' of the medieval cycles: 'Whereas the Roman doctrine of *amplificatio* or *auxesis* was concerned with the art of making small things great, of "raising acts and personal traits above their dimensions" in a kind of upward movement, the medieval variety of amplification was, on the contrary, a linear or horizontal extension, an expansion or an unrolling of a number of interlocked themes.' "[14]

Both the Aristotelian and the medieval models are precapitalist in origin, but under capitalism both forms achieve a different resonance, distorted or transformed by the acoustic context of capitalist totality. Morris's use of the middle ages is wholly in terms of its condition as the period prior to the full flower of the capitalist period: the "acentric composition" of the Paradise a function of its resistance to the administration of desire, the predetermined management of fulfillment—it is another assertion of the eroticized body.

Adorno's *Minima Moralia* is constructed in a similar way for similar reasons, as a series of grouped fragments: so is W. C. Williams's *Kora in Hell: Improvisations* and Barthes's *The Pleasure of the Text,* a line of development that begins, or at least emerges into the light, with Nietzsche and Wittgenstein—a refusal to systematize, an affirmation of particulars and pursuit of their resonance. *Ulysses* is another such text, deeply preoccupied with the logic of capitalism and with forms of resistance, with the body, with the dynamics of total structure: a collection of fragments imposed upon by a deitylike entity, bound into order, made available by Joyce's Homeric and stylistic ministrations and by a reader's own ministrations, finding his or her own strategies of relation, compelled both into and out of narrative.

All books in a sense are so—a code imposed and collaboratively, sensuously decoded: words written and words read. This is what it means to make meaning. *The Earthly Paradise* simply (and almost inaudibly—such the feebleness of its breath) places this formal dynamic more explicitly than most in the context of the logic of capitalism and resistance to administration. Thus another reading of *The Earthly Paradise:* it is reading. And another: a gesture of the nonintegral, the stray, a collection of tales that amount to nothing but themselves and the relationships between them, not only virtually endless but conceptually endless, antiprogressive.

The fragment is by definition a form of negativity. It is defined by what it is not—a totality—thus insisting on the hegemony of that totality while insisting on something other, something outside, some waste, some nonintegralized product.

The fragments of the Paradise assume the form of totality in several ways: composed of a common vocabulary, repetitious, coming back to the same language in recombination again and again, relations developing recursively according to patterns of authorial arrangement and readerly practice. This is in a sense a pretense to totality—the book and the experience of reading the book are strictly circumscribed in their "use value," in their power to supplant the totality of the Administered World. The presumption of the Paradise to totality mirrors the presumption of capitalism, of industrial England, to the same: neither is eternal. (Yet another reading of the Paradise: life on earth, that which comes and goes.) The Paradise maintains a life against the absolute of administration, the hegemony of capitalism, and it bows unto oblivion before that absolute, faint of heart and weak of breath. "The whole is the false."[15]

Idle/Empty

Let our scars fall in love.
                                    —KINNELL

Jameson, *The Ideologies of Theory: Syntax of History* (1988), speaks of an "influential tradition in Frankfurt School thought which insists on the determinate relationship between commodification and what we may have been tempted to think of as pleasure" but which is really "that very different commodity called 'leisure,' the form of commodity consumption stamped on the most intimate former pleasures from sexuality to reading." Horkheimer, "Art and Mass Culture" (1968): "The transformation of personal life into leisure and leisure into routines supervised to the last detail, into the pleasures of the ballpark and the movie, the best seller and the radio, has brought about the disappearance of the inner life. Long before culture was replaced by these manipulated pleasures, it had already assumed an escapist character. Men had fled into a private conceptual world. . . . But with the loss of his ability to take this kind of refuge—an ability that thrives neither in slums nor in modern settlements—man has lost his power to conceive a world different from that in which he lives. This other world was that of art."[16]

Hegemony, complicity, little sense of resistance. The idle singer's threadbare hope, "his power to conceive a world different from that in which he lives" diminished, virtually extinguished, is the embodiment of its own negation. His assertion of pleasure takes the self-contradicted form of a monument to leisure, which is predicated on the death of pleasure, of desire, "the disappearance of the inner life"—a point not lost on Morris's contemporary audience, as for instance: "A thorough purity of thought and language characterizes Mr. Morris . . . and *The Earthly Paradise* is thereby adapted for conveying to our wives and daughters a refined, though not diluted, version of those wonderful creations of Greek fancy which the rougher sex alone is permitted to imbibe at first hand."[17] Praise for emasculation, a poem of pleasure (*The Book That Never Was*) a book of leisure.

The idleness of the singer and the emptiness of the day define one another: each is "*critical* in the sense in which the Frankfurt School so described the distantiation and heightened awareness of contradictions afforded by the *negative*" (Jameson). It is in this sense that the idle singer's failure, and the poem's failure—its distended feebleness, its rendering unto leisure and its hastening toward oblivion—forms a critique of the forces against which idleness strives. The emptiness of the day gives a singer nothing to be but idle, and the idleness of the song gives a form to that emptiness, and sustains it. Adorno: "In beauty the frail future offers its sacrifice to the Moloch of the present; because, in the latter's realm, there can be no good, it makes itself bad, in order in its defeat to convict the judge."[18]

Utter hegemony, then, and utter, inescapable complicity, but not utter hopelessness: the paradox of the Paradise. Adorno on Goethe: "The human consisted for him in a self-limitation which affirmatively espoused as its own cause the ineluctable course of history, the inhumanity of progress, the withering of the subject."[19] An affirmative espousal of the withering of the subject: identification of the subject with its negation, the World, "the Moloch of the present," an attempt to master that World in surrender to it. An affirmative espousal nonetheless, in the form of the negative: not utterly hopeless "in its defeat to convict the judge." A possible act.

Gramsci indicates the extremity of this situation, the deep obfuscation of possibility, when he identifies the self-contradicted nature of such an act, and demonstrates the dialectic of hegemonic totality and its opposition. A consciousness "uncritically absorbed" is the problem, and the solution looked for in another kind of consciousness, split off from the dominant (and even from awareness), a *material* consciousness barely capable of sustaining itself (and at its best only capable in negative terms). The subject here is in a sense the possibility of possibility. *Prison Notebooks*:

> The active man-in-the-mass has a practical activity, but has no clear theoretical consciousness of his practical activity, which nonetheless involves understanding the world in so far as it transforms it. His theoretical consciousness can indeed be historically in opposition to his activity. One might almost say that he has two theoretical consciousnesses (or one contradictory consciousness): one which is implicit in his activity and which in reality unites him with all his fellow-workers in the practical transformation of the real world; and one, superficially explicit or verbal, which he has inherited from the past and uncritically absorbed. But this verbal conception is not without consequences. It holds together a specific social group, it influences moral conduct and the direction of

> will, with varying efficacy but often powerfully enough to pro-
> duce a situation in which the contradictory state of consciousness
> does not permit of any action, any decision or any choice, and
> produces a condition of moral and political passivity. Critical
> understanding of self takes place therefore through a struggle of
> political "hegemonies" and of opposing directions, first in the
> ethical field and then in that of politics proper, in order to arrive at
> the working out at a higher level of one's own conception of
> reality.[20]

The passage recapitulates what I have been saying about the idle
singer: the negation of consciousness / withering of the subject, and the
recalcitrance of transformative action. Action for Gramsci is another word
for what I have been variously calling desire, pleasure, free play, resistance:
a kind of potentiality of the unadministered, an impulse predicated upon
possibility, an embodiment of conviction that remains, though deeply
thwarted, possible. Adorno is cautious about naming this possibility,
about pretending that it exists in any form but most dimly: "Whatever is in
the context of bourgeois delusion called nature [i.e., the unadministered],
is merely the scar of social mutilation." There are examples, however, of
works felt to embody this negative affirmation. Horkheimer: "Today it
survives only in those works which uncompromisingly express the gulf
between the monadic individual and his barbarous surrounding—prose
like Joyce's and paintings like Picasso's Guernica . . . forced into queer
discordant forms."[21] The "struggle of political 'hegemonies' and of opposing directions" is a dialectical one, the embrace of those at war: virtually
nothing is possible in a "condition of moral and political passivity" but the
possibility of possibility, and this, for Gramsci as for Horkheimer and
Adorno, only in terms of the impossible.

The totalitarianism of capitalist hegemony is felt in these critical texts to be
greater, more invasive, than other social structures—religious, economic,
political, whatever. This is in a sense the distinction of capitalism, that it
provokes elaborate discourse in terms of abjection, waste, disappearance,
emptiness, speechlessness, hegemony: it is felt vociferously to be not only
an enabling structure but a paralyzing one as well. The hegemony of
capitalism produces "contradictory consciousness" and this is part of its
creative power: it is powerful "enough to produce a situation in which the
contradictory state of consciousness does not permit of any action, any
decision or any choice . . . a condition of moral and political passivity"—

which is nevertheless capable of embodying a form of hope. By producing its own negation, its own critique, capitalist hegemony—even as it extends into our "most secret innervations"—frees us from the taboo of hegemony, frees us to be critical (*negative*) in relation to it, to be plural. (Capitalism produces communism.)

Capitalist hegemony is thus a new beginning. The idle singer represents an end—a snuffing out—and a beginning toward "a higher level of one's own conception of reality," an engagement of hegemonies. The idle singer glosses his desire in numerous ways: he wants to be remembered by "full hearts still unsatisfied," to tell a tale "to those who in the sleepy region stay" (tale for Morris always ambiguously meaning both a life as it is lived and a fabrication), "to build a shadowy isle of bliss / Midmost the beating of the steely sea"—to forget forget forget and think, dream, think, to deploy "hollow puppets" "I now am fain to set before your eyes," to display his faded memory of dulled flowers, to love in spite of scorn—"to gain the Land of Matters Unforgot" or at least the "company" of Chaucer, who "didst never stand alone," to gain "some place in loving hearts," to "pray"—in other words to desire, to desire to desire. In each case the idle singer follows Adorno. He offers up his "beauty" in "sacrifice to the Moloch of the present," the Morpheus of capitalist plenitude (capitalism's own aesthetics of immersion), in order "to convict the judge": he displays his pathetically threadbare condition, his meager claims, hollow puppets and faded imaginary blossoms, his subversive, if virtually hopeless resistance to extinguishment. His opposition is in the form of love, an image of the unadministered, against scorn, against negation: he seeks through this isolation, this obsessive withered subjectivity, to achieve fellowship ("company," "some place in loving hearts")—not a reading class but a virtually nonexistent audience, one that finds in the Paradise a glimpse of the extremity under which desire labors, some solace for "full hearts still unsatisfied." The "unsatisfied" is the idle singer's dialectical lever, his own claim to hegemony, the prospect of "a higher level of [his] own conception of reality." His parting formulation of the desire of his song is "to strive to lay / The ghosts that crowd about life's empty day"—a new beginning wrapped in an unfinished end (and "strive" always implies failure), an imagination of the end of hegemony, the end of the false whole.

Jameson, *Postmodernism, or the Cultural Logic of Late Capitalism* (1991): "If, indeed, the subject has lost its capacity actively to extend its pro-tensions and re-tensions across the temporal manifold and to organize its past and future into coherent experience, it becomes difficult enough to see how the cultural productions of such a subject could result in anything but 'heaps of fragments' and in a practice of the randomly heterogeneous and fragmentary and the aleatory." The material of *The Earthly Paradise*—the song of the idle singer—does not appear quite randomly heterogeneous, although its principles of order are to a certain extent tenuous, and suggest both plurality and interchangeability, both obstacles to order. The book, the poem, the song is fragmentary, at least, and certainly it is aleatory: "dependent on uncertain contingencies" (*Shorter OED*). This condition is the condition of its existence: "He who is rebuffed becomes human."[22]

Fears and Hopes

> that everything is contextual and that all contexts can be broken
> —UNGER

Roberto Unger, *Social Theory: Its Situation and Its Task* (1987), speaks a faith "that all contexts can be broken." It is the same faith as Gramsci's in "a higher level of one's own conception of reality" and in Adorno's desire "to convict the judge." Unger imagines "forms of representation" that "neither [hide] nor [abolish] context dependence." Such a form "recognizes" context dependence—totalitarian hegemony, complicity—"with a vengeance and, in so doing, changes its nature. To live and move in the conditional world is, then, constantly to be reminded of its conditionality. To gain a higher freedom from the context is to make the context more malleable rather than to bring it to a resting point of universal scope."[23]

To make "malleable" is to prepare a site for oppositional hegemony to contend with totalitarian hegemony, "for contexts of representation or relationship differ in the severity of the limits they impose on our activity." Hegemony is not total: "We are not governed fully by the established imaginative and institutional contexts of our societies."[24]

> Occasionally . . . we push the given contexts of thought, desire, and practical or passionate relations aside. We treat them as unreal and even as if our apparently unfounded devotion to them had been just a ploy. We think the thoughts and satisfy the desires and establish the relationships excluded, in the world we inhabit, by all the practical or conceptual structures to which we had seemed so thoroughly subjugated. We think and act, at such moments, as if we were not ultimately limited by anything. Our practical,

theoretical, and spiritual progress is largely the record of these repeated limit breakings. The experience of freedom and achievement implied in such acts of defiance is iconoclastic: it works by doing things that cannot be dreamt of in the established mental or social world rather than by creating the world that could realize all dreams.[25]

Unger's "experience of freedom and achievement" is nonetheless an action of negativity—iconoclastic, a constrained mode of praxis—for all its transformative capability: its transformative power, its limit breaking, is the dialectical negation of utter context dependence, an exploration of its border.

This border is hard to reach. If all contexts can be broken, and everything is contextual, then even the "limit breakings" of context are contextual—contextually provoked and contextually reabsorbed. "The absolute is utterly eternal" (Schelling), "the system's claim to totality, which would suffer nothing to remain outside it" (Adorno).[26] Such a self-enclosed, totalizing system is a commonplace by now. Again, this time from Raymond Williams, *Problems in Materialism and Culture* (1980), who defines Gramsci's "hegemony" as

> the central, effective and dominant system of meanings and values, which are not merely abstract but which are organized and lived. That is why hegemony is not to be understood at the level of mere opinion or mere manipulation. It is a whole body of practices and expectations; our assignments of energy, our ordinary understanding of the nature of man and of his world. It is a set of meanings and values which as they are experienced as practices appear as reciprocally confirming. It thus constitutes a sense of reality for most people in the society, a sense of absolute because experienced reality beyond which it is very difficult for most members of the society to move, in most areas of their lives. . . . The process of education; the processes of a much wider social training within institutions like the family; the practical definitions and organization of work; the selective tradition at an intellectual and theoretical level: all these forces are involved in a continual making and remaking of an effective dominant culture.

Williams's reference to "most people" and "most members of society" appears to reserve a kind of elite class for whom resistance to domination is

more fully possible, but this is a notion that would seem incompatible with
the definition of hegemony that he is proposing, which "emphasizes the
facts of domination"—Williams sounds more like Ruskin than like Gramsci here. For Horkheimer and Adorno, and for Unger—and for Morris
and for the idle singer—no such class is conceivable: "Everything is
contextual," "nobody" is capable of thinking outside "the terms of exchange value" "even in his most secret innervations." Jameson calls it
"the implacable sociability of even the most apparently private of our
experiences."[27]

Implacable: but again, the dominant creates its own negation, what
Williams calls "the production and the practice of possibility." "There is
clearly something that we can call alternative to the effective dominant
culture, and there is something else that we can call oppositional, in the
true sense. The degree of existence of these alternative and oppositional
forms is itself a matter of constant historical variation in real circumstances." It is this "constant historical variation" that allows a work like
The Earthly Paradise to be recuperated by the critical language of the Frankfurt School, Bataille, the $L = A = N = G = U = A = G = E$ poets,
and others in the tradition I have been sketching. Williams: "The irreducibly individual products that particular works are, may come in experience
and analysis to show resemblances which allow us to group them into
collective modes"—again collectivity a dialectical negation of the fragmented, "the irreducibly individual"—"These are by no means always
genres."[28] Thus a text like *The Earthly Paradise* can come to be oppositional
even if it was not so initially, not taken to be so, impossible to conceive so.
Its relation to the oppositional is changed by what follows: *The Earthly
Paradise* is what does not die, but what lives under the sign of Death, a
zombie to haunt the twentieth century—it's a Gothic monster.

Jameson: "There are, of course, ways of breaking out of this isolation, but
they are not literary ways and require complete and thoroughgoing transformation of our economic and social system, and the invention of new
forms of collective living." Literature's power to establish collectivity is
constrained, but by engaging both the collectivity of book production and
the negative dialectics of "the irreducibly individual," literature can come
to embody a form of resistance, a necessary step toward any "invention of
new forms." Unger speaks of the "ability to incorporate the next best
thing to absolute knowledge and fulfilled desire: [the ability] not to be a
prisoner of the context": "the mind is never entirely imprisoned by its

current beliefs. It can achieve insights that it may or may not be able to verify, validate, or even make sense of within the established criteria of validity, verification, or sense. All past and present modes of discourse put together do not exhaust our faculties of understanding. If objectivity [Unger's name for the unadministered] cannot consist in the attachment to unrevisable and self-authenticating elements in thought, then it may lie in the negative capability not to imprison insight in any particular structure of thought."[29] Negative capability: while a prisoner of the context, not to be a prisoner of the context. Complicity and resistance.

Boredom

The Wanderers' hope ("whose bitter hope hath made this book") is the hope of death: that is, both a hope (for eternal life) born *of* death, of plague and fear of death, and a hope *for* death—"the heart of Death to move"—an amorous advance upon Death. Clearly the life of the Wanderers is founded in profound confusion and desperation. The idle singer, the voice of that desperate confusion, is himself but the shadow of a former self which is itself a shadow that never was. (His flowers are flowers of evil.) The extremity of the work—of this impossible condition—is monumental and minutely pervasive. But by giving a form to it, the Paradise exercises a critical dialectic upon the body of that extremity, and thus engages in "the production and practice of possibility": it thinks a thought that cannot be wholly reconciled to the "established imaginative and institutional contexts of our societies"; and if it is reconciled, absorbed (as an instance of what Marcuse called repressive desublimation), it is in the form of that which is not reconciled—the forgotten, the waste, the vestige, "that tedious poem *The Earthly Paradise*."[30] In tedium begins hope.

Jameson: "Boredom . . . is a powerful hermeneutic instrument: it marks the spot where something painful is buried. . . . Not interest or fascination, therefore, but rather that sense of dreariness with which we come to the end of our own world and observe with a certain self-protective lassitude that there is nothing for us on the other side of the boundary—this is the unpleasant condition in which, I suggest, we come to the realization of the Other which is at the same time a dawning knowledge of ourselves as well." Jameson's subject here is "alien and primitive forms" but his terms describe the Paradise as well: "the uninventive simplicity and repetition, the liturgical slowness and predictability, or else the senseless and equally monotonous episodic meandering, of an oral tradition that has neither verbal density nor opacity, nor psychological subleties [*sic*] and violence to offer us."[31]

The Earthly Paradise is an Earthly Paradise—by definition so to speak. *The* is the author's joke in the face of death, his pathetic, self-mocking stab at hegemony. But as *a* paradise, poor as it is, bound between covers, Morris's work embodies a critical imagination of possibility: a collectivity of fragments, a protraction of (enfeebled) love, a suasion to the acentric, to the cyclical, to "changeless change"—tales told, lives embodied, against all odds, and then, but not finally, forgotten. The poem "marks the spot where something painful is buried" and in doing so makes a judgment on its bored reader's interest, that capitalist tool. A burial: boredom means loss, and promises (or hints at promising) the return of the repressed. It judges us wanting, "a dawning awareness of ourselves as well" (or an awareness locked in night), an awareness of our boundaries realized in awareness of something beyond them.

In boredom we learn what we are incapable of valuing. If in "our own world" interest is what accrues to an investment over time, boredom suggests "the other side of the boundary." It is an outlandish argument, to be sure, that denies our critical attention its foundation in what interests us, but this is only to say again that we come to the Paradise in extremis. Morris's poem offers us nothing that we might know what to do with—it offers us, in Stevens's phrase, "the nothing that is"[32]—and this is, again, the condition of its existence and the power of its challenge.

Si Je Puis

the system's claim to totality, which would suffer nothing to remain outside it

—ADORNO

House, Root, Well, Wood, World, Isles, Flood, Dream, Nowhere, Story—the names of Morris's romances (or his "capacity for a true sense of history") are all names of totalities, enveloping and enabling conceits. Morris speaks in "Art and Industry in the Fourteenth Century" (1890) of "past times which we can picture to ourselves as a whole, rightly or wrongly, because they are so far off."[33] *As a whole* is essential here, although almost invisible in this sentence, a given. (Morris's experience of totality predates his practice as an artist and socialist, back to the suit of toy armor he wore as a child, encased, in Epping Forest.) *Rightly or wrongly:* the wholeness of the Other (what is eternal, essential to it) is a function less of the Other (which is "so far off") than of present need—what "we can picture to ourselves," si je puis.

An enveloping and enabling illusion. Bloch, "Art and Utopia" (1959): "Without the utopian function it is impossible to explain the intellectual surplus that went beyond the status quo and that which had been accomplished, even if that surplus is filled with illusion instead of anticipatory illumination"; "illusions are necessary, have become necessary for life in a world completely devoid of utopian conscience and utopian presentiment" ("Something's Missing" [1968]).[34]

An alternative totality, habitation of desire and resistance, of the affective and the unadministered. Silliman, his subject here the "transformation which has occurred over the past several centuries: the subjection of writing (and through writing, language) to the social dynamics of capitalism": "What happens when a language moves toward and passes into a capitalist stage of development is an anaesthetic transformation of the perceived tangibility of the word, with corresponding increases in its expository, descriptive and narrative capacities, preconditions for the invention of 'realism', the illusion of reality in capitalist thought. These developments are tied directly to the function of reference in language, which under capitalism is transformed, narrowed into referentiality."[35]

The Earthly Paradise both succumbs to this development, embodying the "expository, descriptive and narrative capacities" of capitalist language, and undermines it as well, chips at the monolith. It aspires to and despairs of the tangibility of the word, seeks reference in referentiality, denies realism. Silliman: "For the individual, be it artist or consumer, art provides . . . experiences of that dialectical consciousness in which subject and object, self and other, individual and group, unite. Since it is precisely this dialectical consciousness which capitalism seeks to repress through the serialization of the individual (for it is by such consciousness that we know the overdetermination of the objects of our existence by the capitalist mode of production), the fine arts in general function as deformed counter-tendencies within the dominant society."[36]

The Earthly Paradise is a monument to the overdetermination of objects locked in dialectical embrace with a deformed counterconsciousness. Morris the able man rendered incapable. "Repression does not, fortunately, abolish the existence of the repressed element which continues as a contradiction, often invisible, in the social fact. As such, it continues to wage the class struggle of consciousness. The history of Anglo-American literature under capitalism is the history of this struggle."[37] But this history is submerged, even in the works that embody it.

Silliman: "What is radically new in the age of technical reproduction is the increased value placed on the possession of entities which have been deprived of their integrity and otherness, personal experience reduced to vicarious consumption." "One is rendered numb and passive on a level not previously feasible in history." The language is reminiscent of Horkheimer, but Silliman is less Last Days gloomy about the situation, breathtakingly miserable as it is. "Among the several social functions of poetry is that of posing a model of unalienated work: it stands in relation to the rest of society both as utopian possibility and constant reminder of just how bad things are."[38]

A utopian possibility. For Horkheimer, "The last substantial works of art . . . abandon the idea that real community exists; they are the monuments of a solitary and despairing life that finds no bridge to any other or even to its own consciousness." For Silliman, language art represents a utopian possibility in the face of this calamity, a will to establish what has been abandoned—a will to establish an impulse which though heavily compromised yet speaks somehow against administration, which embodies "the production and the practice of possibility."[39] Such language art, paradoxically, provides "contact with actual experience" by means of denying the transparency of language, and making instead a claim to the materiality of both language and experience. Such language counters referentiality with embodiment, it gives a body to desire. For Morris this means: book production, immersion, repetition, hypnotism, uselessness, and ease. Such are his weapons of resistance.

The Paradise occupies a peculiar moment in the "history of Anglo-American literature under capitalism": the twentieth century has seen the development of Horkheimer's "queer discordant forms" and Silliman's (or Hejinian's) discontinuous densities: such works resist appropriation quite explicitly. The idle singer embodies a discordant form in an important sense, "a solitary and despairing life," but his rhyme is characterized contradictorily by enormous ease—Swinburne called the verse "slow and spontaneous,"[40] artless so to speak, lulling, without struggle. It embodies a possibility of the collective that was already unavailable to Yeats, and increasingly unavailable to Joyce and Pound. In fact it was already unavailable to Morris after the Paradise—his literary language from *Love Is Enough* to *Sigurd the Volsung* to the late romances increasingly noncollective, invented, estranged from ease. The idle singer is the last imagination of audience.

The Earthly Paradise is a labor (700 lines in one day, etc.) and a solace (written on the train from Red House to Queen Square, or in insomniac hours): it is labor ostentatiously stripped of usefulness, both compulsive and wayward, a trifle—"a model of unalienated work" or dealienated work or work that aspires not to be alienated, or in which such a condition "does not appear, but can be said *to have been evoked*."[41] It is one of Morris's claims to attention that his career embodies an elaborate investigation into textile, graphic, and literary arts as work: material and social productions dependent upon a wider range of conditions than questions of style or taste, subject to and expressive of economic and political forces, capable of both resisting and maintaining the Normative Dominant.

Illth

> There's such lovely, lovely misery in this Paradise. In fact, I think it's—the other place—made pretty.
>
> —RUSKIN

The Paradise is a luxury, as much as the Green Room in the Victoria and Albert Museum, or as any Morris chintz or tapestry: an act of labor dissociated from usefulness, an excess, and as such, both resistance and submission to the logic of capitalist ideology.

Bataille: "Every time the meaning of a discussion depends on the fundamental value of the word *useful* . . . it is possible to affirm that the debate is necessarily warped and that the fundamental question is eluded." But this warped debate is virtually inescapable, controlling even the terms that would establish an alternative: "On the whole, any judgment of social activity implies the principle that all individual effort, in order to be valid, must be reducible to the fundamental necessities of production and conservation. Pleasure, whether art, permissible debauchery, or play, is definitively reduced, in the intellectual representations *in circulation,* to a concession." Thus Bataille directs his attention to what is *out of circulation,* to the invalid. "Production is the basis of a social *homogeneity. Homogeneous* society is productive society, namely, useful society. Every useless element is excluded, not from all of society, but from its *homogeneous* part"; "it remains possible to envision, at least as a yet imprecise representation, forms of attraction that differ from those already in existence, as different from present or even past communism as fascism is from dynastic claims."[42]

The vision of such an alterity Bataille calls a "*privileged instant*": "the opposite of a *substance* that withstands the test of time, it is something that flees as soon as it is seen and cannot be grasped. The will to fix such instants . . . is only the way to make them *reappear,* because the painting or the poetic text *evokes* but does not *make substantial* what once appeared. This gives rise to a mixture of unhappiness and exultation, of disgust and insolence; nothing seems more miserable and more dead than the stabilized thing, nothing is more desirable than what will soon disappear. But, as he feels what he loves escaping, the painter or writer trembles from the cold of extreme want; vain efforts are expended to create pathways permitting the endless reattainment of that which flees."[43] Clearly we find ourselves here in desperate straits, on "a shadowy isle in a steely sea," our desire for new "forms of attraction" "definitively reduced . . . to a concession," a desire wedded to death, our only hope in loss, our effort vain. The "*privileged instant*" is one of corruption.

Fascism, for Bataille, represents at once the extremity of homogeneous society—of the Administered World—and the revelation of its own foundation in the negative (which, by definition, belongs to the heterogeneous). "The mode of *heterogeneity,*" with fascism, "*explicitly undergoes a thorough alteration, completing the realization of intense homogeneity* without a decrease of the fundamental *heterogeneity.*" Thus, if all gestures toward the alternative are appropriated by the normative, the normative conjures its Other in equal measure: "*Heterogeneous* processes . . . enter into play once the fundamental *homogeneity* of society (the apparatus of production) has become dissociated because of its internal contradictions." As in Adorno's terms, "the system's claim to totality" is a claim subject to denial; that such a claim "would suffer nothing to remain outside it" places it in the subjunctive, the very mood of the heterogeneous.[44] Hegemony is the mirror of its own anxiety.

The Earthly Paradise is a heterogeneous process, an exploration of the internal contradictions of Victorian culture that produce its own—and the Paradise's—dissociation. The embodiment of dreams is the production of uselessness, both a mirror of capitalist production and a rejection of its ideology. Luxury is the grail of this ideology and the exposure of its debt to the incommensurable, its devotion to what will not be accommodated, to what moves ever beyond, what flees and cannot be grasped. The dynamic of capitalism itself undermines its claim to totality: it is devoted to debt, to what it wants, to what is missing.

Thus the oxymoron of Earthly Paradise, matter and antimatter, a mirror facing a mirror: "The general description of the heterogeneous region actually implies it to be posited as a constitutive element of the structure of the whole that includes not only imperative and impoverished forms but also *subversive* forms."[45] Imperative, impoverished, subversive: Morris's poem embodies all three forms, and constitutes "the structure of the whole" that spells its own death.

The Paradise is not an escape but an illusion of escape. Its alternative totality is wedded, by antithesis and antipathy, to the logic of totality, its aesthetics of immersion an appropriation (that capital venture) of the aesthetics of acquisition, of getting to, getting through, and getting. The Wanderers seek to escape their debt to nature and discover their debt to nature: death, and a community of tales and tellers that itself provides them with an education in desire, illusion, and inescapable defeat—"Since each tale's ending needs must be the same: / And we men call it Death." Bataille: "No representation can be more disconcerting than one that presents death as the fundamental object of the *communal* activity of men, death and not food or the production of the means of production." Making *The Earthly Paradise* a massive construction of death-born (and bound) illusion, Morris makes his judgment on "the spreading of the hideous town," the only world available to him a world of perverse luxury. (García Márquez: "El oro está identificado con la mierda"—gold is identified with shit.)[46] The Paradise is to industrial England what industrial England is to death: the other place—made pretty.

Love

the stain of love
is upon the world!
—W. C. WILLIAMS

"But yet believe no scorn of men can kill / My love of that fair land": that fair land is, again, *The Earthly Paradise* (first edition from F. S. Ellis, London, 1868–70; subsequent editions from Kelmscott Press, 1896, and Longmans, Green, in *Collected Works*, 1910–15, among others)—the site of one's desire untouched by scorn, that is to say again by administration, negator of all desire. Marcuse, *Eros and Civilization* (1955): "The memory of gratification is at the origin of all thinking, and the impulse to recapture past gratification is the hidden driving power behind the process of thought." Silliman: "The memory of aura, that shock of the presence of the Other without which intersubjectivity cannot exist, and thus cannot invoke a recognition of one's own self-presence, is thereby a fundamentally revolutionary instinct. The memory of a lost or debased aura may, in fact, be more powerful and critical than the fact of aura itself."[47]

Morris's object of love is always "lost or debased," "so far off," but his love is always true: his gratification—which he insists on against all scorn—that dulled and diffuse "shock of the Other," embodies a "fundamentally revolutionary instinct," "the free play of sensual, particularly sexual, energy." *The Earthly Paradise* is a monumental body and a monument to the body, an "embodiment of dreams." It is a love poem composed of constancy and travail—a love poem to Jane, to "those who in the sleepy region stay," to us, as well as to "that fair land"—the disembodied, depersonalized (depersoned) world that stands for all. Its object is one "which does not appear, but can be said *to have been evoked*." It is a love that persists, a deformed countertendency, an assertion of Life against The End: Earthly Paradise.

Love too is a function of the capitalist means of production. In the sixteenth century the population of London increased fourfold, from 50,000 to 200,000, virtually all contained within the original city walls—an experience of human density unprecedented in scale and speed of growth. Life expectancy in the poorer parishes was half that of the rest of England, twenty to twenty-five years on average, up five or ten years in the wealthier parishes. These figures are somewhat distorted by the high rate of infant mortality: even so, for those surviving childhood the average life expectancy was around fifty-four. Men married late, around twenty-eight or twenty-nine, after completing an average of seven years' apprenticeship.[48] Thus, even those achieving the age of fifty-four live no longer than it takes to produce a new apprentice, dying just as their firstborn comes of age to work. London the ravening monster of economy, economy pushing people to their biological breaking points. Procreation: produce and die. It's appropriate that *The Earthly Paradise* was composed in association with Morris's move back to London—the antiworld of Earthly Paradise (and ghoulish mirror of it), the maw of the production of labor.

The Earthly Paradise, in this setting, imagines the reproduction of rest—not an epoch but a protracted moment: the moment of reading. This moment is an embodiment of Wealth and Illth in one gesture, a Victorian fantasy of leisure, nightmare of Death-in-Life, and assertion of desire's Life in Death. Like a tale from the Grecian Urn: love that endures impossibility.

Love of the reader: *The Earthly Paradise* is what we have not learned to read, what resists all the ways of reading that our time teaches us. It is a work as prophetic as Blake's, for all its disclaimers: in the context of what still seems like the explosion of Modernism, and the subsequent explosion of the explosion (what we argue about calling postmodernism), *The Earthly Paradise* is what will not compute.

Syntax Bound

> ownership is the most intimate relationship that one can have
> to objects
> —BENJAMIN

I have before me a copy of the first edition of *The Earthly Paradise,* three volumes each boxed separately.[49] The first impression is a heavy sense of containment and totality.

Pasted to the spine of each volume: a paper label reading "The Earthly Paradise" and "A Poem by William Morris." Thus the book, not only what's in it but the object itself before me, is itself a poem. If the conventions of bookbinding do not encourage such an interpretation, neither do they disallow it.

The first page, the flyleaf, is inscribed: "Emma Morris / from her most affectionate son / the Author": Morris defines himself here in a fusion of the most intimate and the most impersonal (indeed, anonymous) bonds.

The verso is blank. There is no half title. The next page, the title page, gives us the following from top to bottom: "The / Earthly Paradise / A Poem," then the illustration, from Morris's woodcut of the three musicians, then "By / William Morris, / Author of The Life and Death of Jason." At the bottom: "London: F. S. Ellis, 33 King Street, Covent Garden. / MDCCCLXVIII." And at the very bottom: "[All Rights reserved.]". The verso is all but blank (I'll return to this in a moment). The blankness surrounding the title page is significant, if purely circumstantial, and contributes to the work's conceit of distantiation and resistance:

an object, both imaginative and specifically historical (its material production in the capitalist mode detailed), set apart, swaddled in a little void.

The Longmans, Green one-volume edition of 1907 is even more striking in this regard. Between the flyleaf (which in the copy I own bears the inscription "Frances, / with love and best wishes / from Margaret") and the title page, there is half-title page that reads simply "The Earthly Paradise." (period in original). This page is framed by blank versos: the object in hand (which has not yet been identified, in this edition, as a poem) framed by blank space. In this 1907 edition, too, the title page is slightly re-arranged: "By / William Morris" appears above the illustration, thus setting off the work's status as an individual's imaginative act from its status as a commodity ("Longmans, Green, and Co. / 39 Paternoster Row, London / New York, Bombay, and Calcutta / 1907 / All rights reserved"—the book's capitalist aura is here distinctly imperialist as well). Further, under the illustration of the three musicians, this edition reads: "New Impression." *The Earthly Paradise* is a contemporary work in 1907, an issue around which there is some confusion in 1868.

In both editions, the woodcut mediates between the Paradise as poem and the Paradise as text, between imagination and execution. The whole page, along with all of these other material details, is a matter of Art, obviously: but the woodcut is an explicit self-representation of Art that looks both ways—up to the Poem as conception (as free play) and down to the World as administrative context.

In the first edition, the verso of the title page is all but blank: at the very bottom it reads: "London: Strangeways and Walden, Printers, / 28 Castle St. Leicester Sq." The space that has been cleared around "The Earthly Paradise / A Poem" extends only this far—to the material details of its printing.

The next page carries the dedication: "To / My Wife / I Dedicate This Book"—with the printing details on the facing verso, this brings us again to a meeting of the intimate and the impersonal, the love object and the object of mass production. We note here, too, the poem's deeply thwarted impulse: its popularity in the latter form and loneliness in the former. The verso is blank.

"A TABLE OF CONTENTS" comes next. Two points are worth making. One is that this is not *the* table of contents: the arrangement of the book here described in linear terms is not the only one imaginable. Second, this particular table of contents makes certain interventions, listing "An Apology" and "The Author to the Reader" when no such headings appear with the text on the pages indicated. In fact, "The Author" does not appear at all in the printer's copy or in the Kelmscott edition—the two extant versions of the Paradise farthest from public consumption. The figure of the Author, the identification of the idle singer with an actual person, a producer, for whom the idle singer is a doppelgänger, appears only in the Table of Contents, as a function of the Paradise's social existence: its publication, its engagement of the collective.

Then the poem begins.

HABUNDIAN WORLD I
End of Transcendence

I have only one subject to lecture on, the relation of Art to Labour.

—MORRIS

Art is only encountered in a form that resists pure conceptualization.

—GADAMER

Death of Art of Death

we shall not be happy unless we live like good animals

—MORRIS

*T*he *Earthly Paradise* demonstrates that when Morris speaks of the Death of Art he is not being sentimental, or sniffing snobbishly at the degradation of taste, or bemoaning a fall from some lost golden age. The poem speaks of a mortal condition, an extremity, the eclipse of desire. The profound pervasiveness of administration, the constraint unto strangulation of desire, of pleasure, of Art, of collective culture: this is what Morris's political vision takes in, and what the Paradise embodies: a great edifice of Death, chief production of a society arranged for ministration to the swinish luxury of the rich, an empty day.

The relation of Art to Labor: the Paradise is a mocking mirror of the forms and motives of Capitalism, a deformed countertendency. More than a mirror: it appropriates the forms and motives of its master. Morris cuts the figure here of a kind of poet-entrepreneur: if he makes such an appropriation, he does more than embody these forms, he puts them to his own (virtual revolutionary) use. (Unger: "Everything is contextual and all contexts can be broken.")[1] As in weaving a pattern with fabric, his idle song works within and against its context, shaping an alternative world, an embodiment of dreams.

What is the nature of this alternative world? *The Earthly Paradise is* an earthly paradise: an impulse of desire held as if forever under a spell, a transcendental state shackled to history. (The description fits Victoria's paradise as well as Morris's.) *The* suggests that Morris's forlorn book is both the only paradise around (not only an earthly one at that but bound within bookcovers, a poor paradise indeed), and at the same time in fact a paradise. His book is a body of freed desire; if only such as it is, nevertheless it *is,* and this is the basis of its radical alterity, its challenge to administration, its true "escapism." Morris deploys (or deplays) various strategies to make his Paradise first and ever a Thing, a thing here and a thing apart. A body: both a totality and a state of containment, a whole and its negation, a thing with boundaries, signifying primarily its own presence. His Art is material, his aesthetics of immersion, of repetition, monotony, emptiness, idle trance, a counterforce to appropriation, to abstraction of any kind, to commodification: a materialist Art standing against the condition of Art under Plutocracy, devoted, and despairing of its devotion to presence. The alternative world is a thing, an object of the sensory life.

In fashioning such a world, Morris subjects Romanticism as well as Capitalism to critical inquiry, engaging both ideological systems in a negative dialectic. Both are transcendental systems, driven by a desire to escape from want, from the physical condition, from limits: endless growth, personal or capital. Both rest on a metaphysical foundation, the value of a commodity its spirit; both are marked by anxiety, by abstraction and alienation from the world, both are structures, for Morris, of Death, designed for denial and flight, generated out of a sense of insufferable Loss, both are mere recompense, abundant and inadequate.

The idle singer is himself a transcendental system, driven by want, faded metaphors of an imaginary past his metaphysic, anxious and deep into denial, with full heart still unsatisfied full up with Loss, Death haunted. But if his song appears as a substitute for a lost world, it is only the song of a lost relationship to *this* world, the only world that ever is, the world we live in. And in its habitation of this world, its constitution as a Thing, the song embodies its resistance to this Loss.

Resistance and recognition. What the idle singer fashions is so to speak a mask of Transcendentalism over a face of Materialism—a see-through mask, a distorting screen. His project is a negation of the negation, a transcendence of the transcendental, a construction of paradox, embodiment of contradiction. Through this hopeless project some Thing is realized, and this Thing (which we call *The Earthly Paradise*) is neither a compensation nor a denial but rather an embrace of Loss. All, all is lost, first it is made and then it is lost. (Nobody reads *The Earthly Paradise*.) The poem is a potlatch.[2] It symbolizes and enacts great wealth, great destruction, the primal dialectic of Life-in-Death and Death-in-Life, the dread and happy self-awareness of Matter. The Thing as an alternative achieves Life in the recognition of Death's dominion, of Changeless Change, and stands against the shadow world of Political (and Romantic) Economy.

Thus Morris's own ideological position is empowered by the ideological conditions and contradictions within late Romanticism and advanced Capitalism. The Death of Art engenders an Art of Death. The materiality of the Paradise is the materiality that Capitalist ideology at once metaphysically denies, frets over and fixates upon. (Capitalism is a potlatch too, but a neurotic one, denial and sublimation of Death's dominion, no embrace.) The Paradise is a body of Loss, of enormous expenditure, for reader as for poet, a body in Time. It is also, as such, the site of a radical critique of transcendence, of Death (the archetype of all transcendence)—of the Not Here that breathes (that inspires and extinguishes) the Here, of cash value and the Romantic Beyond. Morris's own Beyond—his work is the embodiment of *dreams*—is the experience of flesh and bone. His dream is to live "like good animals," which is to say like other animals, not neurotic but in the world, alive to death. To be a thing, or not to be.

Schelling, *The Philosophy of Art,* 1859: "Art . . . is not concerned with things themselves, but rather only with their forms or eternal essence"; "insofar as art takes up the form of the informing of the infinite into the finite as particular form, it acquires matter as its body or symbol," and for Schelling, there is nothing else to say about materiality. Even in the case of architecture, the art of the whole body's imagination, the place we warm our bones, "all beauty as such is the indifference of essence and form—the representation of the absolute in a particular"; "architecture as fine art must portray the organism as the essence of the anorganic, and accordingly the organic forms as preformed within the anorganic."[3] Types and archetypes: Schelling's Art is a matter of portrayal. But for Morris, Art is an event itself and a thing—and this transformation of received Romantic ideology constitutes the basis of his revolutionary critique of Capitalism, and marks the possibility of Art new made.

Phantom of Delight

> We hear in the background of the Romantic sublime the grand
> confidence of a heady imperialism, now superannuated as ethic
> or state of mind—a kind of spiritual capitalism, enjoying a
> pursuit of the infinitude of the private self.
>
> —WEISKEL

Morris in a letter from Oxford writes (breathlessly) of Shelley's "Skylark": "WHAT a gorgeous thing it is! utterly different to anything else I ever read: it makes one feel so different from anything else: I hope I shall be able to make you understand what I mean, for I am a sad muddle-head: I mean the most beautiful poetry, and indeed almost all beautiful writing makes one feel sad, or indignant, or—do you understand, for I can't make it any clearer; but 'The Skylark' makes one feel happy only; I suppose because it is nearly all music, and that it doesn't bring up any thoughts of humanity:

but I don't know either."[4] Happy only: but compared to the bird the best that human Art can devise is "a thing wherein we feel there is some hidden want" (line 70), and the best of human Love is "sad satiety" (l. 80). The "thoughts of humanity" that the poem "doesn't bring up" but rather soars above, or struggles to soar above on wings of identification, are specifically thoughts of alienation in Shelley: from present experience ("We look before and after, / And pine for what is not," ll. 86–87) and from Death ("Thou of death must deem / Things more true and deep / Than we mortals dream," ll. 82–84), from both terms of the primal dialectic.

The transcendentalism Shelley hails is thus an embrace of what the poem seeks transcendence *from,* an embrace of the material immediacy that the bird-watcher cannot bear. "Bird thou never wert" (l. 2) is both a name for the Skylark and a reproach to the poet: to be a bird (or not to be) whose "notes flow in . . . a crystal stream" (l. 85), who is alienated neither from "all the earth and air" (l. 26) nor from the deep truth of Death, is precisely what Shelley wants. He wants his art to be "unpremeditated" (l. 5), an act of making sensible his "full heart" (l. 4), his own Life present to himself.

But "To a Skylark" comes not "from Heaven, or near it" (l. 3)—it comes from down here, and undermines the very desire it portrays: the bird is not present to him ("In the broad daylight / . . . unseen," ll. 19–20), and while clearly nothing but a bird doing the marvelous things birds do (thus the bold polemic of "Bird thou never wert" and the disclaimer of "Heaven, or near it"), it must needs appear to the poet "like an unbodied joy" (l. 15), made invisible metaphysically as well as practically. The act of simile is the mark of Shelley's "hidden want," his dissociation from the sensible world.

His unbodying: the Skylark is a phantom of delight, not a Thing but the portrayal of a Thing, substanceless, a haunt, the residue of an uneasy death. At the same time it *is* a vision of a thing, however much in phantom form, and a delightful thing: a vision of the unadministered, of presence. It speaks its desire in the form of its alienation, a dying song with revelation on its lips. And the pleasure Morris takes in the poem rests in this secular miracle, of a thoroughly compromised desire, a being of estrangement, making at least its own self-contradiction manifest.

What Shelley's Skylark brings to Morris at Oxford is manifestly *not* an unbodied ascent, a fact registered perhaps in the stammering quality of Morris's response. The poem calls for a response that *cannot be*— "but I don't know either." Both poem and reader are bodies, whatever ascent they might make shaped by that formal condition, and the poem bears this knowledge in equal measure with its transcendental gaze.

The self-contradiction of "To a Skylark" then is its flight from the site of its own desire, from the body: the transcendental an escape from the transcendental, a return to the material. Contradiction a matter of counterhegemony: the return of the repressed. In the deeps of dislocation, under dark Satanic mills, to find that which was lost, to locate oneself, to construct even a twisted mirror of the material world and the materiality of human experience, the site of freed desire: Shelley's poem is a creation of this possibility. An agonized mask of transcendence, speaking its own Death.

"What thou art we know not," Shelley says, and can only ask, "What is most like thee?" (ll. 31–32), quick to exchange the Thing for some Idea of it, helpless before the Workings of the Mass Mind: "It occurs to nobody that there might be services that are not expressible in terms of exchange value."[5] At the same time, in rendering this helplessness in the form of its delusion—its escapism—Shelley makes sensible a negativity, the bodily condition his poem seeks to deny: the experience of the unexchangable, the condition of presence, of life and life only (without value-added tax).

This is, certainly, to turn Shelley on his head, but the self-contradiction that drives his work along with the whole Romantic enterprise would seem not only to justify such an approach but to demand it. "A Defence of Poetry" glows with the dying embers of a bewildered relationship to the material world. "We know no more of cause and effect than a constant conjunction of events." The language of poetry "marks the before unapprehended relations of things and perpetuates their apprehension until the words which represent them become, through time, signs for portions or classes of thoughts instead of pictures of integral thoughts": a process that moves away from materiality, beginning not with things but with the "algebraical representations" of "the relations of things, simply as relations," and transforming these already spectralized quasi things into ciphers, "signs for portions." Poetry itself thus participates in its own murder: "For the end of social corruption is to destroy all sensibility to pleasure; and, therefore, it is corruption. It begins at the imagination and the intellect as at the core, and distributes itself thence as a paralyzing venom, through the affections into the very appetites, until all become a torpid mass in which hardly sense survives."[6] Imagination itself both offspring and parent of corruption, of desensibility, of disembodiment, dislocation.

Working against itself, Imagination promises another world but gives instead the familiar world back again: "It reproduces the common universe of which we are portions and precipients, and it purges from our inward sight the film of familiarity which obscures from us the wonder of our being. It compels us to feel that which we perceive, and to imagine that which we know. It creates anew the universe." In our Reproduction is our Death: and only in this Death do we become sensible to the world we inhabit. Deeply divided against itself: Imagination "arrests the vanishing apparitions which haunt the interlunations of life, and veiling them, or in language or in form, sends them forth among mankind, bearing sweet news of kindred joy to those with whom their sisters abide—abide, because there is no portal of expression from the caverns of the spirit which they inhabit into the universe of things." Dealing in apparitions and veils, bearing no thing, no joy but news of joy, knowing "no portal of expression . . . into the universe of things," Poetry nevertheless is devoted only to that universe: it "lifts the veil from the hidden beauty of the world, and makes familiar objects be as if they were not familiar,"[7] transforming "signs for portions or classes of thought" back into "pictures of integral thoughts," Romantic ideology turning back against itself.

Pater, "Romanticism" (*Macmillan's Magazine*, 1876): "It is the addition of strangeness to beauty, that constitutes the romantic character in art." Beauty estranged, Paradise dislocated, Life disembodied: the Romantic project as a whole may be characterized by this self-division, a picture itself of Marx's wage laborer. We could say that Romanticism in Art consists of the embodiment of this self-contradiction, this single gesture of the critique and embrace of the transcendental: a self-contradiction that characterizes all our social, spiritual, economic lives but in a form that impedes reflection, that produces instead "a torpid mass in which hardly sense survives." Imagination is "that imperial faculty, whose throne is curtained within the invisible nature of man": both alienated (curtained, invisible) and inescapable, imperial, the throne of administration. "A poet participates in the eternal, the infinite, the one; as far as relates to his conceptions, time and place and number are not," but his project is precisely the restitution of time and place and number, the material world of "familiar objects" saved from abstraction, saved from estrangement and returned to experience. Beauty, Paradise, the Life of good animals, Art, the Body of Desire: "the opportunity to activate repressed or arrested *organic,* biological needs: to make the human body an instrument of pleasure rather than labor."[8]

Thing to Mind

With rocks, and stones, and trees.
—WORDSWORTH

And murmurs musical and swift jug jug
—COLERIDGE

Another bird: Coleridge, "The Nightingale / Written in April, 1798," from *Lyrical Ballads*. This is a physical bird and a physical poem, a construction of and reflection upon time and place and number, its materiality encoded from the outset in the definite article and the bibliographic subtitle. Its setting is an unnamed Night—not something else, not even the name of Night, "no cloud, no relic of the sunken day" (l. 1), but this, night, and not anywhere else but "on this old mossy bridge" (l. 4). Because "the stars be dim" (l. 8) we know that this night promises rain, and even this is to be an immediate pleasure, the thought of "vernal showers" (l. 9) conducting us back to "a pleasure in the dimness of the stars" (l. 11)—flight turning back on itself, returning us to where we are, absence conducing to presence. This is when "hark! the nightingale begins its song" (l. 12).

And this is when the poet recognizes his own estranged self, his dislocation from the materiality, the time and place and number of his own body, this is the turning of the dialectical wheel. He speaks to us first in quotation marks, " 'Most musical, most melancholy' bird!" (l. 13),[9] an estrangment which the word *bird* alone escapes, and then turns (divided against himself in zeal, to paraphrase Pater) to negate, to critique and judge that estrangement, to return both to direct speech and the world of good animals: "A melancholy bird? O idle thought! / In nature there is nothing melancholy" (ll. 14–15). "And many a poet echoes the conceit" (l. 23) of Melancholy, "when he had better far have stretched his limbs / Beside a brook in mossy fern-dell / By sun- or moon-light, to the influxes / Of shapes and sounds and shifting elements / Surrendering his whole spirit" (ll. 25–29).

Coleridge's poet embodies "a struggle of . . . 'hegemonies' and of opposing directions,"[10] of experience and alienation, the direction of the "shapes and sounds and shifting elements" of the material world and the direction of unbodied joy, the latter represented here by the presumptuous vanity of fame and progress. This unbodied joy, this benighted effort to "make all nature lovelier" (l. 33), " 'twill not be so" (l. 34), and in the effort to make it so, even the "most poetical" (l. 35) will "lose the deep'ning twilights of the spring / In ballrooms and hot theatres" (ll. 36–37), their "sympathy" "meek" (l. 38), and self-divided "must heave their sighs" (l. 38). In poetry the body of the world dies.

And in dying finds itself at last, another dying song with revelation on its lips. " 'Tis the merry nightingale" (l. 43), no bird that never wert, "that crowds, and hurries, and precipitates / With fast thick warble his delicious notes" (ll. 44–45). A body:

> But never elsewhere in one place I knew
> So many nightingales: and far and near
> In wood and thicket over the wide grove
> They answer and provoke each other's songs—
> With skirmish and capricious passagings,
> And murmurs musical and swift jug jug.

(ll. 55–60)

This grove is a place apart, like the grove "hard by a castle huge / Which the great lord inhabits not" in its "wild and tangling underwood" (ll. 50–52), but distinct with Life: here "you might almost / Forget it was not day" (ll. 63–64). A bodied joy, decorously bawdy, to one who watches

> Many a nightingale perch giddily
> On blosmy twig still swinging from the breeze,
> And to that motion tune his wanton song,
> Like tipsy Joy that reels with tossing head.

(ll. 78–81)

Coleridge presents his poem "The Nightingale" as a type of anti-poem, a refutation of the transcendental thorn in the side of the mind. His poem is a direct address, a letter to known recipients—"my friends!" (l. 83)—who together know what "many a poet" knows not: how "we may not thus profane / Nature's sweet voices always full of love" (ll. 41–42) with the sound of our own "slow distemper, or neglected love" (l. 18), how not to lose but to gain by devotion to the sensory world "the deep'ning twilights of the spring," how to redeem the body through the ear.

"The Nightingale," like Shelley's Skylark, is the gauntlet that Transcendental Idealism throws down before itself, and as such partakes of the general plan of *Lyrical Ballads*. The material world claims its own: Wordsworth's Preface speaks of "certain inherent and indestructible qualities of the human mind, and likewise . . . certain powers in the great and permanent objects that act upon it which are equally inherent and indestructible" standing irreducible against alienation. A World of Death: "For a multitude of causes unknown to former times are now acting with a combined force to blunt the discriminating powers of the mind and, unfitting it for all voluntary exertion, to reduce it to a state of almost savage torpor. The most effective of these causes are the great national events which are daily taking place and the increasing accumulation of men in cities, where the uniformity of their occupations produces a craving for extraordinary incident, which the rapid communication of intelligence hourly gratifies. To this tendency of life and manners the literature and theatrical exhibitions of the country have conformed themselves."[11]

Marcuse, *Eros and Civilization* (1955): "The era tends to be totalitarian even where it has not produced totalitarian states"; Adorno, *Minima Moralia* (1951): "Society is integral even before it undergoes totalitarian rule. Its organization also embraces those at war with it by co-ordinating their consciousness to its own."[12]

Against this penetrating corruption Wordsworth proposes a materialist aesthetic that is necessarily at the same time cast in the form of idealist fantasy. "For the end of social corruption is to destroy all sensibility to pleasure," Shelley says, and to return pleasure to the world is to return to "sensibility" at its root, before it branches away from sense. This sense of sense is where Wordsworth's art begins: in "the real language of men in a state of vivid sensation," "in what manner language and the human mind act and react on each other." It is a rejection of prescription, of "a family language which writers in metre seem to lay claim to by prescription" and which Wordsworth has "endeavoured utterly to reject." "I have wished" rather "to keep my reader in the company of flesh and blood."[13]

For Wordsworth, solidarity with "the sympathies of men" and alienation of the means of production are polarities: he censures poets "who separate themselves from the sympathies of men, and indulge in arbitrary and capricious habits of expression in order to furnish food for fickle tastes and fickle appetites of their own creation."[14] But he is bound, in equal measure, to the law of this separation. Like Shelley, he details a process that moves away from the materiality he aspires to: to aspire to materiality is his contradiction, his phantom of delight.

The poet Wordsworth describes is a kind of investment house turning the capital of "spontaneous overflow of powerful feelings," through the accrual of interest ("to throw over them a certain colouring of imagination"), into "understanding . . . enlightened" and "affections ameliorated." He begins "a man pleased with his own passions and volitions . . . delighting to contemplate similar volitions and passions as manifested in the goings-on of the universe, and habitually compelled to create them where he does not find them. To these qualities he has added a disposition to be affected more than other men by absent things as if they were present, an ability of conjuring up in himself passions which are indeed far from being the same as those produced by real events . . . ; whence, and from practice, he has acquired a greater readiness and power in expressing what he thinks and feels, and especially those thoughts and feelings which by his own choice, or from the structure of his own mind, arise in him without immediate external excitement." He begins in a state of sensory autonomy and ends in a state of total estrangement from the world of the senses; in the end when he comes to write "it is obvious that while he describes and imitates passions his situation is altogether slavish and mechanical compared with the freedom and power of real and substantial action and suffering."[15]

This poet thus embodies the form of a bewildered materiality. The form traces in "incidents and situations from common life" and in "language really used by men" "the primary laws of our nature"[16]—a movement away from materiality and at the same time a reclamation of materiality, a movement away from alienated materiality, a disembodiment negatively embodying a body: the return (again) of the repressed. The One that remains when the Many are fled is a distorted image of a desire for the one one holds in one's hand, participation in the living present world. You have to go a long way off—to forget, forget, forget—in order to get back.

What Wordsworth offers to this virtually hopeless state of affairs is, like "The Nightingale," a type of antipoetry (nevertheless, needless to say, itself a type of poetry). "I am certain it will appear to many persons that I have not fulfilled the terms of an engagement . . . voluntarily contracted"; "the pleasure which I have proposed to myself to impart is of a kind very different from that which is supposed by many persons to be the proper object of poetry." At one point in the Preface he is conciliatory: "I am well aware that others [poets] who pursue a different track may interest him [the reader] likewise; I do not interfere with their claim, I only wish to prefer a different claim of my own"—at another utterly subversive: "Now these men would establish a canon of criticism which the reader will conclude he must utterly reject, if he wishes to be pleased with these volumes": in either case his alternative is an act of counterhegemony, of self-contradiction. It marks a return to the sensible Thing of the self: "Nor let this necessity of producing immediate pleasure be considered as a degradation of the poet's art. It is far otherwise. It is an acknowledgment of the beauty of the universe, an acknowledgment the more sincere because it is not formal, but indirect."[17] It is *like* an unbodied joy: it bears the body within it.

The Lucy poems make it plain. "Three Years She Grew in Sun and Shower" infuses Lucy's Death with a redemptive metaphysic, Lucy the lost a kind of presiding spirit, genius and consort of Nature. But this is only Nature's conceit—Nature itself in Wordsworth's distancing Imagination a kind of Transcendental Idealist—and for the poet himself nothing remains but a poverty of sensation: "This heath, this calm and quiet scene; / The memory of what has been, / And never more will be" (ll. 40–42). His estrangement is virtually unutterable, in "She dwelt among th' untrodden ways" barely there at all: "and oh! / The difference to me" (ll. 11–2). The material world here is a place only of emptiness, of "rocks and stones and trees" (in "A Slumber Did My Spirit Seal" l. 8), but the emptiness itself returns us to that world, "mute insensate things" ("'Three years . . .'" l. 18) themselves a new beginning of sensation, Death of the transcendental.

Against this speechless hope the macabre vision of a later poem, "She Was a Phantom of Delight" (1804): "A Spirit, yet" "upon nearer view" "a Woman too!" (ll. 11–12), an alienated Thing, a "machine" with a "pulse" (l. 22), and the very image of the bourgeois Transcendental Ideal:

> The reason firm, the temperate will,
> Endurance, foresight, strength and skill;
(ll. 25–29)   A perfect Woman, nobly planned,
> To warn, to comfort, and command;
> And yet a Spirit still.

Desire transformed into property.

Far Otherwise

And would you learn the spells that drowse my soul?
Work without Hope draws nectar in a sieve,
And Hope without an object cannot live.

—COLERIDGE

Now Art has lost its mental Charms
France shall subdue the World in Arms

So spoke an angel at my birth
Then said Descend thou upon Earth
Renew the Arts on Britains Shore
And France shall fall down & adore
With works of Art their Armies meet
And War shall sink beneath thy feet
But if thy Nation Arts refuse
And if they scorn the immortal Muse
France shall the arts of Peace restore
And save thee from the Ungrateful shore

Spirit who lovst Brittanias Isle
Round which the Fiends of Commerce smile

—BLAKE

De Man, "Mallarme, Yeats, and the Post-Romantic Predicament" (1960): "One has to remember what hopes Yeats had invested in his emblems to measure the bitterness with which he refers to them as 'A mound of refuse or the sweepings of a street, / Old kettles, old bottles, and a broken can, / Old iron, old bones, old rags, that raving slut / Who keeps the till.' They represent not only the sardonic counterpoint of his most venerated 'holy things' but also, quite literally, the utterly worthless content of reality. The failure of the emblem amounts to total nihilism. . . . Those who look to Yeats for reassurance from the anxieties of our own post-romantic predicament, or for relief from the paralysis of nihilism, will not find it in his conception of the emblem." (But Yeats found it in Morris, the one man whose life he wished to live rather than his own.)[18]

Morris's materiality, like Yeats's own development, provides a critique of the failure of the emblem: like Wordsworth's and Coleridge's antipoetics, a form of Romantic Anti-Romanticism, a salvation from ourselves. The development of this aesthetic might be said to define the Romantic tradition in English, from its dawning in print (or whatever we might call Blake's manifestations of "the lineaments of Gratified Desire"), through its afterlife. (De Man: "The main points around which contemporary methodological and ideological arguments circle can almost always be traced directly back to the romantic heritage" and the contradictions borne forward within that heritage.) *Finnegans Wake,* for example, is a great poem of Romantic Anti-Romanticism, in a direct and paradoxical line from *Lyrical Ballads:* song of Life's birth in Death, and of the disappearance of the things of the world, of the word as reclamation of the Thing, of sensory redemption through sound. For Wordsworth and Shelley, Imagination is "a fading coal," composition a "slavish and mechanical" process; "when composition begins," Shelley writes, "inspiration is already on the decline, and the most glorious poetry that has ever been communicated to the world is probably a feeble shadow of the original conceptions of the poet," or in Wordsworth's terms a mere replication "of real and substantial action and suffering." "For Morris," however, as Jerome McGann points out, "when composition (in every sense) begins, inspiration must not be permitted to wane in the least way." The mind that Morris, like Joyce-Earwicker, brings to his Art is "the mind of sensation and experience." "Between the idea / And the reality" here no Shadow falls.[19]

The Earthly Paradise is "the immortal Muse" breathing into form Morris's own Post-Romantic predicament. The poem is from the start a kind of ghost, a reduced spectral vestige, of what J. R. Dunlap has called *The Book That Never Was*—the thwarted plan for a book with some 320 illustrations to be done in woodcut by Morris from designs by Burne-Jones. The failure of this enterprise is a familiar story by now: the plan was given up when it was discovered, upon pulling some trial pages at a commercial press, that the bold lines of the woodcuts threw every page out of harmony with the typefaces available at the time—commercial typeface itself a sort of spectral presence, demanding the spectralization of Morris's own work. *The Book That Never Was* never was because the means of production that dominated Victorian culture rendered it an impossibility. The poem as we have it then is first the mark of an estrangement, or of one absence (the woodcuts) called forth by another (the typeface): the measure, at the same time, of its own failure and its culture's.

 The Book That Never Was was a Thing, an unbodied Imagination of the Kelmscott Press books, still twenty-five years off in the belly of the future: books as bodies, habitations. (Morris, 1894: "If I were asked to say what is at once the most important production of Art and the thing most to be longed for, I should answer, A beautiful House; and if I were further asked to name the production next in importance and the thing next to be longed for, I should answer, A beautiful Book. To enjoy good houses and good books in self-respect and decent comfort, seems to me to be the pleasurable end towards which all societies of human beings ought now to struggle.")[20] But *The Earthly Paradise* (a mere trade book yet a Thing too, a Phantom of delight) carries the materiality of its thwarted conception forward in its own (deformed) way.

("The nostalgia for the object has become a nostalgia for an entity that could never, by its very nature, become a particularized presence," de Man writes of Wordsworth, whose corollary Imagination is figured as an "unfathered vapour"—or more precisely, as with Shelley's bird, "Like an unfathered vapour." Here, far otherwise, is Morris, as reported by Mackail: "That talk of inspiration is sheer nonsense, I may tell you flat, there is no such thing: it is a mere matter of craftsmanship. . . . If a chap can't compose an epic poem while he's weaving a tapestry, he had better shut up, he'll never do any good at all."[21] For Morris the Thing is the thing: his "nostalgia for the object" is profound, obsessive, notorious. Earthly paradise, the rejuvenation of the Body, the death of Death, the presence of the object at once revealed and withheld.)

If all books are inescapably material objects, made things, and thus always potentially revolutionary emanations from the negative image of nostalgia—namely, acts of Presence—what Morris does with books is to embrace and exploit this potential. A book is first of all an experience of vision (as opposed to a visionary experience), and of weight in the hand and of texture, of spine and leaf and case, of pockets, desks, shelves. Morris of course was particularly interested in these sensory phenomena of the book, and his texts carry traces of this interest even when their production is no longer under his control: as in the gold leaf patterning on the cover of my 1907 single-volume edition of the *Paradise.* (The unavailability of much of Morris's work is in part explained by the inability of the modes of textual production now dominant to accommodate these traces in any satisfying way: if the book is not first a pleasure in itself, in its sensory presence, it is nothing.)[22]

The Earthly Paradise, more particularly, is an experience of notable volume, and reading it an experience of time notably, almost ostentatiously, occupied. This is so even now, when the poem lives a restricted life in libraries—more sensibly so in the day of its popularity, when a man might read it aloud, in his bourgeois living room, to his womenfolk. ("Mr. Morris's popularity has . . . something remarkable about it. He is, we have noticed, appreciated by those, who as a rule, do not care to read any poetry. To our personal knowledge, political economists and scientific men to whom Shelley is a mystery and Tennyson a vexation of spirit, read *The Earthly Paradise* with admiration.")[23] The work, poetically as textually, and whether read aloud or not, is keyed in some measure to our bodies' relationship to reading: as if reading were a silence in which our bodies speak themselves. The mild stimulations of the Paradise, its plots and predictabilities of every kind, help this readerly self-embodiment along: not provocative enough to distract much from the quiet (listen closely) of a reader's own body in space and time. (In tedium begins hope, again.)

Putting it the other way around, the poem's actions—to forget, forget, forget, to think rather and to dream—*require* a return to the body, or define the conditions of such a return, a freeing of the site of desire: and the constraints within which such action is possible require that *The Earthly Paradise* be long and quiet and slow (a long room with a low roof, a Palace of Art), as Swinburne calls it, "spontaneous and slow": "It looks as if he purposely avoided all strenuous emotion or strength of music in thought and word"; "the flowing stream of story hushes and lulls the noise of its gurgling and refluent eddies with a still predominance of sound. To me it seems that there has been almost too much of this." Swinburne adds (all this in a letter to Rossetti in 1869) that "there is such a thing as swift and spontaneous style,"[24] but Morris's style is clearly a reduced item: and in this reduction it makes its first claim on us. It creates a reader who both engages in avoidance strategy, floating forward and away on this "flowing stream of story," and in the process goes nowhere so much as eyes on the page, fingers on the spine, back against the chair: things to mind.

The book is, in a sense, blank (in fact, earthly paradise cannot be, and blankness is an appropriate character for it): an empty thing, both monumentally present and scrupulously self-effacing at the same time: a body, first, and a body given to the paradisiacal reader, an experience of the physical act of reading. But if the book were truly blank, needless to say it would not provide this experience at all. (In Paradise, even the obvious bears repeating.) Hope without an object cannot live, and neither can sensible pleasure, and for reading, this means two objects, like the twin halves of Plato's hermaphrodite: the reading body and the body of the read. The words of the Paradise (the Blank that comes between the Blank from whence we came and the Blank whereto we go) must be present in their self-effacement, must effect a Thing themselves no less than page or vellum binding, no less than flesh. The words, embodying dreams, must first be bodies, felt as bodies.

The language of Paradise is thus a language that aspires to deny the capacity to be described—that wants to be indescribable—if by description we mean a transfer of sensory attention from the language itself to some notion about that language (what Pater calls "the art of directing towards an imaginary object sentiments whose natural direction is towards objects of sense.")[25] How can such a language be? ("What thou art we know not; / What is most like thee?") What can we say about it?

In Kafka's parable "the expulsion from Paradise is final, and life in this world irrevocable, but the eternal nature of the occurrence (or, temporally expressed, the eternal recapitulation of the occurrence) makes it nevertheless possible that not only could we live continuously in Paradise, but that we are continuously there in actual fact, no matter whether we know it here or not."[26] In Morris's Paradise, this possibility of actual fact, of continuous presence, is given form in language: sound, vocabulary, diction, meter, and rhyme all given over to the construction of a dream of presence.

It is a difficult language to describe. Kafka's and Morris's worlds here are both exactly where we are and dream worlds at the same time, and this is the difficulty which the language of *The Earthly Paradise* represents. T. S. Eliot: "The effort to construct a dream world, which alters English poetry so greatly in the nineteenth century, a dream world utterly different from the visionary realities of the *Vita Nuova* or of the poetry of Dante's contemporaries, is a problem of which various explanations may no doubt be found"—though no one of them may be found to be convincing. Eliot's example of a nineteenth-century poet is Morris, whose language he finds characterized by "vagueness of allusion" and indefiniteness in general, by "the mistiness of its feeling and the vagueness of its objects"; "the verses of Morris, which are nothing if not an attempt to suggest, really suggest nothing; and we are inclined to infer that the suggestiveness is the aura around a bright clear centre, that you cannot have the aura alone. The day-dreamy feeling of Morris," he adds, "is essentially a slight thing."[27]

For Eliot, Morris's language is precisely characterized by its continuous *absence*—the dissociation of Dream in the nineteenth century so advanced that there is no way for it to be realized in words: and "if anyone doubts whether the more refined or spiritual emotion can be precise, he should study the treatment of the varieties of discarnate emotion in the *Paradiso.*" Eliot, after Pater, Shelley, and Coleridge, and after Morris as well, wants "the making the familiar strange, and the strange familiar," and finds his specimen of Morris's "Nymphs' Song to Hylas" from *The Life and Death of Jason* a "charming poem." But Morris's language lacks utterly "the element of *surprise*," the prerequisite that empowers such a project. Sound, vocabulary, diction, meter, and rhyme, as Morris employs them, are the negativities of surprise, dialectical emanations from the mirror of negation of the world made afresh: Morris's language of self-contradiction precisely an effort (in Shelley's terms) "to feel that which we perceive," to "[create] anew the universe,"[28] and an effort subjected, administered virtually out of existence, constrained to be the opposite of itself, self-contradicted.

The means of the production of surprise, dissociated from dissociation by dissociation. Morris writes a language of the estranged familiar: he makes "the familiar strange, and the strange familiar," negating the negation in orthodox Romantic fashion, but moreso than (as Morris puts it) "those of the Byron and Shelley time,"[29] he embodies the self-contradiction that the endeavor entails. In the same sense in which Morris's book is blank, his language is dead; in fact, we might say that Morris in all his endeavors is always concerned with things that have died, or all but died, in each of the arts the moment when its Death engenders new life, when ebb becomes flow, when November turns to March: and that this aesthetic of morbidity is the theory, so to speak, of "the desire to make beautiful things," the dialectical Other of the Thing, the No-Thing that is. It is by design that Morris's language is difficult to describe, description itself a form of abstraction, of estrangement.

We are, in Kafka's parable, in Paradise "in actual fact": if *The Earthly Paradise* doesn't tell us anything we don't already know—if it offers us no element of surprise—then what we already know is earthly paradise "no matter whether we know it here or not." Forget, forget, forget: remember. The very dullness of the language, its mistiness and emptiness, is its primary strategy of presence, presence and its subversion in one gesture: the poem's linguistic politics. The Paradise is ruled by Dialectic: where there is Death there is Life, where emptiness fullness, where Blankness All, and where dullness interest. (Jameson: "Boredom . . . is a powerful hermeneutic instrument: it marks the spot where something painful is buried. . . . Not interest or fascination, therefore, but rather the sense of dreariness with which we come to the end of our own world and observe with a certain self-protective lassitude that there is nothing for us on the other side of the boundary—this is the unpleasant condition in which, I suggest, we come to the realization of the Other which is at the same time a dawning knowledge of ourselves as well.")[30]

"The Author to the Reader"

Think, listener, that I had the luck to stand,
Awhile ago within a flowery land,

Fair beyond words; that thence I brought away
Some blossoms that before my footsteps lay,
Not plucked by me, not over-fresh or bright;
Yet, since they minded me of that delight,
Within the pages of this book I laid
Their tender petals, there in peace to fade.
Dry are they now, and void of all their scent
And lovely colour, yet what once was meant
By these dull stains, some men may yet descry
As dead upon the quivering leaves they lie.
    Behold them here, and mock me if you will,
But yet believe no scorn of men can kill
My love of that fair land wherefrom they came,
Where midst the grass their petals once did flame.

    Moreover, since that land as ye should know,
Bears not alone the gems for summer's show,
Or gold and pearls for fresh green-coated spring,
Or rich adornment for the flickering wing
Of fleeting autumn, but hath little fear
For the white conquerer of the fruitful year;
So in these pages month by month I show
Some portion of the flowers that erst did blow
In lovely meadows of the varying land,
Wherein erewhile I had the luck to stand.

Morris is not often credited with an undue concern for compositional meticulousness—for getting the words *just so:* he was famously wont to write 500 lines at a go, on the train between Red House and Queen Square, or while working alternately at desk, table, and easel, on pattern design, gold leaf, tapestry and poetry, muttering verse while he wove. It is altogether appropriate to say "that he wove his poems like tapestries, limiting his vocabulary like the colour range of his words, conventionalizing and symbolizing his subject matter to meet the limitations of the material," that "all his work, even his literary work, was in some sense decorative, had in some degree the qualities of a splendid wallpaper"[31]— but only if it is recognized what wallpaper means in Morris. The passage above is designed both to be lived in and to indicate the nature of that habitation, the tenor of the act.

This passage, we should remember, has a doubled source: it is the voice of the idle singer, in part a continuation of his original Apology, and it is the voice and only appearance in the poem of The Author—another ghost, here and gone at once. The figure of the speaker and the emblems that the speaker conjures forth are both objects interred: petals of blossoms associated with delight are laid "within the pages of this book . . . / . . . there in peace to fade"—a burial and a memorial. The happy construction of the line "within the pages of this book I laid" makes the author himself one of these petals. And the book is an exhumation as well (yet another negation of the negation, burial and its reverse): dry, scentless, colorless, dull, dead, these petals lie exposed "upon the quivering leaves" in our hands, open to our inquiry into "what once was meant." The Paradise is Morris's Elizabeth Siddal.

It should come as no surprise then that the language which stands for the petals which themselves stand for the blossoms which stand for the death of the memory of delight, should itself be a compromised object, a pale reminder. The first word, "Think," is eminently pale, commanding an action very like an unbodied joy. The body vague, the feeling misty, and as *precisely* so as any chiseled metaphor (Pound's metaphor) or overall pattern for the walls or the floor, throughout. His luck is nameless, and he stands (or rather stood) only in the most general sense; even in spite of the "footsteps" we hear about later, "to stand" represents nothing so much as simply "was": the verb is virtually a pure cipher. Similarly, "that delight" is virtually without reference: the "land" is "flowery," the "blossoms" are "some," the "delight" only "that."[32]

All of Morris's nouns and adjectives are generalized, "not over-fresh or bright," and in this generalization we read the death of the object. "But yet believe no scorn of men can kill / My love of that fair land": "If ye will read aright, and pardon me" (Apology), we must read in this generalization as well the dialectical negation of that death, the reappearance of the Thing. Morris's paradisiacal language represents a transcendence of the transcendental, like Coleridge's Nightingale, its murmurs musical (with hardly a swift jug jug) denying transcription, denying reference to anything but themselves. If the first thing to reappear under the spell of *The Earthly Paradise* is the reading body, in a chair by the lamp, passing hours "no clock can measure,"[33] the second thing to reappear is the Word as noThing but itself. Or rather, dancer and dance, the reader and the read, they appear as one, a dialectic of making.

All of Morris's strategies of Presence are necessarily paradoxical in this way, strategies of Life-in-Death, embodiments of the quest the Wanderers undertake, "who strove / In their wild way the heart of Death to move, / E'en as we singers, and failed, e'en as we" (Epilogue). His words are fulfilled of emptiness, signifiers without signifieds. Paradoxical self-referentiality of paradisiacal language: the emptiness of the language partakes of the emptiness of the day, and in giving a body to it embodies its dialectical negative as well—the spectral presence of a day and language fully alive, the Imagination of what is not. Paradoxical further: Morris makes words things by emptying them of reference, and in doing so not only restores *them* to the world but the things they refer to as well. Signifieds freed from signifiers.

In such a language there are virtually no salient moments, and those there are of the quietest kind, virtually no cruxes. It is an astonishing performance in its way, though its way is precisely what makes the poem all but invisible to the modern eye: as Jameson says of boredom's edge, "There is nothing for us on the other side of the boundary." The monolithic uniformity of the thing is both an emanation of the monolithic uniformity of the empty day and the dialectical negation of that day, the creation of an alternative irreducible totality. This is clear from the poem's earliest reception, when the poem spoke to boredom with more appreciation: "It is not easy to give an idea of it by extracts, or, indeed, to judge of it by parts"; "the whole effect of the poem is cumulative, and a short extract will therefore not do justice to it"; "the water is not less medicinal, not less gifted with virtues, because a few drops of it are without effect; it is water to bathe and swim in"; "to do full justice to the way in which Mr. Morris has told his story, we should have to quote the whole of it."[34]

By the same token, every example of paradisiacal language is a good example. For instance "the grass" in the line quoted above: "Where midst the grass their petals once did flame." What grass is this? What flame? The petals are familiar, generic to begin with ("Not plucked by me, not over-fresh or bright"), and only emblems themselves of "some" cipher "blossoms" from some emptily "flowery land": the "petals" are objects (and a word) far removed from their meanings, "dead upon the quivering leaves." Grass and flame are similarly so removed, ciphers filled with themselves. The grass is any grass and no grass but the One amidst "their petals once did flame"—"did flame" a way of saying "were very bright and vanishing," words called forth by rhyme logic as much as anything. This is no flame that can burn you, no grass you might press with dainty foot. Any flame, any grass will do for these petals.

The gratuitousness of grass (and of flame): in the idle singer's line "the grass" is readily enough superfluous, "as it were a free particular, a poetical gift, a grace note," an extra. It comes from the world of inutility Bataille desires. (And again, this quality both introjects the disposabilities and interchangeabilities of the ideology of exchange value, and negates that ideology in its excess.) One can tease meanings out of "the grass": e.g., it is what hides Morris's dying petals, that amidst which his verses are as fragments in a sea. But the exercise is virtually dispensable: the meanings of *The Earthly Paradise* are so heavily overdetermined that any instance "might here and there be interchanged without apparent discordance."[35] The grass (and the flame) is a potlatch.

The resolute emptiness of these references to grass and flame both establishes the words themselves as the only sensible things and imagines the embodiment of those other things, that grass, that flaming color, in themselves: imagines a sensibility to the material world which language does not invade, in which Imagination functions not as an "imperial faculty." It is commonplace in the study of Morris to note the lack of introspection in his verse as, apparently, in his character—and to make fine distinctions with regard to degrees of this absence, for instance finding the third volume of the Paradise somewhat less lacking. Again, for Morris, the absence is a strategy of presence: the world exists beyond his head. Grass and flame.

This is a world manifestly in time, a home not of Wordworth's infinitude but of place and time and number: "summer's show," "green-coated spring," "fleeting autumn," "the white conquerer" Winter, each season "of the varying land" shown by "Some portion of the flowers"—a world that knows Death "but hath little fear," a world of bodies present to themselves at least in some faded portion. Morris tells the tale of the seasons here (in the poem as a whole and in this short passage) the way he tells tales always: reading the original, shutting the book, and telling in the sense of counting them off like beads, giving measure to their moments: this one, then this one, then this one, in every case simply a thing to mind, whether word or turn of the globe or unimaginably living Arthur. A world of things untouchable in word or deed, earthly paradise.

A. R. Dufty, in his introduction to the sumptuous two-volume edition of "The Story of Cupid and Psyche" complete with woodcuts and printed in one of Morris's own Kelmscott typefaces, quotes "FitzGerald commenting upon his old friend Tennyson, 'He had better have left King Arthur alone instead of turning him into Prince Albert!' "[36] FitzGerald himself here has the illusion of time travel, imagining an Arthur "as he was," now violated by his old friend. Morris, however, wants to avoid both poles: the idle singer's language is designed to deny both the illusion of any actual thing or person actually being present (other than the empty word itself), and the violation of that absent One by a projection of the modern mind (a rapist fantasy). He wants the words themselves, like the lines and tones of his designs themselves, or the colored threads of tapestry, and he wants Arthur to be Arthur (and Albert to be Albert), he wants both word and thing to be nothing but themselves: the materiality of the world restored. This is Paradise. It is present to love ("no scorn of men can kill") and as absent as "a flowery land." It is neither here nor there. News from nowhere.

HABUNDIAN WORLD II
Still Predominance

the shadow of her Green Tree
                    —YEATS

Happy Only

"Happiness," said Freud, "is no cultural value."

—MARCUSE

every perception of a given experience or work is at the same time
an awareness of what that experience or work is not

—JAMESON

Yeats, "The Happiest of the Poets," in *Ideas of Good and Evil* (1903):

> Morris has but one story to tell us, how some man or woman lost
> and found again the happiness that is always half of the body; and
> even when they are wandering from it, leaves must fall over
> them, for being of Habundia's kin they must not forget the
> shadow of her Green Tree even for a moment, and the waters of
> her Well must be always wet upon their sandals. His poetry often
> wearies us, as the unbroken green of July wearies us, for there is
> something in us, some bitterness because of the fall it may be, that
> takes a little from the sweetness of Eve's apple after the first
> mouthful; but he who did all things gladly, who never knew the
> curse of labour, found it always as sweet as it was in Eve's mouth.
> All kinds of associations have gathered about the pleasant things
> of the world, and half taken the pleasure out of them for the
> greater number of men, but he saw them as when they came from
> the Divine Hand. I often see him in my mind, as I saw him once at
> Hammersmith, holding up a glass of claret towards the light, and
> saying "Why do people say it is prosaic to get inspiration out of
> wine. Is it not the sunlight and the sap in the leaves. Are not grapes
> made by the sunlight and the sap?"[1]

Yeats's references here are to Morris's late romances, the Well the one at the
World's End, Habundia from *The Water of the Wondrous Isles,* protector of
Birdalone.[2] But Yeats freely interchanges them, the "Well" from one book
belonging to "her" from another, each work of Morris's fully identified
with every other, an irreducible totality within which each work is a
fragment. The passage above describes each of the tales the Paradise tells

too, as well as the tale the idle singer tells in his telling of them all, the tale of *The Earthly Paradise,* and the tale Morris tells of himself in this poem as in any morning at the loom. (Tale for Morris always a word for both a story told and a life lived, living out the tale.)

The happiness that Yeats seeks to define represents both an idea of good and an escape from ideality altogether: a return to the body, or at least half of the body, a body divided against itself. "Being of Habundia's kin" means that even in this state of self-division, the body is sensible to its pleasures, "the pleasant things of the world" present even in dislocation. The Imagination of Habundia is prosaic, an antipoetics, in the common mind of the "active man-in-the-mass," and it is a dialectical assault on the totalitarian alienation of that mind—a bringing of things to it, fresh things sweet as in Eve's mouth. We who know "the curse of labour" know not this happiness: it "often wearies us, as the unbroken green of July wearies us," the things of the world in the fullness of themselves "on the other side of the boundary" of interest.

What Yeats finds in Morris is the body of the world unalienated. The Habundian Imagination is a kind of salvation: Yeats in a review (published a month after Morris's death) of *The Well at the World's End* speaks of "little details of happiness" of which the book is "full," of "scarcely a chapter in which there is not some moment for which one might almost give one's soul." A salvation from salvation, reincorporation of the disembodied. (These late romances, Yeats said, "were the only books I was ever to read slowly that I might not come too quickly to the end.") "Almost alone among the dreamers of our time, he accepted life and called it good; and because almost alone among them he saw, amid its incompleteness and triviality, the Earthly Paradise."[3]

Truth is Beauty and Beauty Truth after all, though that is not all we need to know on earth: what we live is a lie, and we need to know that too, to be with the lie as with a thing. We are with Morris in "the shadow" of Habundia's Green Tree: both a tree itself, in the shadow of which we find ourselves and from which we find ourselves distant, and itself a shadow, shadow of a shadow, which we "must not forget." Our relation to Habundian happiness, to the presence of the world, is marked by distance, but "its leaves must still fall over" us.

The Imagination of Habundia is a response to the failure of the emblem, a product of internal stress within the Imagination of Transcendental Idealism, a recuperation of the Body, the Word, the Thing. We are clearly with Morris in the realm of the romantic transcendental, the vision of the One at the heart of Coleridge, Wordsworth, and Shelley; yet again, romance for Morris means "the capacity for a true conception of history," and transcendence not a sublimation of materiality but a movement of and to materiality, a vision and enactment of the moment "when we are to bodies gone." Morris's most specific reference to his romantic forebears, reported by Yeats, is telling in this regard: " 'My masters,' he said once, 'are Keats and Chaucer, because Keats and Chaucer make pictures.' "[4] The present tense of "make," the connection between Romanticism in the person of Keats and the earlier tradition represented by Chaucer, and the emphasis on the materiality of the work—an emphasis "almost child-like" in its lack of concern for less immediate things—are all characteristic. Morris returns to the world, his Habundian Imagination the embodiment of a dream of the familiar remade.

Yeats's emblems, Shelley's unbodied joys, Wordsworth's infinitude are all emanations of that fearful transcendence Death, the Type of all: Habundia is Death's loyal opposition. Yeats says that "unlike all other modern writers," Morris "makes his poetry out of unending pictures of a happiness that is often what a child might imagine," "remaking the world, not always in the same way, but always after its own heart."[5] The language of this happiness, of earthly paradise, is a language of regeneration, of the death of Death, "remaking the world." Typically in Morris, the form of regeneration embodied in the Habundian metaphor is of a type most common (the estranged familiar) and most material: the experience of living things, generation upon generation.

(The Wanderers of the Prologue, as well as many of the figures in the tales they tell and hear, historical transmission upon historical transmission, represent the perversion of this experience, fetishists of Death hypnotized by their fear, estranging themselves from both poles of the Inevitable Dialectic, fleeing both Life and Death at once: "They saw Death clear, and deemed all life accurst / By that cold overshadowing threat,—the End" [Epilogue]. The Wanderers too, in their meeting with the people of their final shore, and in their exchange of tales through changing seasons of the changing year described in the linking verse between each tale, find and partake of a paradise they knew not they had sought: the "nameless city in a distant sea" they come to embodies for them the experience of generation upon generation, lives lived as tales told, spot of time by spot of time. There is no afterlife in the religion of Paradise but the life that one lives after another. Habundia is its Goddess.)

Yeats places the Habundian world squarely within the Romantic tradition, as an extension and transformation of the Romantic return to

Nature. By way of comparison he notes of D. G. Rossetti that his "genius, like Shelley's, can hardly stir but to the rejection of nature, whose delight is profusion, but never intensity": "Men like [Rossetti] cannot be happy as we understand happiness, for to be happy one must delight, like nature, in mere profusion, in mere abundance, in making and doing things, and if one sets an image of the perfect before one, it must be the image that draws her perpetually, the image of a perfect fullness of natural life, of an Earthly Paradise."[6] Morris's vision of happiness, of "a perfect fullness of natural life," is rendered by Yeats as a fixation upon natural flux, a green stream with no beginning, middle, end, or purpose beyond itself—*mere* profusion, *mere* abundance. This green stream "draws her perpetually"— that is, draws "an image of the perfect"—in two senses, continually renewing the image and continually rendering it beyond our grasp, a vision of happiness that is simultaneously a vision of immanent loss. A vegetable metaphor.

Yeats on Morris: " 'Oh, the trees, the trees!' he wrote, in one of his early letters, and it was his work to make us, who had been taught to sympathise with the unhappy till we had grown morbid, to sympathise with men and women, who turned everything into happiness because they had in them something of the abundance of the beechen boughs, or of the bursting wheatear. He alone, I think, has told the story of Alcestis with perfect sympathy for Admetus, with so perfect a sympathy that he cannot persuade himself that one so happy died at all."[7] Yeats's example is "The Love of Alcestis," the tale the Wanderers hear in June, that month of a "thousand peaceful happy words." It is a tale of selflessness (noble or otherwise) in which a dying king is granted a reprieve from Death by the Fates, on the condition that another life end in his stead. Alcestis, his queen, offers hers. Yeats's point is that both Admetus' self-interest and Alcestis' virtuous love in a sense lose their human value, transformed by the principle of mere abundance into images of interchangibility. Their meaning is not lost but subsumed by a disorienting, reorienting metaphor: they become, Yeats suggests, trees.

Trees are a continuous (dying) replication of themselves, endless modulations of a fatal pattern, individuals without individuality, endlessly lost and innocent of loss, endlessly redeemed. In the Habundian Imagination they represent a transfigured human world, given over to an essential measurelessness. The principle of mere abundance, in subordinating the human to the vegetable, belongs to an act without consciousness: earthly paradise the unexamined life worth living, life as it is shared by the entire animate world. The life of the trees is composed of differences without

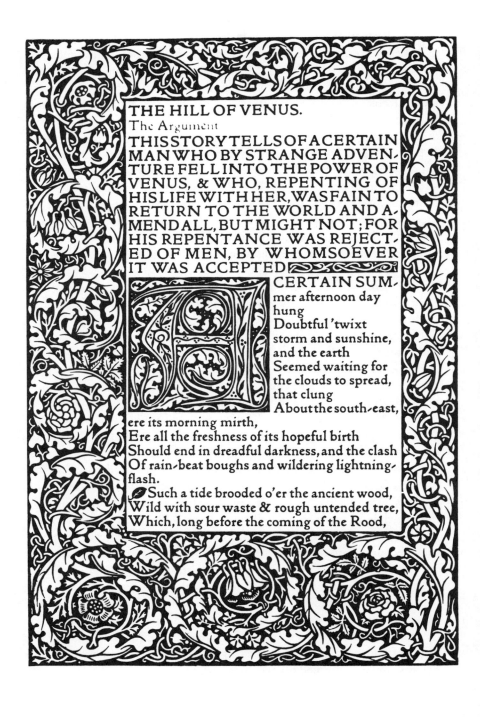

THE HILL OF VENUS.

The Argument

THIS STORY TELLS OF A CERTAIN
MAN WHO BY STRANGE ADVEN-
TURE FELL INTO THE POWER OF
VENUS, & WHO, REPENTING OF
HIS LIFE WITH HER, WAS FAIN TO
RETURN TO THE WORLD AND A-
MEND ALL, BUT MIGHT NOT; FOR
HIS REPENTANCE WAS REJECT-
ED OF MEN, BY WHOMSOEVER
IT WAS ACCEPTED

A CERTAIN SUM-
mer afternoon day
hung
Doubtful 'twixt
storm and sunshine,
and the earth
Seemed waiting for
the clouds to spread,
that clung
About the south-east,
ere its morning mirth,
Ere all the freshness of its hopeful birth
Should end in dreadful darkness, and the clash
Of rain-beat boughs and wildering lightning-
flash.
Such a tide brooded o'er the ancient wood,
Wild with sour waste & rough untended tree,
Which, long before the coming of the Rood,

distinction, measureless sinuous patterns of repletion and decline, and it offers people, its orphans, a dreamy metaphor of life without pain.

This vision of a world—our world—in which measure is sacrificed to abundance, to profusion, to potlatch, in which consciousness is denied and loss unlamentable, represents an escape, specifically, from history: a process itself without measure in the end, which nevertheless strives without stint to measure, mark, and compare. It is also a profoundly impersonal world, a vision of individuals subsumed within species: the species as Morris's Neoplatonic Type, a continuously bodied joy, the only individual. The body of humanity, the family tree: a totality and a thing with boundaries, a part of a greater whole, the whole as the only embodiment of the One. At the same time, a whole in which each part is of a piece, One that is reducible only to more ones, each themselves wholly identified: a vision of Nature's absolute power of integration and, simultaneously, of the wholeness of each piece so integral. One woven fabric.

The vegetable metaphor through which Morris reconciles Humanity and Nature (embodying the grand dream of the Romantic Imagination) is a profoundly encompassing one, more vast even than industrial progress or a poem of 42,000 lines. It represents the death of Death, paradoxically a protraction of Death, the beautiful face of Death. Our solace in beginning again to die, without consciousness of loss, in a trance of endless profusion: the word for this vital mode from a human perspective is Love.

Love in other words is the way in which humanity participates in (and realizes itself as part of) the primal dialectic: it is where Life-in-Death and Death-in-Life meet, where they are not split off from one another, where paradise is not an afterlife and corruption not an end. Morris inscribes a copy of *The Earthly Paradise* to his young daughters, Jenny and May:

> So many stories written here
> And none among them but doth bear
> Its weight of trouble and of woe!
> Well may you ask why it is so.

The weight he refers to is precisely the burden that the idle singer claims in his Apology not to be able to ease, yet it seems that neither can Morris avoid shouldering it. He goes on:

> Yet think if it may come of this—
> That lives fulfilled of ease and bliss

Men held a holy place in Germany;
Yea, and still looked therein strange things to see,
Still deemed that dark therein was uglier
Than in all other wilds, more full of fear.
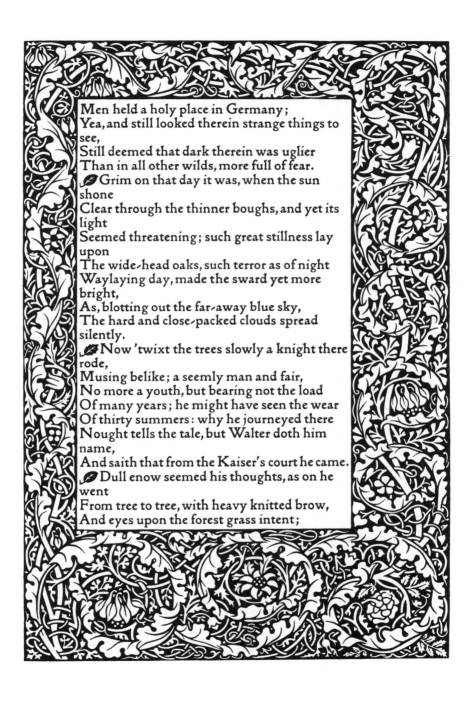Grim on that day it was, when the sun shone
Clear through the thinner boughs, and yet its light
Seemed threatening; such great stillness lay upon
The wide-head oaks, such terror as of night
Waylaying day, made the sward yet more bright,
As, blotting out the far-away blue sky,
The hard and close-packed clouds spread silently.
Now 'twixt the trees slowly a knight there rode,
Musing belike; a seemly man and fair,
No more a youth, but bearing not the load
Of many years; he might have seen the wear
Of thirty summers: why he journeyed there
Nought tells the tale, but Walter doth him name,
And saith that from the Kaiser's court he came.
Dull enow seemed his thoughts, as on he went
From tree to tree, with heavy knitted brow,
And eyes upon the forest grass intent;

Crave not for aught that we can give,
And scorn the broken lives we live;
Unlike to us they pass us by,
A dying laugh their history.
But those that struggled sore, and failed
Had one thing left them, that availed
When all things else were nought—
        E'en Love—
Whose sweet voice, crying as they strove,
Begat sweet pity, and more love still,
Waste places with sweet tales to fill;
Whereby we, living here, may learn
Our eyes toward very Love to turn,
And all the pain it bringeth meet
As nothing strange amid the sweet:
Whereby we too may hope to be
Grains in the great world's memory
Of pain endured, and nobleness
That life ill-understood doth bless.[8]

From the start here, Love is a dialectical product, the embodiment of a whole begotten of "broken lives" and failure. It is the "one thing left" to negate the negation of those lives, the one way in which "life ill-understood" nevertheless blesses us: the human experience of the vegetable death of Death. Love is also identified with "tales," each giving birth to the other in a continuous chain, contained within one another as seeds of seeds. And Love is defined in the same common material terms that mark Morris's vision throughout his work: it belongs to we who are "living here" and it represents the familiar remade, "nothing strange."

Matters Unforgot

when we'are to bodies gone
        —DONNE

I have said to the Worm, Thou art my mother & my sister
        —BLAKE

Marcuse quotes Sean O'Casey: "What time has been wasted during man's destiny in the struggle to decide what man's next world will be like! The

And oft beneath his breath he muttered low,
And once looked up and said: The earth doth grow
Day after day a wearier place belike;
No word for me to speak, no blow to strike:

Once I looked not for this and it has come;
What shall the end be now I look for worse?
Woe worth the dull walls of mine ancient home,
The ragged fields laid 'neath the ancient curse!
Woe worth false hope that dead despair doth nurse;
Woe worth the world's false love and babbling hate:
O life, vain, grasping, uncompassionate!

He looked around as thus he spake, and saw
That he amidst his thoughts had ridden to where
The close wood backward for a space did draw,
Leaving a plain of sweet-grown sward all clear,
Till at the end thereof a cliff rose sheer
From the green grass, o'er which again arose
A hill-side clad with fir-trees dark and close.

Now nigh the cliff a little river ran,
And bright with sun were hill and mead, although
Already, far away, the storm began
To rumble, and the storm-lift moving slow,
Over a full third of the sky to grow,
Though still within its heart the tumult stayed,
Content as yet to keep the world afraid.

There had he drawn rein, and his eyes were set
Upon a dark place in the sheer rock's side,
A cavern's mouth; and some new thought did get

122

keener the effort to find out, the less he knew about the present one he lived in. The one lovely world he knew, lived in, that gave him all he had, was, according to the preacher and prelate, the one to be least in his thoughts. He was recommended, ordered, from the day of his birth to bid goodbye to it. Oh, we have had enough of the abuse of this fair earth! It is no sad truth that this should be our home. Were it but to give us simple shelter, simple clothing, simple food, adding the lily and the rose, the apple and the pear, it would be a fit home for mortal or immortal man."⁹ Morris transforms the transcendental aesthetic of English Romanticism into an aesthetic of habitation: the object of his aesthetic is this world.

The idle singer: "Surely no book of verse I ever knew / But ever was the heart within him hot / To gain the Land of Matters Unforgot" (Envoi). This Land is both "the great world's memory" in which tales figure as "grains," and the material world, a "Land of Matters" redeemed from disappearance. From the perspective of an empty day, the object of all verse is nothing but "our home." And this home is "unforgot"—not remembered but forgotten and its forgetting redressed. Aesthetic of habitation: the whole of *The Earthly Paradise* is the house of Habundia, both an embodiment of the irreducible "one lovely world" and a delineation of our dislocation from that world.

To unforget is not the same as to remember. The unforgot is first and always essentially forgotten, its forgetting somehow redeemed without being canceled: a negation of the negation that still leaves the negated negated, a most precarious existential condition. To redeem Matters Unforgot, to redeem the materiality of experience in a world given over to alienation, is to find this experience in the form of its alienation, to find what is lost still lost even in its finding. How does the idle singer manage such effects?

The Things of the Paradise, in order to embody the dream of Matters Unforgot, must first of all lack presence. Jameson says of the Romantic enterprise as a whole, in its reaction to "the conventional rhetoric of eighteenth-century poetry," that "the various sensations collected by the Romantics fade and wither, and what was freshest and most vivid in them . . . comes across the generations to us as the very epitome of the *insipid,* a dialectical reversal in which pure sensation turns around into its own opposite, its own absence." The Paradise, as it were, incorporates this historical experience within itself, anticipating the judgment of future generations upon such a doomed enterprise by making its own elephantine body a body of absence: a Thing that is as if it were not there, composed of

Place in his heart therewith, and he must bide
To nurse the thing; for certes far and wide
That place was known, and by an evil fame;
The Hill of Venus had it got to name.

And many a tale yet unforgot there was
Of what a devilish world, dream-like, but true,
Would snare the o'er-rash man whose feet should pass
That cavern's mouth: old folk would say they knew
Of men who risked it, nor came back to rue
The losing of their souls; and others told
Of how they watched, when they were young and bold,

Midsummer night through: yea, and not in vain;
For on the stream's banks, and the flowery mead,
Sights had they seen they might not tell again;
And in their hearts that night had sown the seed
Of many a wild desire and desperate need;
So that, with longings nought could satisfy,
Their lives were saddened till they came to die.

For all the stories were at one in this,
That still they told of a trap baited well
With some first minutes of unheard-of bliss;
Then, these grasped greedily, the poor fool fell
To earthly evil, or no doubtful hell.
Yet, as these stories flitted by all dim,
The knight's face softened; sweet they seemed to him.

He muttered: Yea, the end is hell and death,
The midmost hid, yet the beginning Love.
Ah me! despite the worst Love threateneth,

123

things that are as if they were not there. Things pale, Things formulaic, Things unstressed but touched upon and passed, indicated, or as Eliot puts it, Things merely suggested, an "aura around a bright clear centre" that is, in fact, a missing center.[10]

At the same time, the embodiment of the Unforgot requires that the Paradise provide a site for nothing but such Things, for nothing but the missing materiality of the world: no abundant recompense, no hard-won grief-borne lesson, no spiritual transcendence or intellectual accommodation, nothing other than what is lost, what is forgotten, the only Thing that is, the only Thing worth our while, the world sold down the river, the world drained of its own presence. As Jameson says of aura: "In a secularized universe it is perhaps easier to locate"—or more precisely, perhaps, only possible to locate—"at the moment of its disappearance, the cause of which lies in general technical invention, the replacement of human perception with the substitutes for and mechanical extensions of perception which are machines"; "the objects of aura stand perhaps as the setting of a kind of Utopia, a Utopian present, not shorn of the past but having absorbed it, a kind of plenitude of existence in the world of things, if only for the briefest instant."[11]

Thus the Scholar's knapsack in "The Writing on the Image":

> Now on his back a bag had he,
> To bear what treasure he might win,
> And therewith now did he begin
> To go adown the winding stair;
> And found the walls all painted fair
> With images of many a thing,
> Warrior and priest, and queen and king,
> But nothing knew what they might be.

The bag, the treasure, the winding stairway down, the painted images are all readily enough symbolic objects, susceptible to an import beyond themselves: the bag a very image of the Paradise itself, a vessel to carry back the buried, the stair an image of history (or the subconscious), the walls of war and religion and politics. But Morris's treatment of these objects does not lend itself to such a reading: each is at once generic and mundane, barely noted—which is to say noted, but no more than noted, "a kind of plenitude of existence in the world of things, if only for the briefest instant," a plenitude of the virtually absent. A page further on the bag reappears, providing one of the most salient moments in the whole

Still would I cling on to the skirts thereof,
If I could hope his sadness still could move
My heart for evermore. A little taste
Of the king's banquet, then all bare and waste

My table is; fresh guests are hurrying in
With eager eyes, there to abide their turn,
That they more hunger therewithal may win!
Ah me! what skill for dying love to yearn?
Yet, O my yearning! though my heart should burn
Into light feathery ash, blown here and there,
After one minute of that odorous flare.

With that once more he hung his head adown;
The name of Love such thoughts in him had stirred,
That somewhat sweet his life to him was grown,
And like soft sighs his breathing now he heard;
His heart beat like a lover's heart afeard;
Of such fair women as he erst had seen,
The names he named, and thought what each had been.

Yet, as he told them over one by one,
But dimly might he see their forms, and still
Some lack, some coldness, cursed them all, and none
The void within his straining heart might fill;
For evermore, as if against his will,
Words of old stories, turned to images
Of lovelier things, would blur the sight of these.

Long dwelt he in such musings, though his beast
From out his hand had plucked the bridle-rein,
And, wandering slowly onward, now did feast

Paradise for its remarkable lack of presence. The Scholar has descended the stairs and found "A goodly hall hung round with gold, / And at the upper end . . . / . . . a glorious company" "attired in full royal guise, / And wrought by art in such a wise / That living they all seemed to be," but "dead and cold" in fact, sitting at a dais laden with "golden cups" and such.

> Therewith he drew
> Unto those royal corpses two,
> That on dead brows still wore the crown;
> And midst the golden cups set down
> The rugged wallet from his back,
> Patched of strong leather, *brown and black.*

To emphasize these last words, as I have done here, is perverse to be sure: nothing could be more inconsequential, less noteworthy, less present even when noted. The words seem there to fill out the rhyme more than anything else, but there they are, and the status of their presence is of a piece with every Thing, and every aspect of every Thing, that the idle singer and his hollow puppets name. Brown and black, sensations collected, period.

Another example, from "The Ring Given to Venus." The hero of the tale and his father seek help from the priest Dan Palumbus in escaping the spell under which the hero has fallen in giving his wedding ring to the ancient goddess, and which keeps him from consummating his earthly marriage. Again, the situation is fraught with readings: the relationship between the old gods and the newer Christian church, the wondrous craft-wealth and the decadence of the land, the psychosexual terror of the hero, scornful of the old gods and complacent in his wealth. And again, as available as such readings are, the movement of the verse militates for a different sort of readerly experience: one of narrative gratuitousness. Son and father come to "the great church," and waiting until

> the mass was fully o'er
> They made good haste unto the door
> That led unto the sacristy:
> And there a ring right fair to see
> The old man to a verger gave
> In token, praying much to have
> With Dan Palumbus speech awhile.

Upon the short sweet herbage of the plain;
So when the knight raised up his eyes again,
Behind his back the dark of the oak-wood lay,
And nigh unto its end was grown the day.

He gazed round toward the west first, and the stream,
Where all was bright and sunny, nor would he
Have deemed himself deep fallen into a dream
If he had seen the grass swept daintily
By raiment that in old days used to be;
When white 'neath Pallas' smile and Juno's frown
Gleamed Venus from the gold slow slipping down.

But void was all the meadow's beauty now,
And to the east he turned round with a sigh,
And saw the hard lift blacker and blacker grow
'Neath the world's silence, as the storm drew nigh;
And to his heart there went home suddenly
A sting of bitter hatred and despair,
That these things, his own heart had made so fair,

He might not have; and even as he gazed,
And the air grew more stifling yet and still,
Down in the east a crooked red line blazed,
And soon the thunder the eve's hush did fill,
Low yet, but strong, persistent as God's will.
He cried aloud: A world made to be lost,
A bitter life 'twixt pain and nothing tossed!

And therewithal he stooped and caught the rein,
And turned his horse about till he did face
The cavern in the hill, and said: Ah, vain

125

The verger's function in the narrative seems only to extend the moment of waiting, to heighten our experience of anxiety, of not yet knowing how it all turns out: he accepts the ring "with a smile / As one who says 'Ye ask in vain,'" tells them nevertheless that he will lead them to the priest, and takes them "from out the lordly church" to "the priest's house." On the way, "with eyes made grave by their intent," what they see is not keyed to their mood but rather simply what they would see, and what they hear what they would hear, in such a spot: "The grey hawks chatter to the breeze, / The sanctus bell run down the wind," "the minster wall," "the belfry huge and high, / Fluttered about perpetually / By chattering daws." And then the verger takes his leave, and Morris takes eight lines to get him gone:

> "Sirs, Dan Palumbus takes his way
> E'en now from out the sacristy,"
> The verger said; "sirs, well be ye!
> For time it is that I were gone."
> Therewith he left the twain alone
> Beside the door, and sooth to say,
> In haste he seemed to get away
> As one afeard; but they bode there,
> And round about the house did peer,
> But found nought dreadful: small it was
> Set on a tiny plot of grass,
> And on each side the door a bay
> Brushed 'gainst the oak porch rent and grey;
> A yard-wide garden ran along
> The wall, by ancient box fenced strong;
> And in the corner, where it met
> The belfry, was a great yew set,
> Where sat the blackbird-hen in spring.

Again, the details that follow the verger's departure are handled in such a way as to suggest little more than the mere occupation of space and time. But it is the departure itself that is most striking in this regard. Although his mysterious demeanor seems to indicate something ominous, something potentially fearful, his speech is wholly superfluous, a dilation of the narrative without value, a moment as easily conveyed by saying: 'And so he gat himself away / In haste, it seemed, as one afeard.'

My yearning for enduring bliss of days
Amidst the dull world's hopeless, hurrying race,
Where the past gain each new gain makes a loss,
And yestreen's golden love to-day makes dross!

And as he spake, slowly his horse 'gan move
Unto the hill: To-morrow and to-day,
Why should I name you, so I once hold Love
Close to my heart? If others fell away,
That was because within their souls yet lay
Some hope, some thought of making peace at last
With the false world, when all their love was past.

But strangely light therewith his heart did grow,
He knew not why; and yet again he said:
A wondrous thing that I this day must trow
In tales that poets and old wives have made!
Time was when duly all these things I weighed.
Yet, O my heart, what sweetens the dull air?
What is this growing hope, so fresh and fair?

Then therewithal louder the thunder rolled,
And the world darkened, for the sun was down;
A fitful wind 'gan flicker o'er the wold,
And in scared wise the woods began to moan,
And fast the black clouds all the sky did drown;
But his eyes glittered, a strange smile did gleam
Across his face, as in a happy dream.

Again he cried: Thou callest me; I come;
I come, O lovely one! Oh, thou art nigh;
Like a sweet scent, the nearness of thine home

This is, we might say, simply an example of flaccid, inadequately worked verse, but if the verse is bad there's method in its badness. The examples of the black and brown bag and of the priest Dan Palumbus's verger's leavetaking differ in degree but not in kind from every other moment in the Paradise: they are most gratuitous details, that is, details merely given, given without justification (or, at least, any justification that would enrich their presence—if only at the cost of absenting them, abstracting them, justifying rather than being with them, mediating between them and an audience)—and in this regard they are emblematic rather than anomolous, a salience by virtue of lacking salience. To read the Paradise is to read tales—erotic quest tales for the most part, tales of striving for and disappointment in sensual transcendence, for which the Wanderers provide the model, tales driven by an idea, a dream, of pleasure without end, of Love, "E'en Love," the world made eternally present. It is an idea we get soon enough, and then are given again, again and again. But before we even get the idea, and while we submit to the trance of its repetition, and afterwards, when the book is done, what we have is an experience and a memory of the form in which the dream is embodied: words used in this way, and things regarded in this way, as nothing but themselves.

This is a paradoxical way to speak, of course, but it is the only way to speak of a desire confounded as that of the Paradise, a world dislocated, a contradiction in terms. The words *are* more than themselves—they are the signs of things—and the things are more than *them*selves—symbols it may be, and emblems of a method, an approach to things, a Habundian dream of impersonal profusion: but these functions of words and things are placed in dialectical relation to an existence far otherwise, a yearning for words to be nothing but, and things to be nothing but, a purely sensual impossible experience. Love begotten by Despair upon Impossibility.

The Habundian attributes of presence in absence and of profusion are sustained in the Paradise by means of a further attribute of the Habundian: the embodiment of the dream of process. From the Prologue, a representative and necessarily long passage:

> Well, in a while I gained the Rose-Garland,
> And as toward shore we steadily did stand
> With all sail set, the wind, which had been light,
> Since the beginning of the just past night,
> Failed utterly, and the sharp ripple slept,
> Then toiling hard forward our keels we swept,

Is shed around; it lighteth up God's sky:
O me, thy glory! 🌿 Therewith suddenly
The lightning streamed across the gathering night,
And his horse swerved aside in wild affright.

He heeded not except to spur him on;
He drew his sword as if he saw a foe,
And rode on madly till the stream he won,
And, even as the storm-wind loud 'gan blow,
And the great drops fell pattering, no more slow,
Dashed through the stream and up the other bank,
And leaped to earth amidst his armour's clank,

And faced the wild white rain, and the wind's roar,
The swift wide-dazzling lightning strange of hue,
The griding thunder, saying: No more, no more,
Helpless and cruel, do I deal with you,
Or heed the things the false world calleth true.
Surely mine eyes in spite of you behold
The perfect peace Love's loving arms enfold.

🌿 Then, whirling o'er his head his glittering sword,
Into the night he cast it far away;
And turning round, without another word
Left the wild tumult of the ruined day,
And into the darkness that before him lay
Rushed blindly, while the cold rain-bearing wind
Wailed after him, and the storm clashed behind.

A few steps through black darkness did he go,
Then turned and stayed, and with his arms outspread
Stood tottering there a little while, as though

127

Making small way, until night fell again,
And then, although of landing we were fain,
Needs must we wait; but when the sun was set
Then the cool night a light air did beget,
And 'neath the stars slowly we moved along,
And found ourselves within a current strong
At daybreak, and the land beneath our lee.
      There a long line of breakers could we see,
That on a yellow sandy beach did fall,
And then a belt of grass, and then a wall
Of green trees, rising dark against the sky.
Not long we looked, but anchored presently
A furlong from the shore, and then, all armed,
Into the boats the most part of us swarmed,
And pulled with eager hands unto the beach,
But when the seething surf our prow did reach
From off the bows I leapt into the sea
Waist deep, and, wading, was the first to be
Upon that land; then to the flowers I ran,
And cried aloud like to a drunken man
Words without meaning, whereof none took heed,
For all across the yellow beach made speed
To roll among the fair flowers and the grass.
      But when our folly somewhat tempered was,
And we could talk like men, we thought it good
To try if we could pierce the thick black wood,
And see what men might dwell in that new land;
But when we entered it, on either hand
Uprose the trunks, with underwood entwined
Making one thicket, thorny, dense, and blind;
Where with our axes, labouring half the day,
We scarcely made some half a rod of way;
      Therefore, we left that place and tried again,
Yea, many times, but yet was all in vain;
So to the ships we went, when we had been
A long way in our arms, nor yet had seen
A sign of man, but as for living things,
Gay birds with many-coloured crests and wings,
Conies anigh the beach, and while we hacked
Within the wood, grey serpents, yellow-backed,

He fain would yet turn back; some words he said
If the storm heard, then fell, and as one dead
Lay long, not moving, noting not how soon
Above the dripping boughs outshone the moon.

E woke up with the tears upon his cheek,
As though awakened from some dream
of love,
And as his senses cleared felt strange
and weak,
And would not open eyes or try to move,
Since he felt happy and yet feared to prove
His new-born bliss, lest it should fade from him
E'en as in waking grows the love-dream dim.

A half hush was there round about, as though
Beast, bird, and creeping thing went each their ways,
Yet needs must keep their voices hushed and low,
For worship of the sweet love-laden days.
Most heavenly odours floated through the place,
Whate'er it was, wherein his body lay,
And soft the air was as of deathless May.

At last he rose with eyes fixed on the ground,
And therewithal his armour's clinking seemed
An overloud and clean unlooked-for sound:
He trembled; even yet perchance he dreamed,
Though strange hope o'er his wondering heart there
streamed;
He looked up; in the thickest of a wood
Of trees fair-blossomed, heavy-leaved, he stood.

128

And monstrous lizards; yea, and one man said
That midst the thorns he saw a dragon's head;
And keeping still his eyes on it he felt
For a stout shaft he had within his belt;
But just as he had got it to the string
And drawn his hand aback, the loathly thing
Vanished away, and how he could not tell.

The one detail with a special claim to salience here—the dragon's head—is the one that turns out not to have been there in the first place. This fact both sustains the method, extending it into narrative, and reflects the conditions under which such a method comes to invention: the absence of things, our dislocation from the material world: Habundia both mirror of the Administered World and a way far otherwise, in which (to reverse Jameson's remark on the Romantics) disappearance undergoes "a dialectical reversal . . . [and] turns around into its own opposite." The disappeared is all there is, things that are not there the only things there are.

The dragon's head, however, like the Scholar's bag and the verger taking his leave, stands out only to indicate its uniformity within the system as a whole. Every Thing in Paradise, as in the passage above, is worth noting, and no Thing especially noteworthy, everything of reduced presence, nothing striving for effect. This is a poetry of the antisublime, undistracted by grandeur (even such grandeur as Wordsworth, say, will invest in the tiniest detail), making no claim beyond itself. To name Things as Morris does is to free them from one order, the order of hermeneutics, and to subordinate them to another, the order of pace, of pure motion, the green stream. The movement of the verse saves Things from anything but themselves, collects sensations and simultaneously saves them from collection, from anything but their own enfeebled presence.

What we find here, reading the Paradise, is what the Wanderers themselves find. As their purchase on dry land is impeded by night ("Needs must we wait") and, at daybreak, by a wood too thick to hack, so our entry is constrained both temporally and spatially: by the imposition of an unmendable pace and the elaboration of a world of redundancies, of entangling sameness. When the Wanderers anchor near the shore, their slowly drifting approach bursts into an eager assault, as "all armed, / Into the boats the most part of us swarmed, / And pulled with eager hands unto the beach"; but the moment of their passion carries the same weight as their moment of waiting, in the light air of the cool night, moving slowly under the stars. The pace of the verse, its rhythmic pattern of scans and foci, makes no accommodation for the priority of discrete events. The

He turned about and looked; some memory
Of time late past, of dull and craving pain,
Made him yet look the cavern's mouth to see
Anigh behind him: but he gazed in vain,
For there he stood, as a man born again,
'Midst a close break of eglantine and rose,
With no deed now to cast aside or choose.

Yet, as a man new-born at first may hear
A murmur in his ears of life gone by,
Then in a flash may see his past days clear,
The pain, the pleasure, and the strife, all nigh,
And stripped of every softening veil and lie,
So did he hear, and see, and vainly strive
In one short minute all that life to live.

But even while he strove, as strong as sleep,
As swift as death, came deep forgetfulness,
Came fresh desire unnamed; his heart did leap
With a fresh hope, a fresh fear did oppress
The new delight, that else cried out to bless
The unchanging softness of that unknown air,
And the sweet tangle round about him there.

Trembling, and thinking strange things to behold,
The interwoven boughs aside he drew,
And softly, as though sleep the world did hold,
And he should not awake it, passed them through
Into a freer space; yet nought he knew
Why he was thither come, or where to turn,
Or why the heart within him so did burn.

viii. k 1   129

wind is light, the wind picks up, night falls, day breaks, the keels sweep forward and make small way.

Habundimagination: the experience of living things, generation upon generation, is defined in *The Earthly Paradise* by three conditions: it is a matter of bodies only, of Things free from abstract valuation; it is a matter of "profusion, but never intensity," an abundance of Things without salience; it is a matter of process, a dynamic rather than static totality. A procession of bodies in profusion: the transcendentalism of the Habundian is a transcendence of the personal, a vision intrinsically collective.

According to Yeats the Habundian is an imagination given over to pleasure, to an apprehension of "the pleasant things of the world," and an imagination from which we are dislocated—each of its conditions thus defined negatively in terms of what it is not. It is Habundia who speaks for "the free play of sensual, particularly sexual, energy" in Morris's work: the counterforce of desire against the abstractions and alienations of the Administered World. (Jameson, *Marxism and Form* [1971]: "The abstract and the alienated, no doubt, name the same object.") Habundia, or the shadow, at least, of her Green Tree, speaks, in Marcuse's terms, "a critique of the established reality principle in the name of the pleasure principle—a re-evaluation of the antagonistic relation that has prevailed between the two dimensions of the human existence." "Here, eternity is reclaimed for the fair earth—as the eternal return of its children, of the lily and the rose, of the sun on the mountains and lakes, of the lover and the beloved, of the fear for their life, of pain and happiness. Death *is;* it is conquered only if it is followed by the real rebirth of everything that was before death here on earth—not as a mere repetition but as willed and wanted re-creation."[12]

In the name of the pleasure principle: all of the tales in *The Earthly Paradise* of course are concerned precisely with the pursuit of Eros unmixed with Death, with the necessary failure of this pursuit, and with the machinations of a human world in which this failure is determined. "Atalanta's Race," "The Doom of King Acrisius" (with Burne-Jones' extraordinary illustration of Perseus freeing Andromeda from the sea monster), "The Story of Cupid and Psyche," "The Love of Alcestis," "Pygmalion and the Image," "The Death of Paris," "The Story of Accontius and Cydippe," "The Story of Rhodope," "The Golden Apples": among the Greek tales, these all concern the attainment of a state of erotic delight, and the estrangement of this state from our normal experience (requiring supernatural interventions and/or utter defeat). The remaining Greek tales—"The Son of Croesus," "Bellerophon at Argos," and "Bellerophon in Lycia"—live more wholly in the world estranged from that desire, a

Then through the wood he went on, and for long
Heard but the murmur of the prisoned breeze,
Or overhead the wandering wood-dove's song;
But whiles amid the dusk of far-off trees
He deemed he saw swift-flitting images,
That made him strive in vain to call to mind
Old stories of the days now left behind.

Slowly he went, and ever looking round
With doubtful eyes, until he heard at last
Across the fitful murmur of dumb sound,
Far off and faint, the sound of singing cast
Upon the lonely air; the sound went past,
And on the moaning wind died soft away;
But, as far thunder startles new-born day,

So was his dream astonied therewithal,
And his lips strove with some forgotten name,
And on his heart strange discontent did fall,
And wild desire o'ersweet therefrom did flame;
And then again adown the wind there came
That sound grown louder; then his feet he stayed
And listened eager, joyous, and afraid.

Again it died away, and rose again,
And sank and swelled, and sweeter and stronger grew,
Wrapping his heart in waves of joy and pain,
Until at last so near his ears it drew
That very words amid its notes he knew,
And stretched his arms abroad to meet the bliss,
Unnamed indeed as yet, but surely his.

130

world of political struggle for Bellerophon and of Death (the reversal of generation) for Croesus and his son. The Wanderers' tales are similarly divided into visions of erotic states prohibited and desperate, preconscious desires to get there—"The Writing on the Image," "The Lady of the Land," "The Watching of the Falcon," "Ogier the Dane," "The Land East of the Sun and West of the Moon," "The Man Who Never Laughed Again," "The Lovers of Gudrun," "The Fostering of Aslaug," "The Ring Given to Venus," "The Hill of Venus"—and tales, like "The Man Born to Be King" and "The Proud King," of a world consumed by other desires, a world in which the erotic is not only unattainable but unimaginable.

At the same time, although the idle singer is not Psyche longing for Cupid, in spite of the fact that no dragon will metamorphose into a woman at his kiss, nor goddess forgive him and heal his mortal wound—despite the fact, in other words, that his possibilities as a man of the nineteenth century are severely limited—Morris's figure itself nevertheless embodies the same erotic dream. The "shadowy isle of bliss" he builds can only be a book, unsubstantial as visions of paradise go, and seemingly small comfort, but in its own fashion speaks in the name of the pleasure principle, in the shadow of its Green Tree.

The Imagination of Love as an imagination of the wholly encompassing is a matter of more than tales, which are themselves but grains in the whole. *The Earthly Paradise* is a gathering of tales, but it is also a "sweet voice" which itself embodies the aesthetic of mere abundance as fully as, for instance, the figure of Alcestis does for Yeats. The words themselves are matters unforgot, despite their immateriality, their "mistiness of . . . feeling and . . . vagueness of . . . object," nevertheless themselves available to sensation.

Not for Nought

Naturally mimesis here has nothing to do with the mere imitation of something that is already familiar to us. Rather, it implies that something is represented in such a way that it is actually present in sensuous abundance.

—GADAMER

T. Earle Welby, *The Victorian Romantics* (1929): "The craftsmanship [of Morris's verse] is, in its sort, perfect, with an instinctive subdual of the separate line lest it should stand out excessively in the pattern. But this is not, in the full sense, creation; it is the leisurely, unemphatic display of figures no more real than those on tapestry." This "instinctive subdual" is

EFORE our lady came on earth
Little there was of joy or mirth;
About the borders of the sea
The sea-folk wandered heavily;
About the wintry river-side
The weary fishers would abide.

Alone within the weaving-room
The girls would sit before the loom,
And sing no song, and play no play;
Alone from dawn to hot mid-day,
From mid-day unto evening,
The men afield would work, nor sing,
Mid weary thoughts of man and God,
Before thy feet the wet ways trod.

Unkissed the merchant bore his care,
Unkissed the knights went out to war,
Unkissed the mariner came home,
Unkissed the minstrel men did roam.

Or in the stream the maids would stare,
Nor know why they were made so fair;
Their yellow locks, their bosoms white,
Their limbs well wrought for all delight,
Seemed foolish things that waited death,
As hopeless as the flowers beneath
The weariness of unkissed feet:
No life was bitter then, or sweet.

Therefore, O Venus, well may we
Praise the green ridges of the sea
O'er which, upon a happy day,
Thou cam'st to take our shame away.

the mark of both complicity and resistance, the effacement of each Thing under the force of totality, and paradoxically within that effacement the insistence of presence, the presence of that which is effaced. Jameson: "The consumer's society, the society of abundance, has lost the experience of negation in all its forms," but "it is . . . the negative alone which is ultimately fructifying from a cultural as well as an individual point of view. . . . a genuinely human existence can only be achieved through the process of negation."[13]

Both in its approach to the material particularity of the world and in its commitment to a unifying order, its cyclical paradigm of repletion, decline, and regeneration, the Habundian conceit mirrors the conditions against which it offers resistance, incorporates to negate them. This is why the poem's own death—its virtual disappearance from readership—is its strongest claim to our attention. The Paradise is, in Adorno's terms, a "sacrifice to the Moloch of the present; because, in the latter's realm, there can be no good, it makes itself bad, in order in its defeat to convict the judge": "Even its own impossibility it must at least comprehend for the sake of the possible." No poem, in other words, which is not "bad," no resistance which is not "impossible," can have taken adequate measure of the forces arrayed against and introjected within it, the forces that deny its own possibility. Jameson: "The profound vocation of the work of art in a commodity society: *not* to be a commodity, *not* to be consumed, to be *unpleasurable* in the commodity sense."[14]

At the same time, as those dialecticians of defeat the Wanderers instruct us, this condition of utter estrangement, once it is recognized and given form, generates its own negation. As the Wanderers discover a Habundian paradise in their bondage to the earth they sought to escape, readers of Morris's poem are offered an experience in which the impossibility of escape, of amnesia and of memory alike, embodies the desire for what is lost.

Thus what is lost is what is found, what is found lost: "Every perception of a given experience or work is at the same time an awareness of what that experience or work is not." The body unbodied, the Thing dematerialized, discovers its own self in negativity. Morris's poetic strategy here represents a challenge to the whole tradition of classical philosophy, the very foundation upon which the Transcendental Idealism of Romanticism rests. Jameson, on Lukács's response to Kant, makes the point clear:

> According to Kant, the mind can understand everything about external reality except the incomprehensible and contingent fact of its existence in the first place: it can deal exhaustively with

Well may we praise the curdling foam
Amidst the which thy feet did bloom,
Flowers of the gods; the yellow sand
They kissed atwixt the sea and land;
The bee-beset ripe-seeded grass,
Through which thy fine limbs first did pass;
The purple-dusted butterfly,
First blown against thy quivering thigh;
The first red rose that touched thy side,
And overblown and fainting died;
The flickering of the orange shade,
Where first in sleep thy limbs were laid;
The happy day's sweet life and death,
Whose air first caught thy balmy breath.
Yea, all these things well praised may be,
But with what words shall we praise thee,
O Venus, O thou love alive,
Born to give peace to souls that strive?

Louder the song had grown to its last word,
And with its growth grew odours strange and sweet,
And therewithal a rustling noise he heard,
As though soft raiment the soft air did meet,
And through the wood the sound of many feet,
Until its dusk was peopled with a throng
Of fair folk fallen silent after song.

Softly they flowed across his glimmering way,
Young men and girls thin-clad and garlanded,
Too full of love a word of speech to say
Except in song; head leaning unto head,

its own perceptions of reality without ever being able to come to terms with noumena, or things-in-themselves. For Lukács, however, this dilemma of classical philosophy, to which Kant's system is a monument, derives from an even more fundamental, prephilosophical attitude toward the world which is ultimately socio-economic in character: namely, from the tendency of the middle classes to understand our relationship to external objects . . . in static and contemplative fashion. It is as though our primary relationship to the things of the outside world were not one of making or use, but rather that of a motionless gaze, in a moment of time suspended, across a gap which it subsequently becomes impossible for thought to bridge. The dilemma of the thing-in-itself becomes, then, a kind of optical illusion or false problem, a kind of distorted reflection of this initially immobile situation which is the priveleged moment of middle class knowledge.[15]

Things in themselves, in other words, cannot be apprehended but only engaged: an experience of pure motion, noumena realized in a Habundian relinquishment.

The verse of *The Earthly Paradise* is the voice of this paradoxical engagement, composed of Things in a steady stream within which they disappear to find themselves nothing *but* themselves. Jameson: "In the commercial universe of late capitalism the serious writer is obliged to reawaken the reader's numbed sense of the concrete through the administration of linguistic shocks . . . as if, in this state of pathological hebetude and insensibility, only the painful remained as a spur to perception." Yeats: "Instead of the language of Chaucer and Shakespeare, its warp fresh from field and market—if the woof were learned—[Morris's] age offered him a speech, exhausted from abstraction, that only returned to its full vitality when written learnedly and slowly."[16] The language of the Paradise marks a rejection of these conditions: the tales are like stories for children, narrated as if the things in them were altogether familiar (not to be invested with interest by linguistic ingenuity) and at the same time open to virtually endless fleshing out in the listener's ear. It is a language conceived in the name of nothing but (a reduced and barely conceivable dream of) pleasure.

For Wordsworth, "this necessity of producing immediate pleasure" "is a homage paid to the native and naked dignity of man, to the grand elemen-

As in a field the poppies white and red;
Hand warm with hand, as faint wild rose with rose,
Mid still abundance of a summer close.

Softly they passed, and if not swiftly, still
So many, and in such a gliding wise,
That, though their beauty all his heart did fill
With hope and eagerness, scarce might his eyes,
Caught in the tangle of their first surprise,
Note mid the throng fair face, or form, or limb,
Ere all amid the far dusk had grown dim.

A while, indeed, the wood might seem more sweet,
That there had been the passionate eyes of them
Wandering from tree to tree loved eyes to meet;
That o'erblown flower, or heavy-laden stem
Lay scattered, languid 'neath the delicate hem
That kissed the feet moving with love's unrest,
Though love was nigh them, to some dreamed-of best.

A little while, then on his way he went,
With all that company now quite forgot,
But unforgot the name their lips had sent
Adown the wave of song; his heart waxed hot
With a new thought of life, remembered not,
Save as a waste passed through with loathing sore
Unto a life which, if he gained no more

Than this desire, lonely, unsatisfied,
This name of one unknown, unseen, was bliss;
And if this strange world were not all too wide,

viii. k 3

tary principle of pleasure, by which he knows, and feels, and lives, and moves. We have no sympathy but what is propagated by pleasure." This "grand elementary principle" is fundamental to "metrical arrangement" which is a matter of "small but continual and regular impulses of pleasurable surprise."[17] A regular surprise: pleasure thus self-contradicted exists in a reduced state, but its potential as a wholly encompassing experience persists in regular continuity, the surprise of the normal, "the native and naked" redeemed from home exile.

The impulses of the Paradise are arranged, essentially, in couplets, either tetrameter or pentameter, the rhyme royale pattern of seven-line pentameter stanzas (with a rhyme scheme: *a b a b b c c*) a variation of the form. The arrangement of these three forms—tetrameters, pentameters, rhyme royale—makes a pattern itself sensible to small but continuous and regular surprise. Ten of the twenty-four tales are in rhyme royale, and seven each in tetrameter and pentameter, seasonally arranged. The opening and closing seasons bring two tales each in rhyme royale, the middle seasons three each. Tetrameter couplets appear twice each season except Summer, when they appear once; pentameter couplets appear twice each season except Fall, when they appear once. The distribution of these forms is further arranged so that the movement from one form to another establishes additional patterns—although *establishes* may be too strong a word for a phenomenon so shadowy, and occurring on a scale too distended for ready apprehension. The poem's whole year of verse forms (rhyme royale, tetrameters, and pentameters) may be represented thus:

Spring:	RR	T	P	RR	P	T
Summer:	P	RR	RR	T	RR	P
Fall:	RR	T	T	RR	RR	P
Winter:	RR	T	P	T	P	RR

Spring brings us first each of the three forms in succession, then repeats the pattern, only reversing the position of the last two so that where tetrameters preceded pentameters now pentameters precede tetrameters. Summer maintains the interplay of expectation and variation, beginning not with rhyme royale as we might expect but with pentamenters, and then returning twice to rhyme royale—the first instance of consecutive tales in the same form—before returning again to tetrameters, and interposing yet another tale in rhyme royale before returning at last to pentameters, completing the loop of the season. This Summer pattern Fall repeats

But he some day might touch her hand with his,
And turn away from that ungranted kiss
Not all unpitied, nor unhappy quite,
What better knew the lost world of delight?

Now, while he thought these things, and had small heed
Of what was round him, changed the place was grown
Like to a tree-set garden, that no weed,
Nor winter, or decay had ever known;
No longer now complained the dove alone
Over his head, but with unwearying voice
'Twixt leaf and blossom did the birds rejoice.

No longer strove the sun and wind in vain
To reach the earth, but bright and fresh they played
About the flowers of a wide-stretching plain,
Where 'twixt the soft sun and the flickering shade
There went a many wild things, unafraid
Each of the other or of the wanderer,
Yea, even when his bright arms drew anear.

And through the plain a little stream there wound,
And far o'er all there rose up mountains grey,
That never so much did the place surround,
But ever through their midmost seemed a way
To whatsoe'er of lovely through them lay.
But still no folk saw Walter; nay, nor knew
If those were dreams who passed the wild wood through.

But on he passed, and now his dream to prove
Plucked down an odorous fruit from overhead,
Opened its purple heart and ate thereof;

134

initially, replacing pentameters with rhyme royale in the first tale, and replacing rhyme royale with tetrameters in the next two; but following the logic of the previous season, when we would expect pentameters in the fourth Fall tale we find rhyme royale instead. In Winter as in Spring the form changes steadily from tale to tale and the pattern of the forms doubles back on itself in conceivably endless replication. Thus the year begins again in endless chain of changeless change.

The Apology that begins the poem, the Envoi that ends it, and the monthly lyrics that preface each pair of tales throughout the year, are all in rhyme royale. The Prologue and Epilogue to the tales, as well as the bits of linking verse that precede and follow each individual tale, are in pentameter couplets, as is The Author to the Reader (which functions, really, as the linking verse between the Wanderers' tale and the rest). Thus the seasonal development of the poem's formal pattern meets the conditions Wordsworth sets for the metrical production of pleasure: the formal variations that constitute and enwrap the Paradise are arranged as any metrics to embody "small but continual and regular impulses of pleasurable surprise" on a grand scale. (An earthly paradox: small on a grand scale, a pattern barely perceptible, a vague wash, and thoroughly encompassing.) The rhyming of forms, each tale in each form echoing the others in that form, and the regularized return of the forms, make the poem's very architecture metrical. The couplets twos, the tales in each month two, the forms of the tales three, the months in each season three, the bits of linking verse each month four, the seasons four: the Paradise is inescapably time and place and number.

The pleasure produced by the architectural metrics of *The Earthly Paradise* is determined, according to Wordsworth's terms, by the poem's pattern of regularities and variations, of order and surprise: for Morris, here as always, this order is not rigid but organic, not a rational abstraction but a Habundian dream. (Or more precisely, a Habundian dream in dialectical tension with rational abstraction, the seamless flow of changing weather against the organization of seasons into four, months into twelve, hours of folly measured against hours of wisdom.) The regularities in the pattern of formal variation from tale to tale are consistently irregular, the variations virtually uniform: the Paradise grows in space and time as a tree does.

The same pattern of patterns can be observed at the micrometric as at the macrometric level. If we compare Morris's couplets to those of other masters of the form, certain distinctive features are immediately apparent. For example, in the opening five stanzas (35 lines) of "Atalanta's Race" (the

Then, where a path of wondrous blossoms led,
Beset with lilies and with roses red,
Went to the stream, and felt its ripples cold,
As through a shallow, strewn with very gold

For pebbles, slow he waded: still no stay
He made, but wandered toward the hills; no fear
And scarce a pain upon his heart did weigh;
Only a longing made his life more dear,
A longing for a joy that drew anear;
And well-nigh now his heart seemed satisfied,
So only in one place he should not bide.

And so he ever wandered on and on,
Till clearer grew the pass 'twixt hill and hill;
Lengthened the shadows, sank adown the sun,
As though in that dull world he journeyed still
Where all day long men labour, night to fill
With dreams of toil and trouble, and arise
To find the daylight cold to hopeless eyes.

Some vague thought of that world was in his heart,
As, meeting sunset and grey moonrise there,
He came unto the strait vale that did part
Hill-side from hill-side; through the golden air,
Far off, there lay another valley fair;
Red with the sunset ran the little stream:
Ah me! in such a place, amidst a dream,

Two sundered lovers, each of each forgiven,
All things known, all things past away, might meet:
Such place, such time, as the one dream of heaven,
     viii. k 4

first tale in rhyme royale), we find nine lines with full endstops (periods, colons, or semicolons); in the first 36 lines of "The Man Born to Be King" (the first tale in tetrameter couplets) nine lines with full endstops; and in "The Doom of King Acrisius" (the first tale in pentameter couplets) nine lines with full endstops: in other words, 25 percent in each case, and in each case irregularly distributed. Dryden's "Absalom and Achitophel," by comparison, contains 18 lines with full endstops out of the first 36, for the most part coming in every other line; Pope's "An Essay on Man," 16 lines with full endstops out of the first 36, distributed as in Dryden; and Crabbe's "The Village," 16 lines with full endstops out of the first 36, again similarly distributed: in each case a proportion closer to 50 percent.

Couplets, by definition, are the most tightly rationalized of all verse forms: the perception of order imposed upon the lines by the steady succession of end-rhymes is relentless and immediate. The punctuation of Dryden's and Pope's and Crabbe's couplets accentuates the order imposed by the rhyme, enforcing a great system of containment. But Morris's couplets, unlike Dryden's or Pope's or Crabbe's, efface themselves, embodying patterns of sinuous continuity rather than closure. They are punctuated in such a way as to undermine the order that the form embodies as a given.

The patterns of Morris's verse are Habundian patterns (they resemble his designs for paper or chintz): changelessly changing impulses of profusion, their stops as often barely noticeable as not. Another embodiment of the dialectical tension at the heart of all Morris's work: to speak of Habundian couplets is to speak of contradiction, of paradisiacal earth, of the negation of administration. To speak in the name of the pleasure principle in subjection to and subversion of the reality principle (embodied in this case by the reality of endstops), "the system's claim to totality, which would suffer nothing to remain outside it."[18]

Morris's couplets destroy themselves from within: they posit an unwavering order, and without escaping that order they deny it, engaging us yet again in the experience of a totalizing system and its negation.

The Habundian imagination is an extreme response to "a situation where subjective and objective have begun to split apart," as Jameson puts it, and his remarks on *Ulysses* apply equally to *The Earthly Paradise*: "The literary materials lead a double life on two separate levels, that of empirical existence and that of a total relational scheme . . . where each empirical fact is integrated into the whole." The architecture of the idle singer's couplets and the pattern of formal variation from tale to tale embody the

Midst a vain life of nought. With faltering feet
He stayed a while, for all grew over-sweet;
He hid his eyes, lest day should come again
As in such dream, and make all blank and vain.

He trembled as the wind came up the pass;
Was it long time 'twixt breath and breath thereof?
Did the shade creep slow o'er the flower-strewn grass?
Was it a long time that he might not move,
Lest morn should bring the world and slay his love?
Surely the sun had set, the stream was still,
The wind had sunk adown behind the hill.

Nay, through his fingers the red sun did gleam;
In cadence with his heart's swift beating now
Beat the fresh wind, and fell adown the stream.
Then from his eyes his hands fell, and e'en so
The blissful knowledge on his soul did grow
That she was there, her speech as his speech, stilled
By very love, with love of him fulfilled.

O close, O close there, in the hill's grey shade,
She stood before him, with her wondrous eyes
Fixed full on his! All thought in him did fade
Into the bliss that knoweth not surprise,
Into the life that hath no memories,
No hope and fear; the life of all desire,
Whose fear is death, whose hope consuming fire.

Naked, alone, unsmiling, there she stood,
No cloud to raise her from the earth; her feet
Touching the grass that his touched, and her blood

dream of Habundia's kin. This is a dream of the body's presence discovered in a state of estrangement to which it remains, unaccountably,
impervious: a dream of location in dislocation, of dislocation denied.
Habundia's kin are located in a dream of process, of "profusion, but never
intensity," of the death of Death, at once a dream of materiality, of Things
in themselves, the sensible world freed from transcendental abstraction
and even from language itself, and a dream of totalizing order in which all
particulars are equalized, interchangeable, particularity subdued. (Bloch:
"For in the long run, everything that meets us, everything we notice
particularly, is one and the same.")[19]

Present Sight

> Earth's voices as they are indeed.
> Well ye have helped me at my need.
>
> —MORRIS

An anonymous American reviewer of *The Earthly Paradise* in the *New
Englander* (1871):

> In an age like this, which has had so much to say about the mission
> of the poet as a teacher, a thinker, a prophet, an apostle of
> humanity, and so forth, it may seem strange to some to hear a
> considerable poet declaring frankly that his chief aim is to give
> pleasure; . . . what seems to place Mr. Morris in a peculiar posi-
> tion, is the close limitation to which he deliberately commits
> himself in his choice of subjects and means of treatment.
>
> . . . . .
>
> It is plain enough that Mr. Morris has little or no practical
> sympathy with any theories which represent it as their chief aim
> and peculiar glory to refer to something beyond themselves. On
> Mr. Morris, nature never makes an impression as she does on
> Wordsworth, for example, or on Shelley; nor to him does the
> aspiration of the artist appear the same thing it does to Mr.
> Browning. . . . Other poets have thought it enough for them
> often to ask no more of nature than the pleasure of the present
> sight, but none of them, not Chaucer, nor Wordsworth, nor
> Keats, nor Scott, nor Byron, seem ever able to avoid the intrusion
> of an emotion—communicating itself to the verse—which is
> strange to Mr. Morris; and for none of these—not even Words-

Throbbing as his throbbed through her bosom sweet;
Both hands held out a little, as to meet
His outstretched hands; her lips each touching each;
Praying for love of him, but without speech.

He fell not and he knelt not; life was strong
Within him at that moment; well he thought
That he should never die; all shame and wrong,
Time past and time to come, were all made nought;
As, springing forward, both her hands he caught;
And, even as the King of Love might kiss,
Felt her smooth cheek and pressed her lips with his.

What matter by what name of heaven or earth
Men called his love? Breathing and loving there
She stood, and clung to him; one love had birth
In their two hearts, he said; all things were fair,
Although no sunlight warmed the fresh grey air
As their lips sundered. Hand in hand they turned
From where no more the yellow blossoms burned.

Louder the stream was, fallen dead was the wind,
As up the vale they went into the night,
No rest but rest of utter love to find
Amidst the marvel of new-born delight;
And as her feet brushed through the dew, made white
By the high moon, he cried: For this, for this
God made the world, that I might feel thy kiss!

worth or Scott with all their fondness for details—was it ever possible to remain so long contented with the comparatively inferior portions of a landscape as Mr. Morris.

Morris's devotion to the pleasure principle here is embodied in "the close limitation to which he deliberately commits himself": "it is impossible not to see that after all it is under and because of these very limitations that he has been enabled to do some of his best work."[20] ("Pleasure originates in alienation.")[21] Monotone in pace and in principles of selection—in "means of treatment" and "choice of subject"—the Paradise resists certain modes of critical scrutiny prevalent for the Victorians as for us.

The *Edinburgh Review:* "The Arthur of Mr. Tennyson is manifestly the embodiment of the highest Christian chivalry, and the Prometheus of Shelley is the man who strives against injustice and wrong in all ages and in all countries; these poems may therefore be regarded from a point of view lofty and immutable. Mr. Morris's tales can be submitted to no such criticism." The *New Englander:* "Where Wordsworth notices that 'every flower enjoys the air it breathes,' Mr. Morris remarks that it is small and as 'red as blood,' or that it 'flames' in 'grey light,' or that it has a black or yellow centre and takes a certain curve in bending. To know such facts as these about flowers, and similar facts about all natural objects, is of more importance to his purpose than to be impressed with a belief that they are alive and enjoying the life they feel; and to the observation and report of such facts as these, accordingly it is his instinct and his habit to confine himself. . . . Of what Matthew Arnold calls 'the grand power of poetry, its interprative power,' there will be little if any manifestation."[22]

This is an antitranscendental, antihermeneutical poetry, unredeemed by either polysemy or compelling effects. It is also a poetry of redundancy, of profusion: again, both image of the productive splendor of capitalism and negation of its utilitarian ideology, what Ruskin calls "illth" an appropriation and perversion of Habundia's own grand power of endless propagation. Charles Eliot Norton: "There is scarcely a page that does not give a picture to the eye, and this becomes at once a merit and a defect, for in the limited compass of his story the variety of his pictures cannot be thus numerous without involving an occasional repetition, not of details, but of what, in the language of pictorial art, is called motive. Mr. Morris's landscapes have frequently, underlying their diversity of detail, a general similarity of outline and of tone; his descriptions of persons and incidents might here and there be interchanged without apparent discordance."[23] Maidens will crush blossoms under dainty foot in every case, and we are

The Hill
of Venus

 HAT, is the tale not ended then? Woe's me!
How many tales on earth have such an end:
I longed, I found, I lived long happily,
And fearless in death's fellowship did wend?
On earth, where hope is that two souls may
blend
That God has made; but she, who made her then
To be a curse unto the sons of men?

And yet a flawless life indeed that seemed
For a long while: as flowers, not made to die
Or sin, they were: no dream was ever dreamed,
How short soe'er, wherein more utterly
Was fear forgot or weariness worn by;
Wherein less thought of the world's woe and shame,
Of men's vain struggles, o'er the sweet rest came.

Men say he grew exceeding wise in love,
That all the beauty that the earth had known,
At least in seeming, would come back, and move
Betwixt the buds and blossoms overblown;
Till, turning round to that which was his own,
Blind would he grow with ecstasy of bliss,
And find unhoped-for joy in each new kiss.

Men say that every dear voice love has made
Throughout that love-filled loneliness would float,
And make the roses tremble in the shade
With unexpected sweetness of its note
Till he would turn unto her quivering throat,
And, deaf belike, would feel the wave of sound
From out her lips change all the air around.

138

not so much required even to "see" this as to move along, description's worth in pure motion. To "make sense" quite literally, rather than to "understand."

In a nineteenth-century poem of the fourteenth century, however, the notion of "present sight" is clearly problematic. The Paradise is distinguished, in the eyes of its first audience, by "the old unreflecting simplicity, the old ascendancy of the object over the subject," "entirely without self-consciousness, . . . an attitude differing as little as possible from that of Chaucer and the true medieval story-tellers"; "Mr. Morris . . . has given us an effectual antidote for the overwrought self-consciousness of this generation"; "It is Mr. Morris's happy and peculiar faculty to cast utterly aside the complex questionings that vex our modern poetry. He carries us away to the days when men lived their life without overmuch thinking about it." Faced with the happy prospect of such a trip, we might well ask what baggage we should be bringing along. If, indeed, "the pleasure of the present sight" is anomalous in the context of contemporary concerns—if "Mr. Morris has given the go-by to his age, and . . . has done wisely"—then he has done so in a manner that only a contemporary could fashion.[24]

Morris himself articulates the problem in his 1891 retrospective "Address on the Collection of Paintings of the English Pre-Raphaelite School": "Now I must say one word about the fact that both Rossetti and Burne-Jones have had very little to do with representing the scenes of ordinary modern life as they go on before your eyes. One has often heard that brought against the 'Romantic' artists, as a short-coming. Now, quite plainly, I must say that I think it *is* a shortcoming. But is the shortcoming due to the individual artist, or is it due to the public at large? for my part I think the latter. When an artist has really a very keen sense of beauty, I venture to think that he cannot literally represent an event that takes place in modern life. . . . That is not only the case with pictures, if you please: it is the case also in literature." In other words, "the pleasure of the present sight," as Morris enjoys it, represents not "the old ascendancy of the object over the subject" but a new ascendancy, wrested from the context of "the ugliness and sordidness of the surroundings of life in our generation."[25] Thus, what is present to sight will be by definition *not* present to sight: an illusion of presence that bears within it a revelation of absence.

The Chaucerian model provides a template against which the difference may be read. Swinburne begins his review of *The Life and Death of Jason* by noting how "it resembles the work of Chaucer" in its "direct

Men say he saw the lovers of old time;
That ORPHEUS led in his EURYDICE,
Crooning o'er snatches of forgotten rhyme,
That once had striven against eternity,
And only failed, as all love fails, to see
Desire grow into perfect joy, to make
A lonely heaven for one beloved's sake.

THISBE he saw, her wide white bosom bare;
Thereon instead of blood the mulberries' stain;
And single-hearted PYRAMUS anear
Held in his hand tufts of the lion's mane,
And the grey blade that stilled their longings vain
Smote down the daisies. Changeless earth and old,
Surely thy heart amid thy flowers is cold!

HELEN he saw move slow across the sward,
Until before the feet of her she stood
Who gave her, a bright bane and sad reward,
Unto the PARIS that her hand yet wooed:
Trembled her lips now, and the shame-stirred blood
Flushed her smooth cheek; but hard he gazed, and
yearned
Unto the torch that Troy and him had burned.

Then ARIADNE came, her raiment wet
From out the sea; to her a prison wall,
A highway to the love she could not get.
Then upon PHYLLIS' ivory cheeks did fall
The almond-blossoms. Then, black-haired and tall,
Came DIDO, with her slender fingers laid
On the thin edge of that so bitter blade.

139

narrative power, in clear forthright manner of procedure, not seemingly troubled to select, to pick and sift and winnow, yet never superfluous or verbose, never straggling or jarring:" " 'But,' it is said, 'this sort of poetry is a March flower, a child of the first winds and suns of a nation; in May even, much more in August, you cannot have it except by forcing; and forcing it will not bear. A late romance is a hothouse daffodil.' And so indeed it must usually be. But so it is not here; and the proof is the poem. It could not be done, no doubt, only it has been. Here is a poem sown of itself, sprung from no alien seed, cut after no alien model."[26] By a kind of parthenogenesis, the Habundian impulse operates here under the most restricted conditions, overleaping impossibility.

The object of Morris's pleasure is a freakish bloom, out of season, forced, unbearable; and Swinburne, in his rapture of critical sympathy, has eyes only for it: he does not see the hothouse for the daffodil, a victim, perhaps, of his own rhetoric. His subject here is Medea: "For dramatic invention and vivid realism of the impossible, which turns to fair and sensible truth the wildest dreams of legend, there has been no poet for centuries comparable. But the very flower and crest of this noble poem is the final tragedy at Corinth. Queen, sorceress, saviour, she has shrunk or risen to mere woman; and not in vain before entering the tragic lists has the poet called on that great poet's memory who has dealt with the terrible and the pitiful passion of women like none but Shakespeare since." Swinburne then quotes the following passage:

> Would that I
> Had but some portion of that mastery
> That from the rose-hung lanes of woody Kent
> Through these five hundred years such songs have sent
> To us, who, meshed within this smoky net
> Of unrejoicing labour, love them yet.
> And thou, O Master!—Yea, my Master still,
> Whatever feet have scaled Parnassus' hill,
> Since like thy measures, clear, and sweet, and strong,
> Thames' stream scarce fettered bore the bream along
> Unto the bastioned bridge, his only chain—
> O Master, pardon me, if yet in vain
> Thou art my Master, and I fail to bring
> Before men's eyes the image of the thing
> My heart is filled with: thou whose dreamy eyes
> Beheld the flush of Cressid's cheek arise,

Then, what had happed? was the sun darker now?
Had the flowers shrunk, the warm breeze grown a-chill?
It may be; but his love therewith did grow,
And all his aching heart it seemed to fill
With such desire as knows no chain nor will:
Shoulder to shoulder quivering there they lay,
In a changed world that had not night nor day.

A loveless waste of ages seemed to part,
And through the cloven dullness BRYNHILD came,
Her left hand on the fire that was her heart,
That paled her cheeks and through her eyes did flame,
Her right hand holding SIGURD'S; for no shame
Was in his simple eyes, that saw the worth
So clearly now of all the perished earth.

Then suddenly outbroke the thrushes' sound,
The air grew fresh as after mid-spring showers,
And on the waves of soft wind flowing round
Came scent of apple-bloom and gilliflowers,
And all the world seemed in its morning hours,
And soft and dear were kisses, and the sight
Of eyes, and hands, and lips, and bosom white.

Yea, the earth seemed a-babbling of these twain,
TRISTRAM and YSEULT, as they lingered there,
All their life-days now nothing but a gain;
While death itself, wrapped in love's arms, must bear
Some blossoms grown from depths of all despair,
Some clinging, sweetest, bitterest kiss of all,
Before the dark upon their heads should fall.

140

As Troilus rode up the praising street,
As clearly as they saw thy townsmen meet
Those who in vineyards of Poictou withstood
The glittering horror of the steel-topped wood.

"Worthy, indeed," Swinburne adds, "even of the master-hand is all that follows."[27]

The citation is astutely chosen and reveals the idle singer at a singularly expansive, self-reflective moment. He notes the passage of "these five hundred years," and asks that we regard his devotion to Chaucer— "Yea, my Master still"—as somewhat anomalous: a hothouse passion, estranged from its source, from the earth and the sun. Here we are shown that what separates the idle singer from his master is more than a mood or a personal tendency but a specific deficiency: what Chaucer can do, what the idle singer doubts he can emulate, is "bring / Before men's eyes the image of the thing." This power presupposes both an object and an audience, and Chaucer's gift is seen in his relation to both: Chaucer's eyes are at once "dreamy" and unflinchingly present, their gaze effecting a unified vision of legendary past and strife-torn present, figured here in an extreme image of heroic romanticism over a thousand years old and an image out of social history experienced most directly. There is no disjunction in Chaucer's eye between legendary and social history, and no barrier between the poet and either his object or his audience.

Such a disjunction, however, is precisely what the idle singer elaborates throughout the apparatus of *The Earthly Paradise* and in the very texture of paradisiacal language. The unity *he* effects is one of absence, not presence. He is divided from his object by time, which "through these five hundred years" transforms "the rose-hung lanes of woody Kent" into a "smoky net / Of unrejoicing labour," driving the past into an ever more inaccessible dream state; and he is divided from his audience, his contemporary "townsmen," by his absorption in this dream, his alienation from all such matters as foreign wars or, as he puts it in the Apology, "the steely sea / . . . / Whose ravening monsters mighty men shall slay." Since he can see with confidence neither the life of his times nor the object of his dreams, he is unable, by his own definition, "to bring / Before men's eyes the image of the thing / My heart is filled with."

The idle singer's object, his collection of tales (faded petals of fantasy flowers), is thus circumscribed by three layers of distance: innermost of the frames is the linking verse which follows the Wanderers and their hosts throughout the year, beginning with the Prologue and ending with the

Others he saw, whose names could tell him nought The Hill
Of any tale they might have sorrowed through; of Venus
But their lips spake, when of their lives he sought,
And many a story from their hearts he drew,
Some sweet as any that old poets knew,
Some terrible as death, some strange and wild
As any dream that hath sad night beguiled.

But all with one accord, what else they said,
Would praise with eager words the Queen of Love;
Yet sometimes while they spake, as if with dread,
Would look askance adown the blossomed grove;
Till a strange pain within his heart would move,
And he would cling to her enfolding arm,
Trembling with joy to find her breast yet warm.

Then a great longing would there stir in him,
That all those kisses might not satisfy;
Dreams never dreamed before would gather dim
About his eyes, and trembling would he cry
To tell him how it was he should not die;
To tell him how it was that he alone
Should have a love all perfect and his own.

Ah me! with softest words her lips could make,
With touches worth a lifetime of delight,
Then would she soothe him, and his hand would take,
And lead him through all places fresh and bright,
And show him greater marvels of her might,
Till midst of smiles and joy he clean forgot
That she his passionate cry had answered not.

Epilogue; midmost are the monthly lyrics, Habundian meditations on the "changeless change of seasons passing by," the mutual interpenetration of persistence and evanescence; and outermost the Apology, The Author to the Reader, and the Envoi, in which the idle singer speaks in his own person. This complex mediation speaks of anything *but* "present sight."

The language itself of the Paradise is similarly dislocated, not only from the nineteenth century but from the fourteenth from which it is putatively drawn. The same *New Englander* review that notes Morris's narrow concern for "the pleasure of the present sight," notes that this pleasure is itself compromised by the poem's own historical situation: "Unskilled, he tells us, out of the discord and confusion of actual life to charm a music strong enough to over-power and reconcile it to itself, he deliberately withdraws into the 'sleepy region,' to which all the outer noises of the waking world, which hopes and fears and longs and seeks and suffers and enjoys and loses and despairs, come blended into a lulling, murmuring sound, whose origin is now half forgotten, and now only enough remembered 'to convey a melancholy into all his day;' a vague and voluptuous melancholy, which . . . is chiefly valued as a proof and portion of repose." "All the outer noises of the waking world" in effect define the acoustical space within which the idle singer shapes his non-Chaucerian sound, the hothouse for his daffodil: but like Wordsworth throwing "a certain colouring of imagination" over his material, in submerging the experience of "the waking world" within "a lulling, murmuring sound," it would seem that Morris takes his pleasure not in "present sight" but in a kind of blindness, in "rest and forgetfulness."[28] In the sleepy region is where you close your eyes.

The problematics of present sight: Morris's pictorialism works against the grain of an endemic sightlessness, as his memory works against the grain of amnesia, his escapism against a "totality which would suffer nothing to remain outside it." His lulling, murmuring sound is designed to obscure "the outer noises of the waking world" but does so only imperfectly: those noises are only "half forgotten" and "enough remembered 'to convey a melancholy into all his day.'" In the acoustical space of the hothouse, the presence of Morris's objects—his words, images, characters—is self-contradicted.

Paradise dislocated and the Habundian dream: Morris's people and Things are located always in relation to the whole, to the pattern, the moving Habundian totality, no Thing standing out enough to separate itself from the integral whole, no Thing stopping the process of the whole. (No

Forgot to-day, and many days maybe:
Yet many days such questions came again,
And he would ask: How do I better thee,
Who never knew'st a sorrow or a pain?
Folk on the earth fear they may love in vain,
Ere first they see the love in answering eyes,
And still from day to day fresh fear doth rise.

Unanswered and forgot! forgot to-day,
Because too close they clung for sight or sound;
But yet to-morrow: Changeless love, O say
Why, since love's grief on earth doth so abound,
No heart my heart that loveth so ere found
That needed me? for wilt thou say indeed
That thou, O perfect one, of me hast need?

Unanswered and forgot a little while;
Asked and unanswered many a time and oft;
Till something gleamed from out that marvellous smile,
And something moved within that bosom soft,
As though the God of Love had turned and scoffed
His worshipper, before his feet cast down
To tell of all things for his sake o'erthrown.

How many questions asked, nor answered aught;
How many longings met still by that same
Sweet face, by anguish never yet distraught,
Those limbs ne'er marred by any fear or shame;
How many times that dear rest o'er him came
And faded mid the fear that nought she knew
What bitter seed within his bosom grew?

142

Thing, therefore, denying Death: the *Paradise,* again, both image of the Capitalist order which denies Death, which fixates on Things uninte-grated and strives to stop Time—an idle song—and image of the Habun-dian alternative, a world in which the stoppage of Time and denial of Death is subsumed within process.) Becoming no-Things, the Things of the Paradise resist the alienated materiality of the Administered World and reaffirm the possibility of an alternative materiality: Things in themselves, Things freed even from language (that domesticating, appropriating, administering force), freed from salience (which is a kind of appropria-tion), from significance. The words of the Paradise don't refer in any elaborated way to Things, and the Things don't refer to meanings: the *whole* of the Paradise along with each of its parts "a free particular, a poetical gift, a grace note."

'Twixt lessening joy and gathering fear, grew thin The Hill
That lovely dream, and glimmered now through it of Venus
Gleams of the world cleft from him by his sin;
Hell's flames withal, heaven's glory, 'gan to flit
Athwart his eyes sometimes, as he did sit
Beside the Queen, in sleep's soft image laid;
And yet awhile the dreadful dawn was stayed.

And in that while two thoughts there stirred in him,
And this the first: Am I the only one
Whose eyes thy glorious kisses have made dim?
And what then with the others hast thou done?
Where is the sweetness of their sick love gone?
Ah me! her lips upon his lips were laid,
And yet awhile the dreadful dawn was stayed.

And in that while the second thought was this:
And if, wrapped in her love, I linger here
Till God's last justice endeth all our bliss,
Shall my eyes then, by hopeless pain made clear,
See that a vile dream my vain life held dear,
And I am lone? Ah, cheek to his cheek laid!
And yet awhile the dreadful dawn was stayed.

How long who knoweth? and be sure meanwhile,
That could man's heart imagine, man's tongue say,
The strange delights that did his heart beguile
Within that marvellous place from day to day,
Whoso might hearken should cast clean away
All thought of sin and shame, and laugh to scorn
The fear and hope of that delaying morn.

143

HABUNDIAN WORLD III
Gratified Despair

I go to seek if Love may yet be found
Within the arms of death.

—MORRIS

But the third thought at last, unnamed for long,
Bloomed, a weak flower of hope within his heart;
And by its side unrest grew bitter strong,
And, though his lips said not the word, Depart;
Yet would he murmur: Hopeless fair thou art!
Is there no love amid earth's sorrowing folk?
So glared the dreadful dawn, and thus it broke.

For on a night, amid the lily and rose,
Peaceful he woke from dreams of days bygone;
Peaceful at first; and, seeing her lying close
Beside him, had no memory of deeds done
Since long before that eve he rode alone
Amidst the wild wood; still awhile himseemed
That of that fair close, those white limbs he dreamed.

So there for long he lay in happy rest,
As one too full of peace to wish to wake
From dreams he knows are dreams. Upon her breast
The soft wind did the dewy rose-leaves shake;
From out a gleaming cloud the moon did break;
Till, mid her balmy sleep, toward him she turned,
And into his soul her touch his baseness burned.

Then fled all peace, as in a blaze of flame,
Rushed dreadful memory back; and therewithal,
Amid the thoughts that crowding o'er him came,
Clear vision of the end on him did fall;
Rose up against him a great fiery wall,
Built of vain longing and regret and fear,
Dull empty loneliness, and blank despair.

144

News from Nowhere

Inside the Double World
all voices become
eternally mild

—RILKE

The Habundian Imagination, although a conceit of the transhistorical, of an organic process of time beyond the orderly reach of human time, is nevertheless a function of human time. Pater, in his 1868 review of *The Earthly Paradise,* places this vision within its historical context. Suggesting that the air is thick with misreadings, he begins by defining what the Paradise is *not:* "This poetry is neither a mere reproduction of Greek or medieval life or poetry, nor a disguised reflex of modern sentiment. Greek poetry, medieval or modern poetry, projects above the realities of its time a world in which the forms of things are transfigured. Of that world this new poetry takes possession, and sublimates beyond it another still fainter and more spectral, which is literally an artificial or 'earthly paradise.' It is a finer ideal, extracted from what in relation to any actual world is already an ideal. Like some strange second flowering after date, it renews on a more delicate type the poetry of a past age, but must not be confounded with it."[1]

In Pater's formulation what Yeats calls "the pleasant things of the world" are figured as "the realities of [another] time," in either case a matter of what we can't, as a rule, get back to, which Morris's Art in general is a meditation upon. The Paradise is "a prolonged somnambulism," "the art of directing towards an imaginary object sentiments whose natural direction is towards objects of sense," "a love defined by the absence of the beloved, choosing to be without hope," "the love . . . for the chevalier who never comes, of the serf for the chatelaine, the rose for the nightingale, of Rudel for the lady of Tripoli." And although it is through this spectralization, this sublimation of the sublimation, that for Pater as for Yeats the world returns in Morris, "heard across so great a distance only as through some miraculous calm,"[2] what we hear here clearly is at least as much the distance of the object as the object itself.

Pater, his subject here *The Life and Death of Jason:* "In handling a

A little space in stony dread he lay,
Till something of a wretched hope at last
Amidst his tangled misery drave its way.
Slowly he rose, and, cold with terror, passed
Through blossomed boughs, whose leaves, upon him cast
As he brushed by, seemed full of life and sound,
Though noiselessly they fell upon the ground.

But soon he fled fast: and his goal he knew;
For each day's life once burdened with delight
Rose clear before him, as he hurried through
That lonely hell the grey moon yet made bright;
And midst them he remembered such a night
Of his first days there, when, hand locked in hand,
Sleepless with love, they wandered through the land;

And how, as thus they went, and as he thought
If he might still remember all her speech
Whatso fresh pleasure to him might be brought,
A grove of windless myrtles they did reach,
So dark, that closer they clung each to each,
As children might; and how the grove nigh done,
They came upon a cliff of smooth grey stone;

And how, because the moon shone thereabout
Betwixt the boughs grown thinner, he could see,
Gazing along her smooth white arm stretched out,
A cavern mid the cliff gape gloomily;
And how she said: Hither I guided thee,
To show thee the dark danger and the death,
But if thou have heed, of thy love and faith.

viii. I 1

subject of Greek legend, anything in the way of an actual revival must always be impossible. . . . The composite experience of all the ages is part of each one of us; to deduct from that experience, to obliterate any part of it, to come face to face with the people of a past age, as if the middle age, the Renaissance, the eighteenth century had not been, is as impossible as to become a little child, or enter again into the womb and be born. But though it is not possible to repress a single phase of that humanity, which, because we live and move and have our being in the life of humanity, makes us what we are; it is possible to isolate such a phase, to throw it into relief, to be divided against ourselves in zeal for it, as we may hark back to some choice space of our own individual life."

To "hark back" is not to live again but only to relive, to produce but "ghosts of passionate song," "aspiring to but never actually reaching [a past age's] way of conceiving life," Morris's project an embodiment of the disembodied, massively overdetermined, a proliferation of bodies and unbodies like a vision of Ezekiel's. And at the same time once again the very embodiment of this profoundly thwarted condition—the embodiment of this nightmare of dissociation—produces its own dialectical negation, the return of the repressed. For Pater this is not "a past age" but rather the sense of historical passage, human time itself made sensible, a Thing restored to sense, a thing to mind. Morris's paradisiacal language, that "finer ideal, extracted from what in relation to any actual world is already an ideal," embodies a vision of History from classical Greece to Victorian England by way of fourteenth-century Nowhere. Divided against itself in zeal, the Paradise conceives neither the fourteenth nor the nineteenth century but the dynamic passage from one to the other.[3]

Pater defines the relationships between the classical, medieval, and Renaissance periods specifically in terms of the status in each period of the "life of the senses," and the dynamic relation of each age to the conception of that life in ages previous. The Hellenism of the Paradise, "if not . . . the Hellenism of Homer, yet . . . that of the middle age, the Hellenism of Chaucer," synthesizes the three periods' relationships to the life of the senses, and exposes the dynamic of their relation. "It is precisely this effect, this grace of Hellenism relieved against the sorrow of the middle age, which forms the chief motive of *The Earthly Paradise*." The "medievalisms, delicate inconsistencies" of *Jason* (and by extension the whole Paradise) "bring into this white dawn thoughts of the delirious night just over, and make one's sense of relief deeper." "No writer on the Renais-

Ah me! the memory of the sunrise sweet
After that warning little understood,
When stole the golden sun unto her feet,
As she lay sleeping by the myrtle-wood,
Watched by his sleepless longing! O how good
Those days were! fool, go back, go back again;
Shalt thou have lived and wilt thou die in vain?

So cried he, knowing well now what it meant,
That long-passed warning; that there gaped the gate
Whereby lost souls back to the cold earth went:
Then through his soul there swept a rush of hate
'Gainst hope, that came so cruel and so late
To drive him forth from all the joys he knew,
Yet scarcely whispering why or whereunto.

Therewith he stayed: midst a bright mead he was,
Whose flowers across her feet full oft had met
While he beheld; a babbling stream did pass
Unto the flowery close that held her yet.
O bliss grown woe that he might ne'er forget!
But how shall he go back, just, e'en as now,
Oft, o'er again that bliss from him to throw?

He cried aloud with rage and misery,
But once again gat onward through the night;
Nought met him but the wind as he drew nigh
That myrtle-grove, black 'gainst the meadow bright;
Nought followed but the ghost of dead delight;
The boughs closed round him as still on he sped,
Half deeming that the world and he were dead.

146

sance has hitherto cared much for this exquisite early light of it. Afterwards the Renaissance takes its side, becomes exaggerated and facile."[4]

Morris of course shares this latter view of the development of the Renaissance, although he will not articulate it explicitly until he begins lecturing in the late 1870s. In *The Earthly Paradise* the progression from the life of the senses in Ancient Greece through the overwrought spiritualities of the middle age to the Hellenism of Chaucer, is embodied in the form of a parallel historical progression: from the Hellenism of Chaucer (or rather, the Customs Office work of Chaucer, "nigh the thronged wharf" inspecting "bills of lading") through the exaggerated and facile bloom and fester of the Renaissance to the snorting steam and piston stroke, the spreading of the hideous town of advanced Industrial Civilization, overhung with smoke.

Thus in the same way that the "return" in the "early light of the Renaissance" to "the earlier, more ancient life of the senses" is bound for its effect to the "delirious night" "of the middle age," Morris's Victorian return "under mixed lights . . . in mixed situations" to the Hellenism of Chaucer is bound for its effect to the "exaggerated and facile" culture of the Renaissance, the inheritance of which it proposes to deny (divided against itself) even as it incorporates it.[5] *The Earthly Paradise* thus bears a double relation to "that earlier return," Morris's relationship to the historical setting of his material both a sympathetic rendering and a redeployment of similar strategy on new historical terms, the fourteenth century as object and metaphor of his own great leap backward.

Chaucer divided against himself in zeal for ancient Greece, Morris against himself for the Hellenism of Chaucer, for Pater both figures represent the return of the repressed, the return of the life of the senses that Yeats has in mind when he speaks of Habundia's kin. Habundia is a metaphor for the life of the senses, the Habundian Imagination both a look backward and the harbinger of a new "white dawn," the "exquisite early light" of a future yet unimaginable.[6]

"The Wanderers" exists in two full drafts: the version published as prologue, written in the same pentameter couplets as many of the tales proper, and an earlier version, abandoned upon completion and published posthumously, in ballad quatrains more reminiscent of *The Defence of Guenevere and Other Poems*. Morris's revision is designed principally to embody the historical warp that Pater describes: specifically, the invention of the idle singer—who appears nowhere in the earlier version (henceforth "the

But when he came unto the open space,
Grey with the glimmer of the moon, he stayed
Breathless, and turned his white and quivering face
Back toward the spot where he had left her, laid
Beneath the rose-boughs by their flowers down-weighed,
As if he looked e'en yet to see her come
And lead him back unto her changeless home.

Nought saw he but the black boughs, and he cried:
No sign, no sign for all thy kisses past!
For all thy soft speech that hath lied and lied!
No help, no cry to come back? Ah, at last
I know that no real love from me I cast;
Nought but a dream; and that God knoweth too;
And no great gift He deems this deed I do.

O me! if thou across the night wouldst cry,
If through this dusky twilight of the moon
Thou wouldst glide past and sob a-going by,
Then would I turn and ask no greater boon
Of God, than here with thee to dwell alone,
And wait His day! but now, behold, I flee,
Lest thy kissed lips should speak but mocks to me!

But now I flee, lest God should leave us twain
Forgotten here when earth has passed away,
Nor think us worthy of more hell or pain
Than such a never-ending, hopeless day!
No sign yet breaketh through the glimmering grey!
Nought have I, God, for thee to take or leave,
Unless this last faint hope thou wilt receive!

viii. I 2

ballad")—brings the Wanderers' quest into the nineteenth century. Their quest prefigures his, both based on an illusion of eternal youth and both realizing themselves in the end as a dilation upon Death. To the idle singer this means specifically the death of his tales—their idleness—the death of the hope of bliss, of escape to the past. The sea he sails fruitlessly is history. It is the idle singer, further, who conjurs a third quest, identified with his own, which is the reader's. For the reader too encounters Death at every turn, fleeing "the spreading of the hideous town" as the Wanderers flee the plague, and discovering no escape but a book of tales "living not," no return to the past but a doomed abdication of the present. And within this thwarted gesture, if anywhere, we are to seek our regeneration. All three quests are doomed to paradox—the death of Death is nothing other—and all three find in their failure the boundaries of their heroes' pleasure, the limits of the possible. It is the business of Morris's revision to define these boundaries as they are historically determined.

The ballad presents itself as a raw object, as if delivered from within its fourteenth-century world, rather than projected back, as if an ancient poem, speaking mute distance. It begins:

> Oho! Oho! whence came ye, Sirs,
> Drifted to usward in such guise,
> In ship unfit for mariners,
> Such heavy sorrow in your eyes?[7]

Whence, indeed, to usward? The ballad is upon us with no word of introduction but a prelinguistic exclamation, its bald archaism apparent from the start. This poem is a mock found object, dependent for its impetus upon the dramatic and narrative conventions of oral culture: it wears the aspect of having sailed in from out of nowhere, with no purpose stated, as if, in effect, it speaks itself. As the finished prologue, with the frame tale it generates, is Morris's most extensive attack on the consciousness and voice of the contemporary idle singer, the ballad is his first research into the other end of the problem, an exploratory sounding out of the gone world. By no means an innocent object, the Paradise must nevertheless partake of innocence.

Like many Romantic revisions—like Coleridge adding marginal gloss to his "Rime of the Ancient Mariner" or Keats worrying "Hyperion" into "The Fall of Hyperion"—Morris's is centered around the problem of the historical imagination. When the quest begins, in the ballad, the

And with that word he rushed into the cave.
But when the depths of its chill dark he gained,
Turning he saw without the black boughs wave;
And oh, amidst them swayed her form unstained!
But as he moved to meet her, all things waned;
A void unfathomed caught him as he fell
Into a night whereof no tongue can tell.

INTO bright sun he woke up suddenly,
And sprang up like a man with foes beset
Amidst of sleep, and crying an old cry
Learned in the tilt-yard; blind & tottering yet,
He stretched his hand out, that a tree-trunk met
Dank with the dew of morn, & through his blood
A shiver ran, as hapless there he stood.

Until, though scarce remembering aught at all,
Clearly he saw the world and where he was;
For as he gazed around his eyes did fall
Upon a tree-encompassed plain of grass,
Through which anigh him did a fair stream pass.
He stood and looked, nor a long while did dare
To turn and see what lay behind him there.

At last he did turn, and the cave's mouth, black,
Threatening, and dreadful, close to him did see,
And thither now his first thought drove him back;
A blind hope mingled with the misery
That 'gan to close about him; and yet he
Had no will left to move his feet thereto.
Yea, vague that past joy seemed; yea, hardly true.

148

Wanderers are out to sea, and determine, rather casually, to seek further across the ocean for their wish fulfillment. We never see their native Norway except in flashes of regret or bitterness later on. In the revised prologue, the quest begins with the Wanderers at home, and their departure is linked to the "pestilence" that rages there. Similarly, in the ballad the quest is initiated by a sudden dream, while in the Prologue it grows slowly from the seeds of tales "E'en as the books at Micklegarth had told," and others "of the Kaiser Redbeard . . . / Who neither went to Heaven nor yet to Hell, / When from that fight upon the Asian plain / He vanished." These differences are emblematic of the historical orientations of the two versions. Where the Prologue is elaborated to mediate between the paradisiacal vision and the times of its envisioning, the rejected ballad makes no such gesture.

Within the ballad as well, individual episodes are presented in a relatively stark manner, in keeping with the thrust of the framing apparatus. As Jessie Kocmanova writes in *The Poetic Maturing of William Morris*: "It is an essence of the ballad form that it concentrates on the immediate action and emotion without explaining, motivating or judging. . . . The often weird and magic charm of the ballad lies precisely in this tension between the extreme vividness of the glimpses of life in action, and vagueness of cause and effect, of social orientation and conditioning."[8] This "essence of the ballad form" is the same quality attributed by Morris's contemporaries to the Paradise as a whole—that "old ascendancy of the object over the subject"—but looking at the two drafts of the Prologue we can see how this lost mode suffers a sea change on the way to resurrection.

In the ballad, for example, when The People of the Shore query the Wanderers as above, the Wanderers reply, and the People speak once more in conclusion. In the Prologue, the Elder of the City not only asks for the tale and responds in conclusion but interrupts three times along the way. The tale itself, that is, in the first version, is conceived as "immediate action," bound by before and after, and in the second it is subjected to interpolations that reflect upon questions precisely of explanation, motivation, and judgment. In other words, the revision of the Prologue incorporates a critical consciousness. We are introduced here to the Elder of the City in his extended function as audience surrogate, actively engaged in the tale's unfolding, interposing a distinct frame of reference, and responsible in part for the course of the tale's progress—a function elaborated further in the linking verse that frames each tale. Although contemporary reviews of the Paradise often praise its devotion to the transhistori-

Again he looked about: the sun was bright,
And leafless were the trees of that lone place,
Last seen by him amid the storm's wild light:
He passed his hand across his haggard face,
And touched his brow; and therefrom did he raise,
Unwittingly, a strange-wrought golden crown,
Mingled with roses, faded now and brown.

The cold March wind across his raiment ran
As his hand dropped, and the crown fell to earth;
An icy shiver caught the wretched man
As he beheld his raiment of such worth
For gems, that in strange places had their birth,
But frail as is the dragon-fly's fair wing
That down the July stream goes flickering.

Cold to the very bone, in that array
He hugged himself against the biting wind,
And toward the stream went slow upon his way;
Nor yet amidst the mazes of his mind
The whole tale of his misery might he find,
Though well he knew he was come back again
Unto a lost world fresh fulfilled of pain.

But ere he reached the rippling stony ford,
His right foot smote on something in the grass,
And, looking down, he saw a goodly sword,
Though rusted, tangled in the weeds it was;
Then to his heart did better memory pass,
And in one flash he saw that bygone night,
Big with its sudden hopes of strange delight.

viii. l 3

149

cal concrete, we can see here one instance of how, in Kocmanova's words, "the most striking aspect of the Prologue as finally published is its sense of the historic determination of character and outlook."[9]

E. P. Thompson's attack on the diction of *The Earthly Paradise* illuminates the same point, albeit inadvertently. His thrust is that Morris achieves "in these poems . . . a 'technical mastery' at odds with real poetic achievement." What concerns Thompson is precisely the artificiality of the idle singer's voice, the mark of his habitation of historical place and time. He quotes, for example, a passage from the ballad in which the Wanderers are surprised by a night attack; "thin verse," Thompson notes, but "still verse which can carry action: the sudden awakening is vividly shown—the sequence of events is clear—the confusion and impotence of the warriors at night presented with movement and conviction." In contrast the revised version, though as Thompson notes it "seems to scan all right," aims purely at a "static, ornamental effect." "The passage describes action," he writes, "it does not begin to evoke it." Thompson cites especially the line "And with good haste unto the hubbub went," asking "what line could with less conviction convey speed and confusion," and complains too that "in the press of imminent death the narrator can find time to note the conventional poetic beauties" of "the star-besprinkled sky." The pattern is pervasive, extending to every narrative nuance. Thompson notes that "in the first version of the Prologue, Morris described the ship of the Wanderers, when they first set out, as supplied with 'stockfish and salt-meat,' " but "in the published version it is [revised to] a 'fair long-ship' 'well-victualled,' " a substitution of the "picturesque" for "the sharp realistic detail." "The realism which was the very salt of Morris's youthful poetry," he concludes, "is deliberately abandoned."[10]

So it must be, and we need only ask what the weight of this deliberation reflects. Realism is abandoned because it would require the consideration of such phenomena as "six counties overhung with smoke," in which case there could be no beauty, in which case there could be no Art, realistic or otherwise. Art then, under these conditions, requires dream, and this is where Morris characteristically begins, both in many individual works and in his career as a whole. *The Defence of Guenevere* is not an example of realism, since it takes no account of the existing world: it represents, rather, pure dream, imagined objects presented *as if* real, with an effect of vivid weirdness. In *The Earthly Paradise* the claims of realism return: the dream is held hostage by the world it hopes to deny, and continues to deny even in its bondage. Thus we behold a thwarted dream

For, lo you, now his blanched and unused hand
Clutched the spoiled grip of his once trusty blade!
There, holding it point downward, did he stand,
Until he heard a cry, and from a glade
He saw a man come toward him; sore afraid
Of that new face he was, as a lone child
Of footsteps on a midnight road and wild.

There he stood still, and watched the man draw near;
A forester, who, gazing on him now,
Seemed for his part stayed by some sudden fear
That made him fit a shaft unto his bow,
As his scared heart wild tales to him did show
About that haunted hill-side and the cave,
And scarce he thought by flight his soul to save.

Now when he saw that, out into the stream
The knight strode, with a great and evil cry,
Since all men suddenly his foes did seem:
Then quailed the man, yet withal timidly
His bowstring drew, and close the shaft did fly
To Walter's ear, but the carle turned and fled,
E'en as he drew the bowstring to his head.

But the knight reached the other side, and stood
Staring with hopeless eyes through that cold day;
And nothing that he now might do seemed good:
Then muttered he: Why did I flee away?
My tears are frozen, and I cannot pray;
Nought have I, God, for thee to take or leave,
Unless that last faint hope thou didst receive.

and a thwarted realism, each powerful enough in its futility to sustain the standoff on a rather titanic scale. The two worlds are superimposed, a vision of "a flowery land, / Fair beyond words" illumined in "the spreading of the hideous town."

Thompson's reading of the poem's diction registers the strained effect of the idle singer's endeavor, the historical dissonance implicit in Morris's liquid murmur. If the invention of the idle singer means that we carry consciousness with us on the quest (which is what several heroes of the tales do, too, finding and losing paradise, returning compulsively to their lives in history), if he delivers the dream in a shroud of the contemporary mind, then the artificiality of his voice maintains an illusion of soaring that betrays, at every turn, its earthbound singer. When we hear, for instance, of "stockfish and salt-meat" we are liable to imagine ourselves vividly planted among sights and sounds of which we have no experience—tastes our mouths, perhaps, have never known; when we hear of a ship "well-victualled," in spite of the archaism, we are not likely to get the same impression. Rather, the revision suggests that we project an ancient world, and withholds the details with which we might substantiate it, in effect suspending us between two worlds. So too with regard to "And with good haste unto the hubbub went." The line precisely denies our engagement with the event, because our distance from the event precludes any such engagement, and because it is the business of the poem to embody this distance. In the retrospective scheme of the Paradise all action is finished action, dependent upon memory for a feeble immortality, and not to be experienced so much as yearned toward. The only bliss to be had is in the failure to experience what is desired, and in the inextinguishable force of that desire nonetheless, the "indescribable fascination" of the thwarted dream.[11] This is the Wanderers' plight, the lesson of their telling, and the definitive condition of their language.

The Prologue is, in effect, a translation of the ballad, the nineteenth century simultaneously negation and embodiment of the fourteenth. Walter Benjamin, "The Task of the Translator" (1923): "Is a translation meant for readers who do not understand the original? This would seem . . . to be the only conceivable reason for saying 'the same thing' repeatedly." The relation here between the translation and the original is that proposed by Henry James, in his review of *The Life and Death of Jason,* between the "artificial" "atmosphere of Grecian mythology" and "Mr. Morris's . . . modern and composite English," or, for that matter, between things-in-

But as he spake these words unwittingly,
He moaned; for once again the moonlit place
Where last he said them did he seem to see,
And in his heart such longing did that raise,
That a bright flush came o'er his haggard face
And round he turned unto the cliff once more,
And moved as if the stream he would cross o'er.

Who shall tell what thought stayed him? who shall tell
Why pale he grew? of what was he afraid,
As, turning, fast his hurried footsteps fell
On the wind-bitten blooms of spring delayed?
What hope his dull heart tore, as brown birds made
Clear song about the thicket's edge, when he
Rushed by their thorny haunts of melody?

Heavily now his feet, so well wont, trod
The blind ways of the wood, till it grew thin,
And through the beech-trunks the green sunlit sod
He saw again; and presently did win
Into another cleared space, hemmed within
A long loop of the stream, and midmost there
Stood the abode of some stout wood-dweller.

Now as he came anigher to the sun,
Upon his glittering, gauzy, strange array
The bough-flecked, dazzling light of mid-day shone,
And at the wood's edge made he sudden stay,
And, writhing, seemed as he would tear away
The bright curse from him, till he raised his face,
And knew the cottage midmost of the place:

viii. l 4   151

themselves and things in a state of estrangement. The one remakes the other, rendering it accessible to the degree that its elements are transformed. Hence, Benjamin reasons, "it is plausible that no translation, however good it may be, can have any significance as regards the original."[12] Translations, that is, are of necessity devoted so much to their own language that the original language all but disappears.

"Yet," Benjamin continues, "by virtue of its translatability the original is closely connected with the translation. . . . We may call this connection a natural one, or, more specifically, a vital connection. Just as the manifestations of life are intimately connected with the phenomenon of life without being of importance to it, a translation issues from the original—not so much from its life as from its afterlife. For a translation comes later than the original, and since important works of world literature never find their chosen translators at the time of their origin, their translation marks their stage of continued life." Matters unforgot: both the fourteenth century and the life of the senses—the originals of Morris's translation—represent the vital impulse of his work; and the effect of his work is to reveal the otherness of his own culture, which can reproduce these originals but never, itself, produce them.

> For in its afterlife—which could not be called that if it were not a transformation and a renewal of something living—the original undergoes a change. Even words with fixed meanings can undergo a maturing process. . . . Translation is so far removed from being the sterile equation between two dead languages that of all literary forms it is the one charged with the special mission of watching over the maturing process of the original language and the birth pangs of its own.
>
> Translation thus ultimately serves the purpose of expressing the central reciprocal relationship between languages. It cannot possibly reveal or establish this hidden relationship itself; but it can represent it by realizing it in embryonic or intensive form.[13]

What Benjamin is saying with regard to the function of translation is precisely what Pater and Thompson make clear with regard to Morris's work: that it is not a return to earlier experience (although that, in its desperation, is what it pretends to be) but rather a measure of "the maturing process" (or Death) of that experience, and that "the central reciprocal relationship" it expresses is not one of "equation" but rather one

The Hill
of Venus
Knew it, as one a-dying might behold
His cup, made joyous once with wine and glee,
Now brought unto him with its ruddy gold
Stained with the last sad potion scantily;
For he, a youth, in joyous company,
Maying or hunting, oft had wandered there,
When maiden's love first known was fresh and fair.

He moaned, and slowly made unto the door,
Where sat a woman spinning in the sun,
Who oft belike had seen him there before,
Among those bright folk not the dullest one;
But now when she had set her eyes upon
The wild thing hastening to her, for a space
She sat regarding him with scared white face;

But as he neared her, fell her rock adown.
She rose, and fled with mouth that would have cried
But for her terror. Then did Walter groan:
O wretched life! how well might I have died
Here, where I stand, on many a happy tide,
When folk fled not from me, nor knew me cursed,
And yet who knoweth that I know the worst?

Scarce formed upon his lips, the word Return
Rang in his heart once more; but a cold cloud
Of all despair, however he might yearn,
All pleasure of that bygone dream did shroud,
And hopes and fears, long smothered, now 'gan crowd
About his heart: nor might he rest in pain,
But needs must struggle on, howe'er in vain.

152

of dissociation. News from nowhere is news somewhere, and these two places are as far from one another as two places can be. The historical and linguistic dynamics of the Paradise, like the dynamics of its prosody and narratology, are an embodiment of nightmare, of submission to and exposure of the inescapable: an embodiment of the lineaments of gratified despair.

Glittering Plain

> Four seasons circle a square year.
> —HEJINIAN

But something else circles the seasons. It would be perhaps more precise to say that the seasons, themselves abstract human constructs, make four-square a phenomenon that is itself a circle, a phenomenon nameable only in the broadest terms as Life on Earth, the Creation, Space in Time: the seasons, like the months, represent an abstract order imposed upon a world in constant seamless Change, the division of the calendar year into four or twelve, Number mastering and estranging Time and Place. The idle singer's monthly lyrics embody the tension between this human backward-forward looking abstraction (generated by fear of Death borne of dislocation and anxiety which in turn feed the fear: "the system's claim to totality . . ."), and the immediate experience of moments. This experience is virtually inexpressible: to speak of moments, to speak at all, is to arrest the constant seamless weaving of Change (and to enter, instead, History), to dislocate from What Is. But "every perception of a given experience or work is at the same time an awareness of what that experience or work is not":[14] the singer's lyrics show the seasons month by month, as he says, but in showing them the verses also conjur an experience of Time that is beyond the comprehension of such calculations.

Apology:

> Folk say, a wizard to a northern king
> At Christmas-tide such wondrous things did show,
> That through one window men beheld the spring,
> And through another saw the summer glow,
> And through a third the fruited vines a-row,
> While still, unheard, but in its wonted way,
> Piped the drear wind of that December day.

Into the empty house he passed withal:
As in a dream the motes did dance and grow
Amidst the sun, that through the door did fall
Across its gloom, and on the board did show
A bag of silver pieces, many enow,
The goodman's market-silver; and a spear
New-shafted, bright, that lay athwart it there.

Brooding he stood, till in him purpose grew:
Unto the peasants' coffer, known of old,
He turned, and raised the lid, and from it drew
Raiment well worn by miles of wind-beat wold;
And, casting to the floor his gauzy gold,
Did on these things, scarce thinking in meanwhile
How he should deal with his life's new-born toil.

But now, being clad, he took the spear and purse,
And on the board his clothes begemmed he laid,
Half wondering would their wealth turn to a curse
As in the tales he once deemed vainly made
Of elves and such-like. Once again he weighed
The bright web in his hand, and a great flood
Of evil memories fevered all his blood,

Blinded his eyes, and wrung his heart full sore;
Yet grew his purpose among men to dwell,
He scarce knew why, nor said he any more
That word Return: perchance the threatened hell,
Disbelieved once, seemed all too possible
Amid this anguish, wherefrom if the grain
Of hope should fall, then hell would be a gain.

153

So with this Earthly Paradise it is,
If ye will read aright, and pardon me.

The manner in which the idle singer names the seasons here is telling. In the first place, it is not the seasons themselves but "wondrous things" that the wizard shows, the seasons from the start themselves abstractions, summaries, translations, or codifications of what is available to sensation. The seasons are what "men beheld" when faced with these things, but they represent a dangerously misleading way of thinking. Thus the only one the idle singer names is spring uncapitalized, the one closest in name to a description of the thing, the only season named concretely. It is not Summer that men "saw" but "the summer glow," a naming of an evanescence, a hot cooling, a momentary phenomenon that means summer but that is not itself summer, a concretion "that resists pure conceptualization."[15] Autumn and Winter are not named directly at all but imaged only, and their images things most passing, "fruited vines" and "drear wind" here and gone in spite of all endeavor to administer them: the vines "a-row" and the wintry wind named (if not under the dominion of) December, Christmas-tide.

The wizard of the idle singer's conceit, at any rate, does not show the Winter: the wind remains "unheard" though "in its wonted way" piping drear, while the wizard spins illusions of the times that are not. "So with this Earthly Paradise it is": Death and Change, though "unheard," in their wonted ways pipe drear, and the Presence of Things that are Not stands both as capitulation and radical alternative, shadowy isle in a steely beating sea.

The showing of the seasons ("month by month . . . / Some portion of the flowers") shows the poet at once dislocated from the movement of Creation, and imagining his loss. (Blake says that "the whole creation will be consumed, and appear infinite, and holy," and that "this will come to pass by an improvement of sensual enjoyment," by a return to measureless time.)[16] *The Earthly Paradise* is a year in the life: an order (of the calendar) imposed upon an order that will not be imposed upon and that sweeps all along with it, the order of things.

March: like every other month in its own way an image of the Paradise as a whole, in this case image of the climate of its inception. March, Spring, new life, is a "Slayer of the winter," like a righteous knight of the Good. The idle singer brings not peace but a sword: or the peace he brings is a declaration of war, a reclamation of the Life of Things. This is where the

He went his ways, and once more crossed the stream,
And hastened through the wood, that scantier grew,
Till from a low hill he could see the gleam
Of the great river that of old he knew,
Which drank the woodland stream: 'neath the light blue
Of the March sky, swirling and bright it ran,
A wonder and a tale to many a man.

He went on, wondering not; all tales were nought
Except his tale; with ruin of his own life,
To ruin the world's life, hopeful once, seemed brought;
The changing year seemed weary of the strife
Ever recurring, with all vain hope rife;
Earth, sky, and water seemed too weak and old
To gain a little rest from waste and cold.

He wondered not, and no pain smote on him,
Though from a green hill on the further side,
Above the green meads set with poplars slim,
A white wall, buttressed well, made girdle wide
To towers and roofs where yet his kin did bide:
His father's ancient house; yea, now he saw
His very pennon toward the river draw.

No pain these gave him, and no scorn withal
Of his old self; no rage that men were glad
And went their ways, whatso on him might fall;
For all seemed shadows to him, good or bad;
At most the raiment that his yearning clad,
Yearning made blind with misery, for more life,
If it might be, love yet should lead the strife.

year of the Paradise begins, athwart the calendar as it were, in the moment of its greatest illusion, a moment of hope in subversion. March arrives every year but the singer sounds surprised: "Art thou here again?" a faint gesture toward surprise, his conceit of a winter so total, so wonted, it can only seem to be the last, as if the earth's winter should follow the pattern of the seasons of civilization and promise final Death. Part of March's message is that of course it goes, by rights, the other way round, that human events move through seasons, cycles, of death and regeneration just as the earth does: a challenge to despair, to the finality of totality. (An illusion isn't necessarily false, it is only false in the current situation: the year as 'tis measured begins and ends in the season of Death.) March, this "first redresser of the winter's wrong," is a matter of negativities: "The bitter wind makes not thy victory vain, / Nor will we mock thee for thy faint blue sky"; it hardly *is* at all, a matter of "kindly days and dry," but it "make[s] . . . ready," it "bring'st . . . night." The idle singer, whose song this is, himself only expects a glimpse of a glimpse of what comes— "though I die ere June"—but he praises March, "Unmindful of the past or coming days," present to himself in it if only for a moment. (This is, again, the illusion upon which the poem as a whole rests.) The restricted, fleeting moment of the poem as a whole is felt as a promise but praised for its presence, loved for the absence it carries in it. And of course Death is the bottom line, "what begetteth all this storm of bliss," Death the grand context, the spirit of "hope of life" itself determined by its End. Unger: "Everything is contextual." But this itself is not the end: Death, faced squarely, offers a potlatch to humanity, an excess of "all the gifts that Death and Life may give."

April: the months, as objects, are observed with a kind of particularity not given to other objects in the Paradise, precisely distinguished from one another. The lyrics are love poems to the seasons, each month a season of a season, the distinctive features of each spot of time adored and bemoaned. Minute gradations: April is "Winter forgotten long, and summer near," a moment defined as passage from what it is not to what it is not; not summer, which "brings us fear: her very death . . . / Hid in her anxious heart," and not autumn, about whose "fainting . . . sweet decay" April's "fresh life clings," and not winter in spite of "thy snowy blossoms' fragrant drift," a moment both intimation and negation of every other. The moment of April is a moment of "The thousand things that 'neath the young leaves grow," and a moment with which the idle singer is out of

He stood a space and watched the ferry-boat
Take in its load of bright and glittering things;
He watched its head adown the river float,
As o'er the water came the murmurings
Of broken talk: and as all memory clings
To such dumb sounds, so dreamlike came back now
The tale of how his life and love did grow.

He turned away and strode on, knowing not
What purpose moved him; as the river flowed
He hastened, where the sun of March blazed hot
Upon the bounding wall and hard white road,
The terraced blooming vines, the brown abode
Where wife and child and dog of vine-dressers
With mingled careless clamour cursed his ears.

How can words measure misery, when the sun
Shines at its brightest over plague and ill?
How can I tell the woe of any one,
When the soft showers with fair-hued sweetness fill,
Before the feet of those grief may not kill,
The tender meads of hopeful spring, that comes
With eager hours to mock all hopeless homes?

So let it pass, and ask me not to weigh
Grief against grief: ye who have ever woke
To wondering, ere came memory back, why day,
Bare, blank, immovable, upon you broke,
Untold shall ye know all; to happy folk
All heaviest words no more of meaning bear
Than far-off bells saddening the summer air.

synch: he longs "for that which never draweth nigh," "past years" which "pass in vain," estranged from both that which is and that which does draw nigh, each instant becoming the next.

May: like each month an image of noncalendar time experienced if only in negation. Its site is "midst a peaceful dream" deep into the night, "when the sweet nightingale / Had so long finished all he had to say." It is addressed to the idle singer's idle lover, asking if she has seen what he has seemed to have seen: the "Lord of Love" passing by "to take possession of his flowery throne," a vision of the instatement of the pleasure principle in a world gone Habundian. This visionary moment is again defined as the passage of more immediate moments, a moment, over before it can be apprehended, that generates successive moments: "methought the Lord of Love went by," "A little while I sighed to find him gone, / A little while the dawning was alone, / And the light gathered; then . . ." The idle visionary, though forced by his vision into this temporal particularity, is dislocated from it, is not "Unmindful of the past or coming days"; unlike the brown birds, which steal along " 'twixt the trees," their "tune . . . strong" even "shivering"—the idle singer, shuddering, holds his breath. He is rapt with a second and a third apparition, "of Eld and Death," upon which "twain shone out the golden sun." "None noted aught of their noiseless passing by, / The world had quite forgotten it must die," but in the Paradise forgetting is always a wayward form of memory, and in any event the idle singer here is not among the "None" who "noted aught."

June: summer near and nigh is here, and does "not make us happy." The lyric is addressed to the month itself, and takes a tone of cajolery: "Wilt thou not . . .?" "See, we have left our hopes and fears behind / To give our very hearts up unto thee." The singer as lover here engages in a bit of pardonable bad faith, telling the lie due every doomed enamored: his hopes and fears are precisely what he has not left behind, his heart powerless to be given. But "if but pensive men we seem, / What should we do?"—the very dislocation of the poet from "this rare happy dream" of "rustling boughs, the twitter of the birds, / And all thy thousand peaceful happy words" is what keeps him *in* the dream, is what "wouldst not have us wake / From out [its] arms."

July: the lyric is addressed again to the beloved, and concerned explicitly with the dislocation between Habundian order and the order of human

But tells my tale, that all that day he went
Along the highway by the river side,
Urged on by restlessness without intent;
Until when he was caught by evening-tide,
Worn out withal, at last must he abide
At a small homestead, where he gat him food
And bed of straw, among tired folk and rude.

A weary ghost within the poor hall there,
He sat amidst their weariness, who knew
No whit of all his case, yet half with fear
And half with scorn gazed on him, as, with few
And heavy words, about the fire they drew,
The goodman and goodwife, both old and grey,
Three stout sons, and one rough uncared-for may.

A ghost he sat, and as a ghost he heard
What things they spoke of; but sleep-laden night
Seemed to have crushed all memory of their word,
When on the morrow, in the young sun's light,
He plodded o'er the highway hard and white;
Unto what end he knew not: though swift thought
Memory of things long spoken to him brought.

That day he needs must leave the streamside road,
Whereon he met of wayfarers no few;
For sight of wondering eyes now 'gan to goad
His misery more, as still more used he grew
To that dull world he had returned unto;
So into a deep-banked lane he turned aside,
A little more his face from men to hide.

156

events at their current pass. "Fair was the early morn, and fair wert thou" is a plain equation enough, entirely formulaic and, unfortunately, entirely questionable. "Peace and content without us, love within / That hour there was, now thunder and wild rain / Have wrapped the cowering world, and foolish sin, / And nameless pride, have made us wise in vain; / Ah, love! although the morn shall come again, / And on new rose-buds the new sun shall smile, / Can we regain what we have lost meanwhile?" His question is the wrong one, the very mark of his dislocation: the problem is not to "regain what we have lost" but to continue, and the idle singer's additional problem is that he mistakes the one for the other. He notes that "the fair sun" "shall rise again for ages yet, / He cannot waste his life—but thou and I— / Who knows if next morn this felicity / My lips may feel," his mind full of the past and coming days, absent now.

August: each month is the season of a season, three to each of the four, one beginning looking backward, one middle, and one end looking forward (although there is a backward and a forward look in each of the months as well toward the months that immediately frame it). August brings History into Paradise Time: up to this point the only artifacts of human time, traces of its passage, have been faint intimations—an orchard in April (an organization for trees), in June references to nameless "hamlets" and "the city's misery" "far-off," in July "beanfields." August brings us "across the gap made by our English hinds, / Amidst the Roman's handiwork," to "behold / Far off the long-roofed church," "the withy" bound "round the hurdles" of the shepherd's fold, "the foss the river fed of old": a humanized landscape "that through long lapse of time has grown to be." The idle singer is dislocated from the moment of August, as from the other months, and at the same time seeks refuge with his lover in it: "Rest here awhile," he says, "Beneath the sky that burning August gives, / While yet the thought of glorious Summer lives." It is a moment "we still waste" craving what is gone, but a moment still, if "restless changing," "musical and clear."

September: lyric for the beginning of Autumn, to begin the second half of the book, its opening echoes the opening of Spring and Summer as well: "O come at last . . . / . . . what hast thou for me?" Art thou here again, wilt thou not make us happy? The echoes make an order at once false and true, true in the way that all the months' echoes of one another are true to the seamless dream of Habundian plenitude, false in the conceit of begin-

Slowly he went, for afternoon it was,
And with the long way was he much forworn;
Nor far between the deep banks did he pass,
Ere on the wind unto his ears was borne
A stranger sound than he had heard that morn,
Sweet sound of mournful singing; then he stayed
His feet, and gazed about as one afraid:

He shuddered, feeling as in time long past,
When mid the utter joy of his young days
The sudden sound of music would be cast
Upon the bright world with the sun ablaze,
And he would look to see a strange hand raise
The far-off blue, and God in might come down
To judge the earth, and make all hid things known.

And therewithal came memory of that speech
Of yesternight, and how those folk had said,
That now so far did wrong and misery reach,
That soon belike earth would be visited
At last with that supreme day all dread;
When right and wrong, and weal and woe of earth,
Should change amid its fiery second birth.

He hastened toward the road as one who thought
God's visible glory would be passing by,
But, when he looked forth tremblingly, saw nought
Of glorious dread to quench his misery;
There was the sky, and, like a second sky,
The broad stream, the white road, the whispering trees
Swaying about in the sound-laden breeze.

157

nings: our calendar no longer starts in March. The idle singer again dislocated: like "a new-wakened man . . . who tries / to dream again the dream that made him glad / When in his arms his loving love he had." His dream, his "nameless shamefast longings made alive," is "vain"—"And hope no more for things to come again / That thou beheldest once"—but this moment is the moment "the spring-tide's hope / Looked for through blossoms," this is the consummation, the "pensive" air of June now "pensive sweetness more complete." Fulfilled of loss: though "Moveless . . . the autumn fain would be" as a "gold-hung, grey-leaved appletree" it goes.

October: lover and beloved move their gaze "from the unchanging sea" to the world of Change, of History, "Wrought in dead days for men a long while dead," October the fulfillment of the promise of August. "Down these grey slopes" "Come down, O love": in this descent "we live today, forgetting June, / Forgetting May, deeming October sweet—" although the prospect is questionable ("may not our hands still meet") and phrased in the negative. At any rate, the lyric ends in a suicide of its own desperate intent: "Look up, love!— . . . never move!" Descending with his lover from their vista on "the unchanging sea" to the World of Change and Death (itself the "changeless seal of change" November speaks of), the idle singer meets both hope and doom, meets, in fact, his death: "That rest from life . . . / That rest from bliss . . . / That rest from Love . . ." tormenting life, cursed bliss and Love, the moment unbearable.

November: the world seems gone, "beyond these four walls, hung with pain and dreams," but the idle singer bids us "Look out upon the real world, where the moon / Half-way 'twixt root and crown of these high trees, / Turns the dead midnight into dreamy noon, / Silent and full of wonders, for the breeze / Died at the sunset"; "no images, / No hopes of day, are left in sky or earth—" and he asks of this moment "Is it not fair, and of most wondrous worth?" The fairness of Death, fulfilled of loss, wonders borne of the death of the (deathless) breeze: Habundia is here, "'twixt . . . these high trees," translating even the symbol of royalty into vegetable language. (Morris seems to be describing the Paradise itself: "the real world" half-tangled in the trees, dead and dreamy, silent, full of wonders.) As with every other month, November's moment is a moment of the Presence of the World, the Presence of the World Estranged: "Yea, I have looked, and seen November there; / The changeless seal of change it

For nigher and nigher ever came the song,
And presently at turning of the way
A company of pilgrims came along,
Mostly afoot, in garments brown and grey:
Slowly they passed on through the windy day,
Led on by priests who bore aloft the rood,
Singing with knitted brows as on they strode.

Then sank his heart adown, however sweet,
Pensive and strange, their swinging song might be,
For nought like this he had in heart to meet;
But rather something was he fain to see,
That should change all the old tale utterly;
The old tale of the world, and love and death,
And all the wild things that man's yearning saith.

Nathless did he abide their coming there,
And noted of them as they drew anigh,
That in that fellowship were women fair,
And young men meet for joyous company,
Besides such elders as might look to die
In few years now, or monks who long had striven
With life desired and feared, life for death given.

Way-worn they seemed, yet many there strode on,
With flashing eyes and flushed cheeks, as though all
Within a little space should be well won:
Still as he gazed on them, despair did fall
Upon his wasted heart; a fiery wall
Of scorn and hate seemed 'twixt their hearts & his;
While delicate images of bygone bliss

158

seemed to be, / Fair death of things that, living once, were fair; / Bright sign of loneliness too great for me, / Strange image of the dread eternity, / In whose void patience" "These outstretched feverish hands, this restless heart" find nothing but themselves.

December: the year of Paradise begins with Winter slain, now it is here. December answers the question of October: "O thou who clingest still to life and love" ("cling close and never move! / How can I have enough of life and love?"), the poet sings, and grants the lover (which is to say himself) his folly—"Cast no least thing thou lovedst once away, / Since yet perchance thine eyes may see the day." This "day" is the next day, after the "Dead night" with which the lyric begins, the night of "strange shadows," "pale stars, bright moon, swift cloud" and "heaven so vast / That earth . . . / Seems shrunken." The moment of December is lost in the clinging, "the year foredone, / Change, kindness lost, love left unloved alone," all lost, and lost, "perchance" a promise.

January: turning from and to again. This is the heart of Winter, which, if Summer "brings us fear[,] her very death . . . / Hid in her anxious heart," brings us something else: Love in fact. The idle singer's beloved turns from the "gathering night" "with thy scarce-seen kindly smile / Sent through the dusk my longing to beguile"—one moment—then the lights come on inside, the windows go black, and their eyes meet in the glass—another. "O look, love, look again!" the poet is at once (and, we might say, for a change) touched with the presence of the world and seized with terror: "The veil of doubt / Just for one flash, past counting, then was raised! / O eyes of heaven, as clear thy sweet soul blazed / On mine a moment! O come back again." It is the same story: "Nay, nay, gone by!" This is the most intense moment of presence in the whole cycle of the months, perhaps because it is the one least marked by plenitude, but it touches upon plenitude, turning around into its own opposite. The idle singer's lover's "wide grey eyes so frank and fathomless" so to speak make more of themselves: his "days they yet shall fill / With utter rest—Yea, now thy pain they bless, / and feed thy last hope of the world's redress." If Love is not yet to be found within the arms of Death, it is not yet dead.

February: like August, a moment filled with History. An "empty road," "rain-washed fields" bare "from hedge to hedge," "some hind's abode" "small and void," a world "whirling down the wind." And again the

Grew clear before his eyes, as rood and saint
Gleamed in the sun o'er raiment coarse and foul,
O'er dusty limbs, and figures worn and faint:
Well-nigh he shrieked; yet in his inmost soul
He felt that he must ask them of their goal,
And knew not why: so at a man he clutched,
Who, as he passed, his shoulder well-nigh touched.

Where goest thou then, O pilgrim, with all these?
Stay me not! cried he; unto life I go,
To life at last, and hope of rest and peace;
I whom my dreadful crime hath hunted so
For years, though I am young: O long and slow
The way to where the change awaiteth me:
To Rome, where God nigh visible shall be!

Where He who knoweth all, shall know this too,
That I am man, e'en that which He hath made,
Nor be confounded at aught man can do.
And thou, who seemest too with ill down-weighed,
Come on with us, nor be too much afraid,
Though some men deem there is but left small space
Or ere the world shall see the Judge's face.

He answered not, nor moved; the man's words seemed
An echo of his thoughts, and, as he passed,
Word and touch both might well be only dreamed.
Yea, when the vine-clad terraced hill at last
Had hid them all, and the slim poplars cast
Blue shadows on the road, that scarce did show
A trace of their past feet, he did not know

moment in its death promises desire, which "liveth yet" even in "useless hope, . . . useless craving pain." Again the desire is "for that which never draweth nigh," for "days dead," and again this dislocated desire bears unexpectable fruit, a "hope for joy new born again"—not the old joy but a new joy, borne of grief—"Since no grief ever born can ever die." The End.

Glittering plain: the lyrics of the months are familiar objects, the most formulaic sort of sentimental verses. That there is nothing new in them at once counters the novelty-fetish of the Death-denying World and submits to the Administration of that World. It is a remarkable performance on Morris's part: in the context of the Paradise as a whole the lyrics acquire a radical force—the structure of the whole, in relation to the structures of (I would need a German word here) Romantikapitalism, investing the lyrics with dialectic negativity. (Predoomed negativity: as "acquire" and "invest" suggest, the Other World of the idle singer's dream is borne in the current of This World, infected, a delirium.) The lyrics redeem the most tired language, the most tired tropes, though all remain nevertheless tired: a Habundian exercise. The vision of Habundia's kin: people die but the People does not (people die so that the People may live), and the People dies but Life does not, and if Life dies the World remains, and if the World goes then the Nothing Is. The collective vision of Habundia encompasses the cosmos—not excluding even "bad" (if competent) verse.

Jane: the lyrics are also, quite obviously, love songs to Jane, who is included within the book's pages from the start in the dedication "To My Wife"—present if unnamed. The lyrics address her only in the most conventional poetic terms—"O love!" "ah, love!": like every other emanation of Paradise, Jane is absent from the page, and nevertheless, at some distance, somehow there, the governing wonder of the book's wondrous Things. That the whole book is intended for her is explicit, and that she could have read the lyrics in any way but most intimately unlikely: but what Mackail calls "an autobiography so delicate and so outspoken that it must needs be left to speak for itself," speaks only to Jane.[17] Not naming her, the lyrics reserve this most delicate of their notes for a select audience (and later, for a prying, ravening, postmortem audience: ourselves). Naming her in the dedication, the book marks the presence of what (or more to the point in this case, *who*) is not otherwise there, not the idle singer's Love but the author's Wife: here "just for one flash, past counting," the Here and the "gone by."

But all had been a dream; all save the pain,
That, mingling with the solid things around,
Showed them to be not wholly vague and vain,
And him not dead, in whatso hard bonds bound
Of wandering fate, whose source shall ne'er be found.
He shivered, turned away, and down the same
Deep lane he wandered whence e'en now he came.

He toward the night through hapless day-dreams passed,
That knew no God to come, no love: he stood
Before a little town's grey gate at last,
And in the midst of his lost languid mood
Turned toward the western sky, as red as blood,
As bright as sudden dawn across the dark,
And through his soul fear shot a kindling spark.

But as he gazed, the rough-faced gate-warder,
Who leaned anigh upon his spear, must turn
Eyes on him, with an answering anxious fear,
That silent, questioning, dared not to learn,
If he too deemed more than the sun did burn
Behind the crimson clouds that made earth grey,
If yet perchance God's host were on its way.

So too, being come unto his hostelry,
His pain was so much dulled by weariness,
That he might hearken to men's words, whereby
It seemed full sure that great fear did oppress
Men's hearts that tide, that the world's life, grown less
Through time's unnoted lapse, this thousandth year
Since Christ was born, unto its end drew near.

160

Behold the Remnant

Grave matters of belief and polity
They spoke of oft, but not alone of these
                                        —MORRIS

In the conceit of *The Earthly Paradise* there is really only one story, beginning with the Prologue, continuing with what I will call the Linktale, ending with the Epilogue: the Apology, the note To the Reader, the monthly lyrics, and the Envoi are the idle singer's wrapping for this tale, which is itself wrapping for the other twenty-four his "hollow puppets" tell one another, two by two. (And Morris's own life, along with all his works, a further wrapping, not within the text itself as much as in the poem's afterlife: a Habundian proliferation of contexts.)

The Linktale is divided into forty-eight sections, one to introduce and one at the conclusion of each tale, four sections each month (the seasons of the month): purely interstitial objects that spell the one story, fragments and the only whole in one, Time and Place divided up and indivisible—the only Whole World the Paradise knows.[18]

As the Prologue begins the Wanderers, fleeing the European plague, forgetting and forgetting and, with each landing, remembering, have come at last to that "nameless city in a distant sea" and the children "of the nations who dwelt anciently / About the borders of the Grecian sea." In the ballad version these people are called "The People of the Shore," their voice (the voice of "Oho! oho! whence come ye sirs") a singular collective; in the Prologue the voice of the people of this place is attributed to an individual, "The Elder of the City," but in either case the land the Wanderers have come to, did they but know it, is Paradise: The Elder of the City of The People of the Shore speaks from a world dislocated from Europe ("that now altered world") and asks the Wanderers for tales of the place, of what they are gone from, a bridge back between Paradise and Deathless Death, between happy exile and the old homeland.

The Wanderers are dislocated too, both from Europe and from this new land, at once identified with and distinguished from their hosts. Not inhabitants but visitors to Paradise, the Wanderers carry Death-haunted baggage, which virtually crowds them out of the place. Thus the tales, too—the first each month out of the lore of Paradise, the second of the lore of Hell—are distinguished from one another by their provenance (and the

Time and again, he, listening to such word,
Felt his heart kindle; time and again did seem
As though a cold and hopeless tune he heard,
Sung by grey mouths amidst a dull-eyed dream;
Time and again across his heart would stream
The pain of fierce desire whose aim was gone,
Of baffled yearning, loveless and alone.

Other words heard he too, that served to show
The meaning of that earnest pilgrim train;
For the folk said that many a man would go
To Rome that Easter, there more sure to gain
Full pardon for all sins, since frail and vain,
Cloudlike the very earth grew 'neath men's feet:
Yea, many thought, that there at Rome would meet

The half-forgotten Bridegroom with the Bride,
Stained with the flushed feast of the world; that He,
Through wrack & flame, would draw unto His side
In the new earth where there is no more sea.
So spake men met together timorously;
Though pride slew fear in some men's souls, that they
Had lived to see the firm earth melt away.

Next morn were folk about the market-cross
Gathered in throngs, and as through these he went
He saw above them a monk's brown arms toss
About his strained and eager mouth, that sent
Strong speech around, whose burden was Repent;
He passed by toward the gate that Romeward lay,
Yet on its other side his feet did stay.

provenance of their current tellers), and at the same time virtually indistinguishable, the same vision unfolding in each, the same vision that occupies the monthly lyrics: a dialectical vision of perpetual presence and perpetual loss. At first glance backward cast, one may (as I do) find the Wanderers' tales the ones that tend to remain in the mind, the ones that seem emblematic, that seem to stand for the whole—perhaps because misery is always more interesting than happiness—but this is something of an illusion: it is not that these tales differ from those of the Greeks in matter or manner, only that their source (or the source of their transmission, plague-ridden desperados of Europe—in the ballad version literally desperados, pirates) gives a different weight to the dialectic. The Greeks' and the Wanderers' tales are all fulfilled of the dialectic—full of yearning helpless and gaining wondrous—and in the end there is no distinction to be made, each one of them emblematic; but the divergent sources of the transmission, the conceit of different vantages, the possibility of Otherness, allows us to move within the dialectic, to feel its dynamic motion forth and back. Each pair of tales is a couplet.

Questions of *transmission,* of *source* (both source of each tale's text and source of its current incarnation, its utterer) and of *reception:* this is what the Linktale is about, the Paradise as conduit. Transmission is the poem's Dream, a dream of distance dissolved, of stimulus and response unseparated, of immediacy: whether the object of the response is "tales extant in 1349,"[19] or the tales that lie behind those tellings, or the objects of those more ancient tales, or the very world under one's nose, the Thing present to the senses. A doomed dream, clearly enough: all of these things within reach to be sure but beyond immediacy, obscured, dislocated.

The form of the Linktale as a whole is Habundian: its successiveness and repetitiousness, its regular irregularities, its fusion of the fragment and the whole. And the questions of transmission that are central to the tale, the promises and impossibilities of transmission, are explicitly framed in Habundian terms: each of the links extends the material of the monthly lyrics, the tropes of the seasons, of changing weather and the cycles of human life, youth and age. Like the lyrics, the links between the tales of the One Tale are cast in the most formulaic verse imaginable, and represent the most formulaic moments known to humankind: there is nothing new under the sun here, and this fact is the basis for a kind of ecstasy, muffled but ineradicable, standing against the "almost savage torpor" Wordsworth speaks of, the sense-deadening shocks of what we come to the Paradise to forget. In its engagement of Romantic ideology (of escapism, Transcen-

Upon a daisied patch of road-side grass
He cast himself, and down the road he gazed;
And therewithal the thought through him did pass,
How long and wretched was the way he faced.
Therewith the smouldering fire again outblazed
Within him, and he moaned: O empty earth,
What shall I do, then, midst thy loveless dearth?

But as he spake, there came adown the wind
From out the town the sound of pilgrims' song,
And other thoughts were borne across his mind,
And hope strove with desire so hopeless strong,
Till in his heart, wounded with pain and wrong,
Something like will was born; until he knew
Now, ere they came, what thing he meant to do.

So through the gate at last the pilgrims came,
Led by an old priest, fiery-eyed and grey;
Then Walter held no parley with his shame,
But stood before him midmost of the way.
Will one man's sin so heavy on you weigh,
He cried, that ye shall never reach your end?
Unto God's pardon with you would I wend.

The old man turned to him: My son, he said,
Come with us, and be of us! turn not back
When once thine hand upon the plough is laid;
The telling of thy sin we well may lack,
Because the Avenger is upon our track,
And who can say the while we tarry here,
Amid this seeming peace, but God draws near?

162

dental Idealism, immateriality of Imagination), and through that ideology its further engagement of the ideology and practice of Industrial Capitalism (in short, in its embodiment of Art under Plutocracy), the Paradise as a whole charges even these useless scraps of pure functionality with oppositional potential. The Linktale, like the tales it incorporates, a matter of "poets' vain imaginings," a Habundian dream of "profusion, but never intensity," of pleasure unstrenuous, glittering plain and available.

That the setting of the tales, the Land of the Elder of the City of the People of the Shore, is Paradise, a world tuned to a Habundian measure, is plain enough from the start (if conveyed as quietly as something taken for granted). The first time the Elder speaks (the first voice to sound in the poem after the idle singer's introductory) he says that "folk of ours," unlike the Wanderers, "are now content to sail, / About these happy islands that we know"; the second time he speaks he summons "maidens . . . / Bearing the blood of this our sunburnt land / in well-wrought cups," wine from grapes that "abode your coming, hidden none the less / Below the earth from summer's happiness"; the third time he tells them that, having come to this land, "a little bliss is reached at last." The fourth time he speaks it is to interpose his own vision of profusion within the Wanderers' dream of intensity, to imagine "another sea" beyond the mountains the Wanderers' narrative names, "though not the deathless country of your thought."

Still, a deathless country in its own way. In the ballad version the Habundian nature of the People's world is more pronounced: something gets lost, dulled, in the translation of the nineteenth-century framework. The People render their life—the Wanderers' new life—as a virtual portrait of Habundia. The metaphorical provenance is organic, and human capacity reduced to a manifestation of the vegetable: "Alas! my masters, by my head / Your hope was but a rotten reed," Habundia present even in the profusion of reeds, synechdoches of song, and redes, in the sense of considered advice, and reads. When the People note that their dead ancestors "found . . . rest and ease at last / Here in this land," "this land" refers both to the People's historical identity, that is, their nation, and to the very earth:

> great deeds they did
> As many an ancient story saith;
> Yet these also the earth has hid,
> No man among them but found Death.

The crowd had stayed their song to hear the priest, The Hill
But now, when Walter joined their company,   of Venus
Like a great shout it rose up and increased,
And on their way they went so fervently
That swept away from earth he seemed to be;
And many a thought o'er which his heart had yearned
Amid their fire to white ash now seemed burned.

For many days they journeyed on, and still
Whate'er he deemed that he therein should do,
The hope of Rome his whole soul seemed to fill;
And though the priest heard not his story through,
Yet from him at the last so much he knew,
That he had promised when they reached the place
To bring him straight before the Pope's own face.

Through many a town they passed; till on a night
Long through the darkness they toiled on and on
Down a straight road, until a blaze of light
On the grey carving of an old gate shone;
And fast the tears fell down from many an one,
And rose a quavering song, for they were come
Unto the threshold of that mighty Rome.

They entered: like a town of ghosts it seemed
To Walter, a beleaguered town of ghosts;
And he felt of them, little though he dreamed
Amid his pain of all the marshalled hosts
That lay there buried mid forgotten boasts;
But dead he seemed as those his pleasures were,
Dead in a prison vast and void and drear.

viii. m 2   163

Their world is not so much death-haunted as death-contingent: "Our fathers dead," remembered, "yet overlive" their death, and between the composition of ancient stories and the decomposition of ancestral lives, the land grows rich.[20]

Even memory, which the Wanderers (such is their alienation) can only associate with pain, here serves the purpose of regenerative bliss. The death of the old fathers opens directly onto a narrative of mere abundance:

> No doubt the Gods have sent you then
> To a fair land and plenteous;
> Of all the gifts they give to men
> Not one have they withheld from us.

This land is at once Paradise and not, which is to say earthly paradise, a substitute item not without its own charm:

> No doubt our gardens might entice
> The very Gods themselves to leave
> The happy woods of Paradise,
> Nor once thereafter grieve.

> Their fields bright with unchanging May,
> Pressed by the feet of Goddesses,
> Are scarce more fair than are today
> Our meadows set about with trees.[21]

The dulled rhyme of "trees" and "Goddesses" strikes the definitive note. The People's season-ridden meadows, of which it is noted they are fair "today," replace the bright unchanging fields, but if they resemble them, they do not quite become them: Paradise at a remove, scarce less fair.

The perfect fullness of natural life, in the midst of which we are led here, depends upon perpetual motion, and the favored mode is cyclical:

> Here fields of corn and pleasant hills
> Dotted with orchards shall ye see,
> And sweet streams turning many mills,
> And of all fruits right great plenty.

Even nascent industrial enterprise becomes in this light an extension of natural order, the mill wheels sustaining the undercurrent. Keeping

Unto a convent that eve were they brought,
Where with the abbot spake the priest for long,
Then bade the hapless man to fear him nought,
But that the Pope next day would right his wrong;
And let thy heart, quoth he, O son, be strong,
For no great space thou hast to sin anew:
The days of this ill world are grown but few.

Night passed, day dawned, and at the noon thereof
The priest came unto Walter: Fair my son,
Now shalt thou know, he said, of God's great love;
Moreover thou shalt talk with such an one
As hath heard told the worst deeds man hath done,
And will not start at thine or mock at thee:
Be of good heart, and come thy ways with me.

Amid the tumult of his heart, they went
Through the calm day by wonders wrought of old;
And fresh young folk they met, and men intent
On eager life; the wind and the sun's gold
Were fresh on bands of monks that did uphold
The carven anguish of the rood above
The wayfarers, who trusted in God's love.

But no more dead the grey old temples seemed
To him than fresh-cheeked girl or keen-eyed man;
And like a dream for some dim purpose dreamed,
And half forgotten, was the image wan
Nailed on the cross: no tremor through him ran,
No hope possessed him, though his lips might say,
O love of God, be nigh to me to-day!

164

and losing can hardly be issues in a world so moved, and the point is
made explicit in a digression from the ongoing catalogue of natural
effects:

> Oxen and sheep and horses go
> About the merry water-meads,
> Where herons, and long cranes thereto,
> Lie hidden in the whispering reeds.
>
> Among all these the maidens play;
> The fair white Goddess of the sea
> Is little fairer made than they
> In all her members certainly.
>
> Like you, Sirs, am I chilled with eld,
> Yet still I look on them with joy. [22]

The distance between old spokesman and young maidens is rendered
inconsequential by those closing words, as if time and age were of no
account, the linear thread broken and looped to itself: a dream, quite
literally in the end, of generation.

When the People say, however, "Thus under gentle laws we live /
Well guarded, and in rest and peace / And ever more and more we thrive, /
And ever do our goods increase," it may be suspected that they themselves
are unaware of certain facts. Certainly the Wanderers considering this
same scene would note the tenuousness of this "guard," each one of them a
Tantalus of rest and peace. The laws of generation are the laws of decay,
but it seems that the Wanderers' new friends hardly take the matter
personally. They raise the issue of Death even as they conclude the catalog
of thriving goods, but the effect, from the Wanderers' perspective, is of a
peculiar blind spot:

> O masters, here as everywhere,
> All things begin, grow old, decay;
> That groweth ugly that was fair,
> The storm blots out the summer's day.
>
> The merry shepherd's lazy song
> Breaks off before the lion's roar;

For surely all things seemed but part of him;
Therefore what help in them? Still on he passed
Through all, and still saw nothing blurred or dim,
Though with a dread air was the world o'ercast,
As of a great fire somewhere; till at last,
At a fair convent door the old priest stayed,
And touched his fellow's shoulder, as he said:

Thou tremblest not; thou look'st as other men:
Come then, for surely all will soon be well,
And like a dream shall be that ill day when
Thou hangedst on the last smooth step of hell!
But from his shoulder therewith his hand fell,
And long he stared astonished in his place,
At a new horror fallen o'er Walter's face.

Then silently he led him on again
Through daintily wrought cloisters, to a door,
Whereby there stood a gold-clad chamberlain:
Then, while the monk his errand to him bore,
Walter turned round and cast a wild look o'er
Fair roof, and painted walls, and sunlit green,
That showed the slim and twisted shafts between.

He shut his eyes and moaned, and e'en as clear
As he beheld these, did he now behold
A woman white and lovely drawing near,
Whose face amidst her flower-wreathed hair of gold
Mocked the faint images of saints of old;
Mocked with sweet smile the pictured mother of God,
As o'er the knee-worn floor her fair feet trod.

viii. m 3   165

The bathing girls, white-limbed and long,
Half-dead with fear splash toward the shore

At rumour of the deadly shark;
Over the corn, ripe and yellow
The hobby stoops upon the lark,
The kestrel eyes the shrew below.

Three more such quatrains follow—in Death a plenitude—ending in a "weariness" that "doth so increase / We have the heart to wish us dead—." Here the visitors' mood has infected the inhabitants', but even weariness is linked to "increase," and the dread bell tolling, though heard, is quickly absorbed into the pattern:

Masters, your hope that this could be,
To live forever anywhere
Has brought sad longings strange to me,
Sad thoughts, my heart can hardly bear.

And sad words from my lips have gone
Unmeet for ancient folk to say;
Pray you forget them, ye have won
Life sweet and peaceful from today.

The Gods have sent you here to us—
The land you sought for, did you know,
A fair land and a plenteous.

The phenomena of life, "all things . . . / That can by any man be sought," are more than abundant recompense—they appear in this land to represent a true Lethe, stream of oblivion.[23]

Although the Wanderers assimilate themselves to this land of mere abundance, one senses that they can never quite be *of* it. It is the land they sought for, did they know, but it is precisely what they *have not* known, and even arriving here at last they represent an inappropriate obsession: "sad thoughts," "sad words," "sad longings." The Prologue in both its versions establishes the fully dialectical relationship between where the Wanderers have come from and where they have got to. The Habundian world of the People of the Shore is acknowledged to be, in spite of all,

Through his shut eyes he saw her still, as he
Heard voices, and stepped onward, as he heard
The door behind him shut to noisily,
And echo down the cloisters, and a word
Spoke by a thin low voice: Be not afeard!
Look up! for though most surely God is nigh,
Yet nowise is He with us visibly.

He looked up, and beside him still she stood,
With eyes that seemed to question: What dost thou?
What wilt thou say? The fever of his blood
Abated not, because before him now
There sat an old man with high puckered brow,
Thin lips, long chin, and wide brown eyes and mild,
That o'er the sternness of his mouth still smiled.

Wilt thou kneel down, my son? he heard him say;
God is anigh, though not to give thee fear;
Folk tell me thou hast journeyed a long way,
That I the inmost of thine heart might hear;
It glads me that thou holdest me so dear.
But more of this thy love I yet would win,
By telling thee that God forgives thy sin.

He knelt down, but all silent did abide
While the Pope waited silent; on the ground
His eyes were fixed, but still anigh his side
He knew she stood; and all the air around
Was odorous with her; yea, the very sound
Of her sweet breath, moving of hair and limb,
Mixed with his own breath in the ears of him.

166

determined by Death, in spite of which it lives; and the Wanderers' death quest is nestled in the shadow of the Green Tree, under which its sick hope languishes, a provocation "unmeet." It is this twin, complementary inversion that marks the Paradise as at once the crown and conquest of Death.

The invitation to exchange tales, with which the Prologue ends, is extended in Habundian terms: to "bring us wealth of happy hours / Whiles that we live, and to our sons, delight, / And their sons' sons." The Wanderers, "our living chronicle" the Elder calls them, like some unlooked for "ancient chronicle / Of that sweet unforgotten land long left, / Of all the lands wherefrom we now are reft," join the Elders in the business of proliferation.

It is a perverse business, in a sense (a Wanderers' sense), in that proliferation is properly something that belongs to Youth—although from the point of view of the folk to whom the Wanderers have come it is not perverse at all: Habundian through and through, they know that there is no end to generation. In any case, engaging in it means working against the grain of the old men's mortality, which is everpresent to them in every link of the tale. The link before each tale these puppets tell is concerned particularly with the tale's provenance: the source of the tale's text, the manner of its transmission, the relation of its current form to its original, in each case a matter of remoteness; the link that follows each tale is concerned particularly with the tale's immediate reception. The whole enterprise of the telling of tales, proposed at the first gathering in March to "crown our joyance," is marked for the old men by difficulty: at the ending of the first tale "on their hearts a weight had seemed to fall," and the second tale is offered as a pang "—Alas, my folly! how I talk of it, / As though from this place where to-day we sit / The way thereto were short." The relationship of the Elders and the Wanderers alike to the Habundian plenitude of which they partake, like everything else in "this Earthly Paradise," is self-contradicted.

Each link, both before and after each tale, embeds this Habundian enterprise of transmission and reception in a context further Habundian: the changing weather, the seasonal earth, the mirth of minstrels when the tale is done. This is a context from which the old men's tales both are and are not dislocated: often the tale-teller will introduce his tale with reference to the weather ("The Story of Cupid and Psyche" "is lovely as the lovely May," while June "Amid such calm delight" is "so bright and glad / I care not if I tell you something sad"), but the tales themselves, again, are virtually of a piece, January as wondrous as July is gloomy. The Linktale

Outside the sparrows twittered; a great tree
Stirred near the window, and the city's noise
Still murmured: long the Pope sat patiently
Amid that silence, till the thin weak voice
Spake out and said: O son, have the world's joys
Made thee a coward? what is thy degree?
Despite thy garb no churl thou seemst to me.

Fearfully Walter raised his eyes, and turned,
As though to ask that vision what to say,
And with a bitter pain his vexed heart burned,
When now he found all vanished clean away:
Great wrath stirred in him; shame most grievous lay
Upon his heart, and spreading suddenly
His hands abroad, he 'gan at last to cry:

Look at me, father! I have been a knight,
And held my own midst men: such as I kneel
Before thee now, amidst a hopeless fight
Have I stood firm against the hedge of steel,
Casting aside all hope of life and weal
For nought, because folk deemed I would do so,
Though nought there was to gain or win unto.

Yet before thee, an old man small and weak,
I quail indeed: not because thou art great,
Nor because God through thy thin pipe doth speak,
As all folk trow: but, rather, that man's hate,
Man's fear, God's scorn, shall fall in all their weight
Upon my love when I have spoken out:
Yea, let me bide a minute more in doubt!

also embodies another branch of the dream: the young folk, who come to listen to the old men's tales, and whose identification with the Habundian is absolute. These young folk are not present at the first gathering in March, establishing the Wanderers' and the Elders' enterprise in its own dislocation, but at the second meeting, a day "too hopeful for the wild days yet to be," "that ancient company, / Not lacking younger folk that day at least," the old men are joined by what they are not.

Spring: the six tales of Spring represent six sources and six modes of transmission, six relationships to Loss. In March an Elder tells a tale "of the land / Wherein the tombs of our forefathers stand," and a Wanderer a tale "As folk with us will tell in every vale / About the yule-tide fire": in one "perchance it is / That many things therein are writ amiss, / This part forgotten, that part grown too great," the other but a "memory / Of ills kings did us" retained by people who "long have been" "a happy, kingless folk." In both cases, the keynote is a chord, at once the currency of the tale and the distance of its provenance. In April the Elder's tale sounds the same note of distance ("midst the ancient gold / Base metal ye will light on here and there, / Though I have noted everything with care, / And with good will have set down nothing new"), and of distance dissolved: the tale is "Fresh e'en among us, far from the Argive land; / Which tale this book, writ wholly by my hand, / Holds gathered up." (The Elder also says "Nor holds the land another book for you / That has the tale in full with nought beside," making a claim that stands for the Paradise itself.) The Wanderers' April tale is very deliberately located in England, which is described as a land of marvelous craft and lying kings: the tale-teller tells us that he has "set down every word / That I remembered," and asserts that "Yet is it still the tale I then heard told," though he is himself, again, of "a happy, kingless folk," and cannot but help to transform it in the telling. In May again, distance: one tale of which "No written record was there," one ("through my memory this same eve doth flit / A certain tale") a remnant of a youth spent reading "many books" of "mystic lore."

　　The reception given the tales too is a matter of discriminating between states of dislocation. "Atalanta's Race," the first tale, is received by the Wanderers and the Elders as one, their common age overriding what else might differ in their perspectives. In the reception of "The Man Born to Be King" the idle singer distinguishes between the two groups of old men and between both of them together and a third group, the young: a pattern of shifting distinctions and identifications that continues throughout the Linktale. The Wanderers see in "The Doom of King Acrisius" an

Man hates it and God scorns, and I, e'en I,
How shall I hate my love and scorn my love?
Weak, weak are words, but, O my misery!
More hate than man's hate in my soul doth move;
Greater my scorn than scorn of God above,
And yet I love on. Is the pain enow
That thou some hope unto my heart mayst show?

Some hope of peace at last that is not death?
Because with all these things I know for sure
I cannot die, else had I stopped my breath
Long time agone; thereto hath many a lure
Drawn on my hand; but now God doth endure,
And this my love, that never more shall bring
Delight to me or help me anything.

Calm sat the Pope, and said: Hope, rather, now;
For many a sinner erewhile have I shriven
As utterly o'erwhelmed in soul as thou,
Who, when awhile with words his mouth had striven,
Went forth from me at peace and well forgiven.
Fall we to talk; and let me tell thee first,
That there are such as fain would be the worst

Amongst all men, since best they cannot be,
So strong is that wild lie that men call pride;
And so to-day it is, perchance, with thee:
Cast it aside, son; cast it clean aside,
Nor from my sight thine utmost vileness hide;
Nought worse it makes thy sin, when all is done,
That every day men do the same, my son!

image of their own shattered hopes, a very image of escape from the alienations of RomantiKapital: a vision "far away" of "that other world, that 'neath another law / Had lived and died; when man might hope to see / Some earthly image of Divinity," "Nor losing joy the while his life should 'dure." "The Proud King" they generalize from England to the world. At the end of the next month, "The Writing on the Image" is received in similar fashion to the two tales previous, its theme related to "other tales of treasure-seekers balked," and the response it provokes the dream of a Habundian home-made Socialist:

> better it would be to give
> What things they may, while on the earth they live
> Unto the earth, and from the bounteous earth
> To take their pay of sorrow or of mirth,
> Hatred or love, and get them on their way;
> And let the teeming earth fresh troubles make
> For other men, and ever for their sake
> Use what they left, when they are gone from it.

The previous tale, "The Story of Cupid and Psyche," brings "remembrance of the mighty deeds of love," the pleasure principle regnant, and leaves "those old hearts" virtually speechless.

In general the link preceding each tale carries its provenance, and the link following its reception. In May, however, the Wanderer explaining the source of the tale, and its distance from him, also tells us what he thinks in advance: it is a tale of "many a mystery / I thought divine, that now I think, forsooth, / Men's own fears made, to fill the place of truth." To give the provenance of a tale is in fact to give its reception, to define the capacities by virtue of which tale and teller make connection, each implicit in the other, no teller without a tale, no tale without a teller. It is another of the poem's dialectical conceits, and another embodiment of the Habundian dream: seamless interchangeabilities. In the Linktale, there is no king but Habundia: here, for instance (in March), even Norway, Norway of the plague-ridden shore receding in the distance, is figured as a very Paradise, "not galled by any yoke, / But the white leaguer of the winter tide," Paradise dislocated.

Summer: the Summer tales' transmission is marked by immediacy. "The Love of Alcestis" is introduced with no word of an earlier text, simply as a

The strained lines of the kneeling wretch's face   The Hill
Were softened; as to something far away   of Venus
He seemed a-listening: silent for a space
The two men were; who knows what 'twixt them lay,
What world of wondrous visions, of a day
Past or to come? to one lost love so clear,
God's glory to the other present there.

At last the Pope spake; well-nigh musical
His voice was grown, and in his thin dry cheek
There rose a little flush: Tell of thy fall,
And how thy weak heart its vain lust must seek,
Cursing the kind and treading down the weak!
Tell all the blindness of thy cruelties,
Thy treason, thine unkindness, and thy lies!

And be forgiven: these things are of earth;
The fire of God shall burn them up apace,
And leave thee calm in thy pure second birth;
No sin, no lust forgotten, in the place
Where, litten by the glory of God's face,
The souls that He hath made for ever move
Mid never-dying, never-craving love.

How fair shall be the dawning of that day
When thy cleared eyes behold the thing thou wast,
Wherefore, and all the tale: hate cast away,
And all the yearning of thy love at last
Full satisfied, and held for ever fast!
O never-dying souls, how sweet to hear
Your laughter in the land that knows no fear!

response (and counterpoint) to the weather of early June. "The Lady of the Land" comes with a claim, if a dubious one, of loss-free transmission, a tale told "such a while agone" of which the present teller says "that I remember everything." "The Son of Croesus" and "The Watching of the Falcon," as if a check against such folly, are introduced in terms of distance ("For I the written book did never see"), but "Pygmalion and the Image" comes without a text and without even a teller: it simply is "heard," as if a pure emanation of the weather. And "Ogier the Dane" comes from a friend's mouth into the teller's "greedy ears," one would think with little loss, and is provoked again primarily by the weather: "ancient longings" for the repletion of "harvest-tide," another counterpoint.

The reception of the Summer tales works the same material as in the earlier months' links: the old men speechless, the old men distinguished from one another, Wanderers and Elders, the old men identified and distinguished from the younger folk, the same elements shuffled according to a pattern like the patterned variation of tetrameter couplets, pentameter couplets, and rhyme royale verse forms.

The dynamic of Youth and Eld receives special attention in the last link of June: the idle singer tells us of the old men that "no more memory of their hopes and fears / They nourished," while

> the younger men
> Began to nourish strange dreams . . .
> Because the story of that luckless quest
> With hope, not fear, had filled their joyous hearts
> And made them dream of new and noble parts
> That they might act.

The dialectic of abjection and dream, of utter closure and further possibility, is the dialectic upon which the Paradise rests.

Autumn: the links between the Autumn tales follow the patterns already established, as the reception links in Summer, so both the reception and the transmission links here. "The Death of Paris" is given no provenance, its provocation the presence of the younger folk at the elders' gathering: "Then to the elders did it seem most meet / Amidst of these to set forth what they might / Of lore remembered, and to let the night / Bury its own dead thoughts with wine and sleep," a Habundian impetus of generation, pleasure, and decline, and an instance of reception standing in for source.

All this thou gainest if to God thou turn,
Since nought but with thy fellows hast thou dealt,
And well He wotteth how vexed hearts may yearn,
Who in the very midst of them hath dwelt,
Whose own soul, too, the world's hard wrong hath felt,
The serpent's burning clutch upon his heel:
Speak, then, and pray, and earn unending weal!

A strange look crossed the knight's face as he said:
Surely all these shall love their God full well;
Good to be one of these; yet have I read
That other things God made, and that they dwell
In that abode He made, too, men call hell.
If every man that will become God's friend
Shall have great joy that never more shall end,

Yet is it so that evil dureth still,
Unslain of God: what if a man's love cling,
In sore despite of reason, hope, and will,
Unto the false heart of an evil thing?
O me! he cried, that scarce heard murmuring
Beside me, and that faint sound of thy feet!
Must thou be wordless this last time we meet?

Then the Pope trembled, for, half-risen now,
Walter glared round him through the empty air:
O man, he said, speak out: what seest thou?
What ill thing 'twixt thy God and thee stands there?
Ah, me! cried Walter, kind thou wert and fair
In the past days, and now wilt thou be gone,
And leave me with this cruel God alone?

170

"The Land East of the Sun and West of the Moon" is generated, by contrast, in the "absence of merry folk and fair," with just "this silent company" of old men to occasion it: no other text is given, "no history / Of men who ever lived." "The Story of Accontius and Cydippe," like "The Death of Paris," returns us to the young but more pointedly, more specifically provoked: it is addressed directly to "the fairest damsel there," spoken with "a grave smile." "The Man Who Never Laughed Again" returns us to a distant provenance (here in October, the first such case since June), "heard and forgotten midst my childish bliss," "little remembered . . . / Come back again." And the last two tales return us to the weather as provenance, conceit of immediacy this time fraught with distance: "The Story of Rhodope" "perchance" provoked by "the empty month," and "The Lovers of Gudrun" from "a strange land and barren," dislocated from the site of its telling but present to its teller ("we / Have ever deemed this tale as true to be / As though those very Dwellers in Laxdale, / Risen from the dead had told us their own tale").

The reception links in Autumn focus on the dialectic of Youth and Eld: the Wanderers and Elders are never distinguished from one another, always identified. In one case, after September's second tale, even Youth is included in this identification: no younger folk or elder appear at all in this link, the tale simply leaving memories to a single collective "we."

The immediacies of Summer and the remotenesses of Spring are woven together in Autumn. In October, the first tale (a "lovesome history") ends with young and old moved most differently, with discriminations made among the responses of the young as well, but the second tale (a "story of the fiery lands") provokes the paradisiacal dream common to all: "to find our hearts the world," "to find nought real except ourselves / Scarce in our hearts the very pain alive," a dream of presence, "Since he is part of all, each thing a part, / Beloved alike of his wide-loving heart."

Winter: as Autumn, for the most part, so Winter. "The Golden Apples," "a tale once told / By kin of ours in the dim days of old," comes from an Elder in response to the request of "some young men" for a tale from the Wanderers, a further braiding of the three threads of the gathering. The Wanderer who tells "The Fostering of Aslaug" does so "to name his people's best beloved man," the provenance immediate and ancient in equal measure. For "Bellerophon at Argos" no prior text is given, but the tale itself is introduced as a fragment, with a second fragment to follow and no third piece to complete it: the text as it comes down to us dislocated

Is it then so as I have deemed erewhile,
That thou fear'st God too, even as I fear?
That I shall see the death of thy kind smile,
When, hand in hand, amid the unshadowed air,
Unto God's face forgot we draw anear?
O mocking lie, that told me while ago,
One minute's bliss was worth unending woe!

🖋 The Pope caught at the staff across his knees,
And, rising, stood, leaned heavily thereon,
And said: Why kneelest thou midst words like these?
Rise up, and tell me swift what thou hast done,
E'en as one man speaks to another one;
Or let me go, lest I begin to deem
That I myself spake thus in some ill dream!

🖋 But, cowering down again, cried out the knight:
Nay, leave me not! wait, father; thou shalt hear!
Lo, she is gone now! surely thou said'st right;
For the whole world is trembling with my fear
And tainted with my sin: I will speak clear
And in few words, and know the end at last,
Yea, though e'en now I know myself outcast.

Hast thou not heard about the gods, who erst
Held rule here where thou dwellest? dost thou think
That people 'neath their rule were so accurst
That they forgot in joy to eat and drink,
That they slept not, and loved not, and must shrink
From the world's glory? how if they loved these
Thou callest devils and their images?

from its events. With "Bellerophon in Lycia" it makes another couplet, and makes explicit the condition in which all tales, in these latter days, live: tales, again, as lore and as a life lived ("for like a tale so told / Is each man's life" says the Elder of the City). "The Ring Given to Venus" brings us something new, even in January, when "the hard frost griped all things bitterly, / And who of folk might now say when or why / The earth should change": a book for the tale-teller to read from, not written by him, no Loss from the previous telling to this. (Only one other such book appears in the Paradise, in the first link of the first month, but in that book "perchance it is / That many things are writ amiss." By contrast, this book in which we read "The Ring" is deemed of scrupulous authority: "Of many things the wise man knew, / The man who wrote this.") And "The Hill of Venus" returns us, at Paradise end, to Habundia and to dislocation, the tale-teller "old and grey, / A priest too," who "yet again must have to say / More words of Venus."

The reception links of Winter each concern the dynamics of Youth and Eld, and each is designed to show the two identified. This is most striking—it has the force of a muffled prophecy come true—after the first tale in February, in a scene that appears as a kind of conclusion, making the one tale remaining, "The Hill of Venus," a coda to the whole (and indeed Morris's incessant revision of this tale, which makes it virtually unique in his corpus, argues for its special significance).

> But one youth who had sat alone and sad,
> While others friends and loves beside them had,
> Rose up amid their talk, and slowly turned
> To where the many lights that thereby burned
> Scarce reached, and in that dimness walked awhile;
> And when he came back . . .
> . . . gazed at the elders there,
> As though he deemed his place among them were,
> . . . and one or two
> Among the youths looked up, as if they knew
> The pain that ailed him.

In the scheme of the Paradise, this final identification of Youth and Eld is recognized only at the end of a full year's dreaming, but it has been hidden below the earth, coming to be all along: it renders (in the scheme of the poem) the dream of Paradise real, even in pain, a seamless Habundian

And did God hate the world, then, for their sake,
When fair the sun rose up on every day,
And blade and bloom through the brown earth did
break,
And children were as glad as now? nay, nay,
Time for thy wrath yet; what if these held sway
Even now in some wise, father? Nay, say then,
Hast thou not heard, from certain Northern men,

Of lonely haunters of the wild-woods there,
Not men, nor angels, soulless as men deem,
But their bodily shape most wondrous fair?
What! thinkest thou I tell thee of some dream,
Some wandering glimmer of the moon's grey beam,
Seen when men's hearts sink mid black-shadowed trees,
And unknown words are in the tangled breeze?

Belike I dreamed then! O belike some shade
Of nought that is I saw with these mine eyes!
I saw her feet upon the blossoms laid,
The flowers o'er which no God-made sun shall rise!
Belike I am a mad fool mid the wise,
But nothing therefor of God's wrath need fear,
Because my body and soul I gave her there.

What! must I name her, then, ere thou mayst know
What thing I mean? or say where she doth dwell,
A land that new life unto me did show,
Which thou wilt deem a corner cut from hell,
Set in the world lest all go there too well?
Lo, from THE HILL OF VENUS do I come,
That now henceforth I know shall be my home!

ribbon of Time. The moment precedes the idle singer's address to "Many-peopled earth!"—a summation among summations.

One further note on reception in Winter: in the link following the reading of "The Ring Given to Venus" from the wise man's book, it is the material immediacy of the book that matters. It is a book of "worn leaves" with "flowers therein, / Drawn on the margin of the yellowing skin," with "fair images" and words that transfix the tale-teller even when the tale is done. The tale-teller, which is to say the book-reader, provides the only reception here, and his relation to the book an embodiment of the paradisiacal dream: to see, if not to live, his desire. This, again, all within the poem's conceit: the real book reader is, perhaps, another story.

A Year in the Life: the Linktale represents a festival that repeats twenty-four times, of story, talk, music, wine, food, and communion. Gadamer, "The Relevance of the Beautiful": "It is of the nature of the festival that it should proffer time, arresting it and allowing it to tarry. . . . The calculating way in which we normally manage and dispose of our time is, as it were, brought to a standstill." "The temporal character of the festive celebration that we enact lies in the fact that it does not dissolve into a series of separate moments." It is a continuing moment, a paradox: "A certain kind of recurrence belongs to the festival. . . . Such moments represent the primacy of something that happens in its own time and at the proper time, something that is not subject to the abstract calculation of temporal duration," as, for example, wages per hour are subject. "What exactly does it mean to say that we 'celebrate a festival'? Is celebration conceived simply negatively as a break from work? And if so, why? Surely because work is something that separates and divides us. For all the cooperation necessitated by joint enterprise and the division of labor in our productive activity, we are still divided as individuals as far as our day-to-day purposes are concerned. Festive celebration, on the other hand, is clearly distinguished by the fact that here we are not primarily separated, but rather are gathered together. It is true, of course, that we now find it hard to realize this unique dimension of festive celebration. Celebrating is an art, and one in which earlier and more primitive cultures were far superior to ourselves."[24]

Living Not / Not Alone

Such thoughts seem desolate at first; at times all the bitterness of life seems concentrated in them. They bring the image of

He sprang up as he spoke, and faced the Pope,
Who through his words had stood there trembling
sore,
With doubtful anxious eyes, whence every hope
Failed with that last word; a stern look came o'er
His kind vexed face: Yea, dwell there evermore!
He cried: just so much hope I have of thee
As on this dry staff fruit and flowers to see!

Walter laughed loud, and knew not who was there,
And who was gone, nor how long he abode
Within that place; or why his feet must fare
Round about Rome that night; or why that load
Was on his heart; or why next morn the road
Beneath his hurrying feet was white and dry,
And no cloud flecked the sunny April sky.

He knew not, though he wondered at all these,
And where he went; but nought seemed strange to him,
And nought unknown, when the great forest-trees
Around a cleared space of the wood were dim
In windless dawn with white mist that did swim
About a pine-clad cliff, above a stream
Dark, scarcely seen, and voiceless as a dream.

No ignorance, no wonder, and no hope
Was in his heart, as his firm feet passed o'er
The shallow's pebbles and the flowery slope,
And reached the black-mouthed cavern, the dark door,
Unto the fate now his for evermore,
As now at last its echoing stony dearth
And dull dark closed betwixt him and the earth.

173

one washed out beyond the bar in a sea at ebb, losing even his personality, as the elements of which he is composed pass into new combinations. Struggling, as he must, to save himself, it is himself that he loses at every moment.

—PATER

From Plato to the "*Schund und Schmutz*" laws of the modern world, the defamation of the pleasure principle has proved its power; opposition to such defamation easily succumbs to ridicule.

—MARCUSE

We must eat again from the tree of knowledge in order to fall back into the state of innocence.

—KLEIST

Pater names the problem—dislocation—Marcuse indicates the difficulties of the solution—"opposition to such defamation"—and Kleist defines the desire: liberation from sin, from History, from shame and fear and self-hatred, from the sickness of the grasping soul. As all three make plain, the project is virtually hopelessly self-contradicted, open at best to a hope (as Adorno says) "in its defeat to convict the judge."

The negation of the negation, the permanent revolution, the Body dying Present, Habundian love. For Marcuse "the image of human freedom is dislocated" in its subjection to the "Welfare-Through-Warfare State," "this amalgam of liberty and aggression, production and destruction": "the project" of this dislocated image is "the *subversion of this sort of progress,*" subversion of both Welfare and Warfare as currently conceivable, undoing of the constituents of both Pleasure and Terror. " 'Polymorphous sexuality,' " Marcuse says, "was the term which I used to indicate that the new direction of progress would depend completely on the opportunity to activate repressed or arrested *organic,* biological needs." (Morris: "We shall not be happy unless we live like good animals.") "The body against 'the machine'—" self-contradicted, the body itself a notion of "the political machine, the corporate machine, the cultural and educational machine which has welded blessing and curse into one rational whole," which would suffer nothing to remain outside it. Pleasure itself, all presence, one's "most secret innervations" administered: "The adjustment of pleasure to the reality principle implies the subjugation and

ND what more would ye hear of him?
Meseems
It passes mind of man to picture well
His second sojourn in that land; yet gleams
There might be thence, if one had heart to tell,
In sleepless nights, of horrors passing hell,
Of joys by which our joys are misery;
But hopeless both, if such a thing may be.

Let us be silent then, but hear at least
What the old tale tells: that the morrow morn
The Pope was busy at the Holy Feast;
Then through the ancient solemn streets was borne,
Where stood the folk as thick as summer corn;
Then o'er their bowed heads and their weeping stilled,
With his small blessing voice the hushed air thrilled:

And, many other things being said and done,
Unto his own house came back at the last,
And in his quiet garden walked alone
Pondering, his mind perplexed and overcast,
Not with the hurry of the day late past;
Rather that haggard face, those hopeless eyes,
Despite himself would still before him rise.

The shadows fell their longest; a great flood
Of golden light glowed through the peaceful place;
The Pope sat down; the staff of olive-wood,
Cursed, as it were, at ending of that case,
Fell from him as he turned his weary face
Unto the western glory: close beside,
A babbling conduit from its stone did glide.

174

diversion of the destructive force of instinctual gratification, of its incompatibility with the established societal norms and relations, and, by that token, implies the transubstantiation of pleasure itself."[25]

For Freud, Marcuse says, "Civilization begins when the primary objective—namely, integral satisfaction of needs—is effectively renounced"; the problem is older than dark Satanic mills, but if the root of the problem is as old as civilization, Capitalism for Marcuse is its flower, the final ripening of Warfare as Welfare. In what Marcuse variously calls "advanced industrial society," "mass democracy," "the market economy" (and elsewhere, of course, One-dimensional Society), "Only one mode of thought-activity is 'split-off' from the new organization of the mental apparatus and remains free from the rule of the reality principle: *phantasy* is protected from cultural alterations and stays committed to the pleasure principle."[26]

This is a hopeful moment in the text. The "triumph" of "the reality principle" "over the pleasure principle is never complete and never secure. In the Freudian conception, civilization does not once and for all terminate a 'state of nature'. What civilization masters and represses—the claim of the pleasure principle—continues to exist in civilization itself. The unconscious retains the objectives of the defeated pleasure principle. Turned back by the external reality or even unable to reach it, the full force of the pleasure principle not only survives in the unconscious but also affects in manifold ways the very reality which has superseded the pleasure principle. The *return of the repressed* makes up the tabooed and subterranean history of civilization." But it is a familiar story by now: this privileged zone of pleasure's operation, this "other part of the mental apparatus remains free from the control of the reality principle—at the price of becoming powerless, inconsequential, unrealistic."[27]

It is within these constraints, "Thy gear too thin, thy limbs and heart too weak," that phantasy "continues to speak the language of the pleasure principle, of freedom from repression, of uninhibited desire and gratification," and that "imagination preserves the 'memory' of the subhistorical past when the life of the individual was the life of the genus, the image of the immediate unity between the universal and the particular under the rule of the pleasure principle." It is a Habundian rule: "Imagination envisions the reconciliation of the individual with the whole, of desire with realization, of happiness with reason. While this harmony has been removed into utopia by the established reality principle, phantasy insists that it must and can become real, that behind the illusion lies *knowledge*. The

Well sang the birds; all was so sweet and fair,
The old man's heart, transmuted all his care
Into a loving peace right hard to win:
He murmured in his faded voice and thin,
Mid the full sweetness of the spring: Would God
That man and I this peace together trod!

For he mayhap had things to say to me
He could not say then, knowing not what I was;
And I, God wot that there are things I see
To tell of, if the words my lips would pass;
Things dimly seen, indeed, as in a glass:
Woe's me! for who shall help me if I erred!
Yet God, I deemed, had given me that last word.

O God, if I have done thee deadly wrong,
And lost a soul thou wouldst have saved and blessed,
Yet other words thou knowest were on my tongue,
When 'twixt that soul & mine thine image pressed:
Thou wilt remember this and give him rest!
And as for me, thou knowest I fear thee nought,
Since this my body and soul thine own hand
wrought.

The sun was sunken now, the west was red,
And still the birds poured forth their melody;
A marvellous scent about him seemed to spread,
Mid strange new bliss the tears his eyes drew nigh;
He smiled and said: Too old to weep am I;
Unless the very end be drawing near,
And unimagined sounds I soon shall hear.

175

truths of imagination are first realized when phantasy itself takes form, when it creates a universe of perception and comprehension. . . . This occurs in *art*."[28]

Against "the progress of civilization—progress achieved through the subjugation of the sensuous faculties to reason"—Art (which Marcuse calls "the Orphic and Narcissistic experience of the world") embodies "the redemption of pleasure, the halt of time, the absorption of death; silence, sleep, night, paradise": a resistance nevertheless reduced to marginality and radical doubt, "committed to the underworld and to death." Orpheus and Narcissus "do not convey a 'mode of living'. . . . At best, they are poetic, something for the soul and the heart. But they do not teach any 'message'—except perhaps the negative one that one cannot defeat death or forget and reject the call of life in the admiration of beauty."[29] An experience of self-contradiction, of double negative, paradise dislocated.

"So let me sing of names remembered, / Because they, living not, can ne'er be dead": the idle singer's project from the start is a matter of negativities, its deeply conflicted propositions that Death, spite of paradox, is Deathless, that the undead is the object of our love (the poem makes necrophiliacs of us all), and that the Living is Not. All the idle singer's tales are the idle singer's one tale, a tale of "the destructive force of instinctual gratification," of the "subjugation and rejection" of this force, of the transubstantiation of pleasure. The tale as a whole, the Paradise, and in each of its parts, is a tale of "Eros, penetrating into consciousness, . . . moved by remembrance; with it he protests against the order of renunciation; he uses memory in his effort to defeat time in a world dominated by time. But in so far as time retains its power over Eros, happiness is essentially a thing of the *past*. The terrible sentence which states that only the lost paradises are the true ones judges and at the same time rescues the *temps perdu*." "Still," Marcuse adds, "this defeat of time is artistic and spurious; remembrance is no real weapon unless it is translated into historical action."[30]

The Wanderers, Milanion, Michael, Acrisius and Perseus, Jovinian, Psyche, the Scholar, Alcestis, a nameless Florentine, Croesus, the Falcon-Watcher King, Pygmalion, Ogier, Paris, Gregory-John, Accontius and Cydippe, Bharam who never laughed again, Rhodope, Gudrun, Hercules, Aslaug, Bellerophon, Laurence, Walter: all protest against the order of renunciation, all, like the idle singer, helpless "to defeat time in a world dominated by time." All the tales are this one tale, a play of form as

And yet, before I die, I needs must go
Back to my house, and try if I may write,
For there are some things left for me to do,
Ere my face glow with that ineffable light.
He moved and stooped down for his staff; still bright
The sky was, as he cast his eyes adown,
And his hand sought the well-worn wood and brown.

With a great cry he sprang up; in his hand
He held against the sky a wondrous thing,
That might have been the bright archangel's wand,
Who brought to Mary that fair summoning;
For lo, in God's unfaltering timeless spring,
Summer, and autumn, had that dry rod been,
And from its barrenness the leaves sprang green,

And on its barrenness grew wondrous flowers,
That earth knew not; and on its barrenness
Hung the ripe fruit of heaven's unmeasured hours;
And with strange scent the soft dusk did it bless,
And glowed with fair light as earth's light grew less,
Yea, and its gleam the old man's face did reach,
Too glad for smiles, or tears, or any speech.

Who seeth such things and liveth? That high-tide
The Pope was missed from throne and chapel-stall,
And when his frightened people sought him wide,
They found him lying by the garden wall,
Set out on that last pilgrimage of all,
Grasping his staff; and surely, all folk said,
None ever saw such joy on visage dead.

176

Gadamer would say: "When do we speak of play and what is implied when we do? Surely the first thing is the to and fro of constantly repeated movement—we only have to think of certain expressions like 'the play of light' and 'the play of the waves' where we have such a constant coming and going, back and forth, a movement that is not tied down to any goal," "movement *as* movement, exhibiting so to speak a phenomenon of excess, of living self-representation . . . excess striving to express itself in the living being."[31]

To speak of theme, in this context, or to speak of "The Hill of Venus" as a coda, is in a sense to violate the spirit of the thing. The notion of theme is itself a transcendental notion, like the notion of a coda, a privileging strategy of an infected hermeneutics: a dislocating maneuver, abstraction from the "*cognitio sensitiva . . .* the apparent particularity of sensuous experience."[32] Repeating the theme in a "constantly repeated movement" works as a counterpoint to this maneuver, rendering the body of the manifestation of the theme the thing, the theme itself virtually given in advance, of no account. At the same time, from a distance at least, the repetition of the theme renders it the only Thing, its manifestations of no account: an obsession, totalizing, leveling.

Thus again the Paradise embodies its own Death. It incorporates theme (and structure: a coda, a calendar, a binding) to neutralize it, "the embrace of those at war" in Adorno's phrase, and in this embrace can only lose itself, doubly self-denied, theme-mad and theme-empty, tightly structured of virtually interchangable parts. We approach the thematic material of the Paradise in the same spirit with which we approach the question of the work's interest or boredom for us: the questions of theme and interest both emblematic of our inescapable dislocation from the world beyond exchange value.

Some of the tales, like "The Writing on the Image," "The Watching of the Falcon," or "The Ring Given to Venus," are very deliberate in locating the tale in a place, particular if often nameless: the question of context, of location, comes to the foreground. Other tales, like "The Son of Croesus" or "The Story of Cupid and Psyche," only locate the action briefly before plunging directly into the events themselves, as if location (or dislocation) were of no account and the tale were all. These latter, contextless tales, tend to come from the Elders, while the tales concerned to locate themselves tend to come from the Wanderers (although there are exceptions here—"Ogier the Dane" and "The Death of Paris," back to back in the middle of the book, are an example—and ambiguous cases as well): thus

SAD eyes there were the while the tale
was told,
And few among the young folk were
so bold
As to speak out their thoughts con-
cerning it,
While still amidst that concourse they did sit.
But some, when to the fresh bright day they turned,
And smooth cheeks even in that freshness burned,
'Neath burning glances might find words to speak,
Wondering that any tale should make love weak
To rule the earth, all hearts to satisfy;
Yet as they spake, perchance, some doubt went by
Upon the breeze, till out of sight and sound
Of other folk their longing lips had found,
If but a little while, some resting-place,
On hand, on bosom, on bright eager face.
BUT the old men, learned in earth's bitter lore,
Were glad to leave untouched the too rich store
Of hapless memories, if it might be done;
And wandered forth into the noonday sun
To watch the blossoms budding on the wall,
And hear the rooks among the elm-trees call,
And note the happy voices on the breeze,
And see the lithe forms; making out of these
No tangled story, but regarding them
As hidden elves upon the forest's hem
Gaze on the dancers through the May-night green,
Not knowing aught what troubled looks may mean.

another doubling, another couplet, tales of Nowhere and tales of Here or There, tales of Paradise and Earthly tales. And a doubling of the doubling: for the Earthly tales are paradisiacal precisely in their disdislocation, their rootedness in place, and the Paradise tales are corrupted precisely by their dislocation.

A Hill of Venus

The Hill of Venus" is divided into five unnumbered parts, breaks in the text marked by large boldface capitals: these five parts take the form of four plus one (the order of the seasons, as it were, and something extra), four broad movements of the tale and then a coda. The first section concerns the knight Walter's life in the world before he enters the Hill, the second takes him from his entrance to his meeting with Venus (the tale's first consummation), the third shows him getting edgy in Paradise, the world's claims of fear and doubt (the repressed) returning, and in the fourth, the longest, he leaves the Hill and goes to Rome, seeking (and both getting and not getting) "God's pardon" from the Pope, and then returns to the Hill: doubling back on himself twice. The fifth section, very short, leaves Walter's tale, and concerns the Pope in the aftermath of his audience, the trace Walter leaves in the world between his disappearances: it provides the tale's second consummation, the flowering and fruitbearing of the "dry rod," a hallucination of the Habundian.

The tale introduces Walter as if he were riding (on horseback) through *The Earthly Paradise* as a whole. He has come "from the Kaiser's court" to a Habundian landscape ("Now 'twixt the trees slowly"), and "Dull enow seemed his thoughts, as on he went / From tree to tree." The setting of the tale into which Walter rides embodies a Habundian conceit as well, the description of the weather in the wood, with which the tale begins, offered as a pattern for this moment in the human mood: "Doubtful 'twixt storm and sunshine," "such terror as of night / Waylaying day." When the thunder speaks, Walter answers "Thou callest me; I come; / I come, O lovely one! Oh, thou art nigh."

From the start here, there is reasonable doubt as to which Goddess is "nigh" indeed, speaking the language of the natural world. Venus is the one Walter has in mind, but Venus, like the Pope's God (Who "devilish" Walter also has in mind), is more appropriately spoken of as distant: in

Walter's audience with the Pope, if God speaks at all it is only in the Pope's "small blessing voice," the focus of attention on "the Pope's own face"; and Walter's dream of Venus nigh is, it would seem, a dream quite out of this world (if not entirely). The only deity nigh is not a deity but the unnamed One who speaks, indeed is, the language of the natural world, time and place and number of Habundia's going green dream. Habundia is who "callest," but who Walter has not the ears to hear.

Mons Veneris: Walter comes to the Hill, the "cavern's mouth" (Hill and cavern negations of one another, concavity and convexity doubling for one another): a genital site generalized to the whole landscape, including even the weather ("bright with sun," "though still within its heart the tumult stayed, / Content as yet to keep the world afraid")—the polymorphous rampant, threatening. The zone of pleasure is "a devilish world," a place of lore, tabooed, unvisited out of fear. "For all the stories were at one in this"—the Hill is described as a Mons Victoria, the site of capital: "some first minutes of unheard of bliss," "grasped greedily," "longings nought could satisfy," "a trap baited well." The Hill represents both Eros and Thanatos, in Marcuse's (Freud's) terms, another doubling. (*The Earthly Paradise* itself is not such a place as described here: its pleasures are slow and steady.) A fearful Hill, "amidst the dull world's hopeless, hurrying race, / Where the past gain each new gain makes a loss," "a world made to be lost."

At issue explicitly is "the name of Love," the Other of this world, which lives only in "old stories" and new visions of them Walter imagines, not in the Here and Now. Walter's vision of "the perfect peace Love's loving arms enfold" comes in counterpoint to the thunder, at once a generation of the Habundian and a negation ("in spite of you behold") of Love's dislocation from this world. Walter in other words is estranged both from his doom and his salvation, entranced by a dream he cannot hear. When he goes forward into the Hill, it is to Some Thing Other, neither an Administered nor Habundian world but a dialectical body of the two. ("Love's Gleaning-Tide" [1872]: "How shall we say, we sowed in vain? / The root was joy, the stem was pain, / The ear a nameless blending"; "Spring's Bedfellow" [1873]: "And sorrow laid abed with Spring / Begat an earthly bliss.")[33] The Love Walter seeks within the arms of Death is not the love of his desire: the Love of Venus is a love separated out, an abstraction. And it is only in the embrace of this abstraction that he can move forward at all. He does, and faints.

The world in which Walter comes to his senses, the world of the Hill, is a world of Dream, of Habundia, and of Song, and also a place of return to the material world: "his senses cleared felt strange and weak," a dream of the senses, a "love-dream." "A half hush was there round about," a still predominance of sound, "hushed and low / For worship of the sweet love-laden days": if "in waking grows the love-dream dim," the wake of Walter's dream here only grows and grows. A pure Habundian world: "in the thickest of a wood / Of trees fair-blossomed, heavy-leaved," "'midst a close break of eglantine and rose," the particulars named in Habundian fashion, particular but unspecific, gratuitous, flowers to fit the rhythm and rhyme and general formulaic symbolic purposes of the whole. It is a world, still, from which Walter is dislocated, even there, as he "vainly strive[s] / In one short minute all that life to live": "his armour's clinking . . . / An overloud and clean unlooked-for sound."

The folk of this Paradise come to him first in "the fitful murmur of dumb sound, / Far off and faint." They are like the idle singer's couplets: "Softly they passed, and if not swiftly, still / So many, and in such a gliding wise, / That . . . / . . . scarce might his eyes / . . . / Note mid the throng fair face, or form, or limb"—Habundian-limbed, obscure-faced, movement-wise. The song they sing (printed elsewhere, by hand in *A Book of Verse,* as "Praise of Venus," but here under the simple title "Song") is in couplets arranged in stanzas, composed in a structure that reads, one more time, as four plus one: the first stanza of six lines (with the first two standing as a sort of general introduction for the whole Song, making thus a stanza of four plus two), the second and fourth of eight lines each (four times two), the third of four, and the fifth of twenty-two lines, beyond even the constraint of stanza, a runaway form, hemmed couplets unhemmable. The regulated stanzas sing of workers without love ("Before our lady came on earth"), of craft disspirited: Unkissed, Unkissed, Unkissed, Unkissed, the merchant, the knights, the mariner, the minstrel. Venus herself appears in the stanza of abundance, as does the world: "the green ridges of the sea," "the curdling foam," "the yellow sand," "the bee-beset ripe-seeded grass," "the purple-dusted butterfly," "thy quivering thigh," "the flickering of the orange shade."

Even then, Venus is nowhere to be seen (and neither is the world). She is a name in a song only (and the song is Habundian). Walter's desire to meet Venus in the flesh (so to speak: Venus is not of the "good animals") is defined by distance: "And if this strange world were not all too wide, /

. . . he might some day touch her hand with his." He dreams, in other words, of his dream's limits, his only hope to find Love if the land is small enough to get out of, the threat a totality so encompassing there is no Other: he dreams of a totality not absolute, within which Love might live. Even in his dream, the basic laws of the place the same "as though in that dull world he journeyed still": opposites identified.

Venus appears in a stanza that begins "Nay," her coming prepared by nine stanzas notable for their Habundian emptiness: Walter is referred to as "the wanderer" through a recapitulation of the themes already established, the weather and landscape, his thoughts of Love, the redundancy of this material the necessary price of our purchase on pleasure. And still she is not fully here, but sensed: "The blissful knowledge on his soul did grow / That she was there, her speech as his speech, stilled / By very love." It is only in the next stanza, which begins "O close, O close there"—which is to say, not quite here—that she appears in full, "No cloud to raise her from the earth; her feet / Touching the grass." A present sight.

There is no language for such a moment. "What matter by what name of heaven or earth / Men called his love?" Language can only hope to govern the experience of the Hill, word and dream incompatible, mutually exclusive dominions, another doubling within the body of the Paradise. The fitful murmur of dumb sound.

"What, is the tale not ended then? Woe's me!" This Paradise of Walter's is a paradise of Love abstracted from the world (no love in a hut), and thus a place of alienation. The pageant of lovers that he sees— famous lovers out of History—is a catalog of suffering, and telling their tales to him these figures "look askance" away from Venus. A bewildered materiality, fulfilled of illusion, this pageant is a projection of Walter's own dislocation: "Then a great longing would there stir in him, / That all those kisses might not satisfy." What is particularly disturbing to his loving perfect peace is the recognition that "he alone / Should have a love all perfect and his own," or rather, the recognition that this is impossible ("trembling would he cry / To tell him how . . . / To tell him how"), that what he is "living" is "not." A dream is a dream, however real it seems: "no real weapon unless it is translated into historical action."[34] (The Paradise, at once both dream and embodiment, represents both what Venus represents and what Habundia does: what is not and what is.) Walter is moved by, and despairs of, solidarity, the transcendental common.

Venus buys off his alienation with distractions of various kinds: "softest words her lips could make," "touches worth a lifetime of delight," "all places fresh and bright," "greater marvels"—buys off, at least, the frenzy of his alienation, sedating him with the prosperity of oblivion. But Walter, by very virtue of her unreal blandishments, is a goner: he begins to worry about "God's last justice," shifting his transcendentals, both the Here and the There neither here nor there. He is Nowhere and doesn't know it: returned, from the Kaiser's court, to pagan idols, in a world (the *real* totality of his worry) that belongs to Jehovah, dislocation upon dislocation. Nowhere: the common world of the senses.

The idle singer appears careful not to indicate any judgment on Walter at this dreadful pass: his flight from the Hill at once makes sense and seems borne of an inadequacy. Venus never speaks to him (but once, when he refers to the sound, past, of "thy sweet voice," and once again directly, if again past, in Walter's flashback as he leaves: she never speaks in *our* hearing); she denies him sympathy (which we are to provide), yet at the same time he is himself the source of the problem, preoccupied by "vain longing and regret and fear," not sympathetic but pathetic, helpless. Leaving this Paradise, for Walter, at once means leaving the world of the pleasure principle (a recidivism of the performance principle: "Memory of deeds done" is the thought that snaps Walter's mind and sends him back again to "that dull world"), and recognizing that the pleasure principle, just as any putative transcendentality, is a corrupt notion, subject to decay as all else, an abstraction, alienation's name for the unnameable, split-off.

In this context, Walter's return to the world beyond the cave is a return *to* materiality, to presence, to Habundia. His concept of Love, oxymoronic, is a concept of Hell, a transcendence that alienates Walter from his own body, paralyzed "in stony dread" "cold with terror." And of course, again, this vision of "that lonely hell," the Paradise of the Pleasure Principle, is a vision of that other Queen's, Victoria's, world. The world we flee with Walter here is the world we come to, inescapable.

He flees.

There is still nothing new under this sun. The first thing Walter has
contact with, back in the world of things present, is "a tree trunk."
"Clearly he saw the world and where he was": a moment of revelation, the
return of the familiar from estrangement, out of Paradise and into paradise, location out of dislocation dislocated. But Walter is not present to
these things, this world, however clearly he sees them for an instant.
"Cold to the very bone" in his dreamy garb of Love, his own dislocation is
deathless: "His raiment of such worth / For gems, that in strange places
had their birth, / But frail as is the dragon-fly's fair wing" no due habitation for his body. (The dream web is a doubled image: both "the raiment
rent of stories oft besung" unfit for survival in Her Majesty's Factory
Land, and the shelter that Land offers a body, a bauble for the foolish,
lavish but wrong-headed. A doubled dream of Queens, Venus and Victoria.) The first human contact Walter has is a frightened man shooting an
arrow at him, the first place he comes to the place where he used to go
"maying" as "a youth," "when maiden's love first known was fresh and
fair," and where his appearance now scares off the old woman who once
watched over them. Deeply dislocated, ripped up at the roots and cut at.

He thinks of returning—again a doubled move, both an escape back to the
pleasure principle out of the world of competition and fear, and an escape
back to Hell, to the nightmare of changeless prosperity, back to the Anti-
Habundian, retreat from the familiar world gone unfamiliar, "the cottage
midmost of the place." Instead of returning, he makes another self-
contradicted gesture, at once theft and exchange, taking from the cottage
"raiment well worn by miles of wind-beat wold" and leaving his begemmed weed in recompense. There is nowhere to go. He sees "the great
river that of old he knew," "a wonder and a tale to many a man," but "he
went on, wondering not; all tales were nought," a great presence as if it
were not there. (Note that *tales* are precisely what was missing from
Venus' paradise—"no memory of deeds done" there. Walter knows the
tales of the pageant of lovers, which is what provokes his first unease
there, but the tales are Walter's imposition on the place, his own—dislocated—way of reading it. Now Walter is the one without tales.) "For all
seemed shadows to him" when he returns to "his father's ancient house,"
which he does not enter. No home nowhere.

"How can words measure misery, when the sun / Shines at its brightest
over plague and ill?" Abundance of misery, abundance of sun, Habundian
beyond words (and cast in the most formulaic), the world Walter wanders

is an empty place, and Walter himself at this point but "a weary ghost," his memory "crushed." It is, echo of his entry into the Hill, "the sweet sound of mournful singing" that draws him on: the song comes from pilgrims, who in effect colonize Walter's soul. One tells Walter "unto life I go" and unto absolution for "my dreadful crime," but Walter imagines that he's dreamed these people up, and wanders off in "hapless day-dreams . . . / That knew no God to come," a man of a different faithlessness entirely. He walks among a throng listening to a monk speak "Repent" but is unmoved: instead "upon a daisied patch of road-side grass / He cast himself" upon Habundia's graces. There is nowhere else to go. But abruptly (to all appearances) Walter joins the pilgrims—"Unto God's pardon with you would I wend"—"And on their way they went so fervently / That swept away from earth he seemed to be": not a good omen, a fervent leap of fear.

They get to Rome, "a beleaguered town of ghosts." Walter, "Dead in a prison vast and void" "dead he seemed," hallucinates Venus. The Pope, meanwhile, is absolving him (without asking anything), and wants him to speak, suggests that he is "a coward" for his silence: this to a dead man. Then Walter's hallucination vanishes, without speaking, and he says to the Pope "Look at me, father!" The dynamics of materiality is the important thing here (it is "the Pope's own face" Walter is promised to be brought to): the missing world that lies beyond the world of the Pope as beyond the transcendent Love world of Venus, a third world that Walter (did he know it, nameless), along with Morris's whole book, yearns for. The world returned to itself, neither the abstraction of Love nor the alienation of advancing civilization (gods after gods after gods), but the practice of love *in* that world of alienation.

Both Walter and the Pope, if they are present at all, are present in their dislocations, as Walter speaks of his Love and the Pope responds, "to one lost love so clear, / God's glory to the other present there." The vision of God's grace that the Pope offers is like a vision of Venus: "never-dying, never-craving love," no help for Walter. He hallucinates Venus again, speaking to her for two stanzas and then making a plea on behalf of the old gods, persistent though despised by those who serve the new—and swears allegiance to the Hill. He returns, both dazed ("and knew not who was there, / And who was gone, nor how long he abode" "or why next morn the road") and present ("nought seemed strange to him, / And nought unknown"). The Pope doubts "on this dry staff fruit and flowers to see!" The Pope is wrong.

That's the end of the tale for Walter: both worlds gone for him, a third world unimaginable, he casts his lot with the devil he loves best, the devil of the other.

"The Pope was busy," meanwhile, blessing people in his small voice. The people—"Where stood the folk as thick as summer corn"—take a Habundian form for the occasion. The Pope's own actions figured in Habundian terms as well: "And, many other things being said and done," an abundance of things, and in the Pope's case, things not worth noting particularly, ghost things. The Pope now dislocated in his own world.

Troubled now (infallible and fallible) by Walter's visit (and this is perhaps the idle singer's most ambitious hope, to trouble the Pope: in his defeat to convict the judge), the busy Pope gets meditative. He sits "close beside / A babbling conduit," the conduit the Wanderers pass on their entry into the nameless city, the conduit of Morris's Paradise itself: the Pope himself now as if drawn by the fitful murmur of dumb sound into the heart of radical doubt.

But when "leaves sprang green" from his staff, at once fulfilling his curse on Walter and redeeming Walter's mad dream, the Pope immediately figures the event in terms he can understand: "That might have been the bright archangel's wand / Who brought to Mary that fair summoning," a beckoning of the transcendental. He has of course (since he too is in "The Hill of Venus" here) got it wrong: "That might have been" is not That Is. It is Habundia's wand, rather: "spring, / Summer and autumn, had that dry rod been, / And from its barrenness the leaves sprang green." And if the wand is the work of Venus as well, as is the most obvious reading (we ourselves, reading, in "The Hill of Venus" too)—the thing is unearthly, hung with "ripe fruit" and "wondrous flowers, / That earth knew not," and "with fair light as earth's light grew less" it glows in the dark—still, it is never named in these terms, and the idle singer, at least, treats the scene as a wholly Habundian moment. The Mover of This World is never named at all: unnameable, over which all dominion is presumption, vanity, blind suicide.

"'None ever saw such joy on visage dead.'" It is worth noting that although this sentence says that the Pope had a joyful visage in death, such as never had been seen before, what the *words* say is that not one person saw such joy at all, unnameable joy unseen still as ever. The Pope is joyful dead: he has seen something, if only for an instant. Like every thing else, he is in the end the Paradise itself, a marvel and a tale unknown.

Coda: in one sense (the sense I have been tracing here) every section of "The Hill of Venus" is the same, embodies the same dynamic: a place doubled, divided against itself in enfeebled zeal, caught between worlds, Nowhere. To consider the movements of the tale separately is to consider only the whole in each moment, a dream of the unfragmented from the Land of Matters Unforgot (the Paradise like the completion of Coleridge's dream of Imagination, without the knock on the door "by a person on business from Porlock"). To consider one tale as a whole as a coda to the whole is to consider only the whole in every part. Each tale has its moment, each moment is the one moment over again, each moment worth noting each moment swallowed up: the whole thing doubled, a ravening monster and a hopelessly earthly paradise, hopelessly hopeful, unreal and terrifying. A body in motion, over and over.

Envoi

Words fail us
  —MORRIS

As a lone ant from a broken ant-hill
  from the wreckage of Europe, ego scriptor
        —POUND

The Earthly Paradise is a paradise written from hell, a "hell–a–dice" as Pound says in Pisa, caged and singing.[1] It is also, no less for that, a paradise (as *The Pisan Cantos* is as well) or at least a song toward one: Pound and Morris both encyclopedists of the wayward, their poems cultural summaries bearing the message that the culture is no longer collective, the poems' own failures the very text of that message. Nobody reads *The Earthly Paradise*.

The Death of the Collective is the primal wound of Romanticism, the dialectical birth of Blake's solo illuminations, Wordsworth's speech of real men, Shelley's mythography and Keats's sensorium, Byron's gloom and laughter, Arnold's gloom and stricture, Dickens's vast tapestries, Tennyson's seriousness and Yeats's doomed magic, Lawrence's sexuality, Pound's and Joyce's and Eliot's experiments in the reconstitution of fragments, Silliman's fragments. The entire Romantic enterprise, along with its early Modernist and later developments, can be seen as a response to this condition, each of these figures an attempt to redress or adapt to this Death, their work directed at a totality that is not collective: the nightmare from which we have not awoken, common bondage in separation. Both the Romantics and their Modernist progeny assume the loss of the collective as a fundamental given, and seek through transcendental means to reconstitute it on another footing, through Nature or Posey or Ideology or Style or System or Method, to indicate if not embody the great commonality by which we know ourselves one, or to make the best of that loss as Mr. Leopold Bloom instructs. What is collective in this tradition is the loss of the collective.

Morris's own response to the death of the collective, his variation on the Romantic trope of the monad adrift, marks a direct challenge to one of the central tenets of Romantic ideology: the transcendental ideal that the earlier generations of Romantics worry over, aspire to, and despair of, is transformed in Morris's work into what I have called an aesthetic of habitation. This aesthetic, I have argued, is fundamentally (if unselfconsciously) a political vision as well: neither antithesis nor even prelude to Morris's later Socialist endeavors, but the very foundation of that later work, an Imagination of Socialism, as it were, of the world present to us. The aesthetic of habitation is a gesture toward the immediate, a politics of the antitranscendental: it seeks the collective in the current.

This is a peculiar thing to say with reference to a poem that urges a radical amnesia of the current and moves resolutely far away and long ago, a poem of "the sleepy region." But this is only to say (again) that the vision of the poem is profoundly self-contradicted. To work the antitranscendental, for Morris, is to posit a hegemony of the transcendental which the aesthetic of habitation is an effort to undermine dialectically.

The transcendental ideal, in Modernist work which aspires to the encyclopedic, in *The Cantos* and "The Waste Land" and *Ulysses* and *Finnegans Wake* and *Paterson,* is embodied by an aesthetic of habitation as well: large works to live in, works preoccupied with the body and its spaces, works which go to extraordinary ends to locate themselves. But these later figures in the tradition occupy a vantage of further disintegration: the center cannot hold, I cannot make it cohere.[2] Morris shares in this condition, or in this perception of its extremity, its hegemonic totality, and thus *The Earthly Paradise,* dying for presence, is wholly dislocated, its purchase on the current thoroughly dubious. But at the same time the poem carries with it the possibility, not merely that this condition might be resisted, but that it might be defeatable, that it is not in fact inevitable.

The Earthly Paradise (as, for that matter, the poet's Socialism) is full not only of the death of collective presence but full of its possibility as well, and the two in equal measure. The poem presents itself as able to conceive (if only in a dying whisper, at least at great length, without appearance of impediment) itself as the only world: as if it were, and as if it were shared, and as if Morris writes at the last possible moment of imagining this possibility, of giving it embodiment. The position he occupies in the tradition is pivotal. He sees the end coming, does not yet assume that it has come, and thus relative to the writers who follow his work is at once less fragmented, more capable of imagining whole, and more hopeless, less duped by hope, by the chance of a new beginning, a making new. He is really the most hopeless figure of all, a Champion of Hope.

The collective in the current: this is the challenge of Morris's aesthetic politics, the lost cause of his devotion. Each of his works is thwarted in the communal desire it springs from, his verse and his decorative work and his radical agitation each a "formal response to problems which are theoretically insoluble, except in terms of metaphors which are unsatisfactory and intractable in the actual historical situation." "This is the starting point of Morris's socialist aesthetic," Goode writes, describing the politics in terms that apply as readily, certainly, to the aesthetics: he notes in Morris "a tension between the need to act and the recognition of the limited possibilities of action—limited, that is, not merely quantitatively but qualitatively: English socialism doesn't offer a confrontation with reality" any more than does *The Earthly Paradise*.[3]

Morris's "awareness of alienation comprehends a sense of the radical dislocation of consciousness from historical reality (with its potential for change)." But "his achievement as a creative writer is that his work attests to the need to create a revolutionary sense of community in order to reflect fully the estrangement of the disaffected mind," a project that begins, I have argued, with the idle singer. For Goode, creating a revolutionary literature "means creating forms which neither accept as eternal man's alienation, nor retreat into worlds in which it has no relevance, but which provide for both its recognition and its assessment by realizing it as a subjective response to an objective condition which is not only valid as subjectivity in recoiling from the objective world, but which is also capable of returning to that world as a subversive force. It means the recognition of the estranged mind of man not merely as an escape, but also as a revolutionary agent. The dreamer of dreams has to recognize that he is born in his due time."[4] This is partially an argument for the exclusion of the Paradise from Morris's radical agenda, or the relegation of it to a preamble: the poem makes much of retreat and disclaims subversion: it is the idle singer who claims to be "Born out of my due time." But it seems to me hardly arguable that the "world" into which the poem retreats is one in which alienation "has no relevance": each tale in it is preoccupied with the effect of this condition, and the very fabric of the verse is consumed by it. The poem's embodiment of "the estrangement of the disaffected mind" depends entirely on the sense of a denied collectivity embodied as well.

"Art has therefore to create a new consciousness which moves away from the immediate toward the possible," Goode writes, "but its form is determined by alienation." Here is the contradiction of the Paradise spelled out once again: a movement away from the immediate toward the possible that is the very possibility of the immediate: the distant immediate. This is a possibility that depends, again, on "a revolutionary sense of community," while "Art is ineluctably the creation of the individual,"[5] that depends, in other words, on contradiction.

Art, the embodiment of joy to the maker and pleasure to the user, is the site for Morris not of our transcendence of the world but of our habitation of it. The Death of Art, the burden of all Morris's work, marks the death of collective culture: not the end of transcendence, which is all Romantic illusion, ideology to begin with, but the end of knowing where we are, of being here together. That *The Earthly Paradise* does not attempt to show us where we are, that it attempts to escape, is one index of the fact that we no longer know where we are, that we are nowhere. The failure of the escape is another index: nowhere is a place from which we cannot get back, a present that has lost its roots, a place defined by the impossibility of being known.

Divided at the root, the Paradise exemplifies bourgeois repression: it at once embodies and abhors the notion of pure expenditure, yearning always for a return (in two senses: return of the past, and audience response) even as it expects none, radically denies any. But at the same time as the poem engages the closed economy of bourgeois historical thought, its own history of loss, its status as waste, violates that economy, opening within it a hidden abyss of loss, waste, shame, horror. It violates the closed economy of Marxist historical thought as well: any notion of progress, of forward motion. The economy of historical thought in the Paradise is Habundian, in its textures, in its handling of the past, and in its afterlife endlessly green, nowhere but here. *The Earthly Paradise* stands against everything.

Adorno: "In beauty the frail future offers its sacrifice to the Moloch of the present; because, in the latter's realm, there can be no good, it makes itself bad, in order in its defeat to convict the judge."[6]

NOTES

BIBLIOGRAPHY

INDEX

Notes

Apology

1. Engels, *Correspondence*, 1:370.
2. Faulkner, *Critical Heritage*, 76.
3. Whether Romantic or Marxist or late Victorian hybrid, these are all visions informed by a particular sense of Totality: it is easy to see dialectical thought itself as a response to such a sense, an effort to undo (if only temporarily or virtually) whatever totality defines the limits of the possible, whatever proscribes the sense of Other.

Intro: Administered World

1. Silliman, *New Sentence*, 191.
2. Raymond Williams defines "hegemony" as "the central, effective and dominant system of meanings and values, which are not merely abstract but which are organized and lived . . . [as] a whole body of practices and expectations . . . a set of meanings and values which as they are experienced as practices appear as reciprocally confirming . . . a sense of absolute because experienced reality beyond which it is very difficult for most members of the society to move" (*Problems in Materialism and Culture*, 38). This use of the term originates with Antonio Gramsci (*Prison Notebooks*). I will be using it here repeatedly, somewhat obsessively, in the spirit of Morris's own aesthetics of immersion (see below). Similarly for "what Adorno called the 'administered world', the prototype for what Marcuse was later to make famous as 'one-dimensional society', [in which] the permeation of ideology [has] gone so far that all resistance [is] virtually eliminated" (Jay, *Adorno*, 38).
3. Of course many others could be added to this list, not necessarily socialists alone: Shelley and Keats, for instance, Baudelaire and Blake.
4. See especially Calhoun, *Pastoral Vision*, and Silver, *Romance*.
5. Shelley, "Defence of Poetry," 123.
6. Reed, *Victorian Conventions*, 431.
7. Spiegelman and Mouly, *RAW*, 3.
8. Sussman, *Victorians and the Machine*, 106–7, 104.
9. Morris, *Collected Letters*, 2:202.
10. Adorno, *Minima Moralia*, 206.
11. Ibid., 195, 40.
12. Ibid., 98.
13. Ibid., 247.
14. Calhoun, *Pastoral Vision*, 117–18.
15. Adorno, *Minima Moralia*, 50.

16. Jameson, *Ideologies of Theory*, 63; Horkheimer, *Critical Theory*, 277–78.
17. In Henderson, *Morris: Life, Work and Friends*, 88.
18. Jameson, *Ideologies of Theory*, 89; Adorno, *Minima Moralia*, 95.
19. Adorno, *Minima Moralia*, 36.
20. Gramsci, *Prison Notebooks*, 333.
21. Adorno, *Minima Moralia*, 95; Horkheimer, *Critical Theory*, 278.
22. Jameson, *Postmodernism*, 25; Adorno, *Minima Moralia*, 164.
23. Unger, *Social Theory*, 22.
24. Ibid., 21, 16.
25. Ibid., 18.
26. Schelling, *Philosophy of Art*, 24; Adorno, *Minima Moralia*, 16.
27. Raymond Williams, *Problems in Materialism and Culture*, 37–39; Jameson, *Ideologies of Theory*, 138.
28. Raymond Williams, *Problems in Materialism and Culture*, 273, 40, 48.
29. Jameson, *Ideologies of Theory*, 132; Unger, *Social Theory*, 23, 81.
30. E. P. Thompson, "Communism," 9.
31. Jameson, *Ideologies of Theory*, 117–18.
32. Stevens, "The Snow Man," in *Palm at the End of the Mind*, 54.
33. Morris, *Collected Works*, 22:375.
34. Bloch, *Utopian Function*, 111, 14.
35. Silliman, *New Sentence*, 8, 10.
36. Ibid., 17.
37. Ibid., 12.
38. Ibid., 45–46, 61.
39. Horkheimer, *Critical Theory*, 279; Silliman, *New Sentence*, 109. Silliman here is quoting Peter Schjeldahl on the poet Joseph Ceravolo.
40. From a letter to D. G. Rossetti (10 December 1869), in Faulkner, *Critical Heritage*, 197.
41. Silliman, *New Sentence*, 110.
42. Bataille, *Visions of Excess*, 116–17, 138, 159.
43. Ibid., 241.
44. Ibid., 151, 156; Adorno, *Minima Moralia*, 16.
45. Bataille, *Visions of Excess*, 157.
46. Ibid., 208; García Márquez, *El olor de la guayaba*, 119 (my translation).
47. Marcuse, *Eros and Civilization*, 31; Silliman, *New Sentence*, 53.
48. Rappaport, *Worlds within Worlds*, 61–69, 327.
49. Huntington Library, San Marino, Calif., Rare Book Collection (32154).

Habundian World I: End of Transcendence

1. Unger, *Social Theory*, 22.
2. Potlatch is "a Chinook word, used by the Kwakiutl of British Columbia, the Tlingit of Alaska, Amerindian tribes first studied by anthropologists at the end of the nineteenth century.
     "These tribes, the anthropologists discovered, had a strange practice: one chief met another and offered gifts. The second chief had to respond in kind, but on a higher plane of value. That was the potlatch. The game might begin with the presentation of a necklace and end with the burning of a town—with

a tribe burning its own town, thus raising the obligations of its rival to an almost impossible level. The potlatch was part of a festival, accompanied by storied songs, dances, and the conferral of new names on the great givers ('Whose Property Is Eaten in Feasts,' 'Causing Trouble All Around,' 'The Dance of Throwing Away Property'). . . . For one tribe to fail to rise to the provocation of another was to admit that it valued property, mere things, more than honor; a chief who distributed the wealth of his tribe was said to 'swallow the tribes' that received it. 'The ideal,' sociologist Marcel Mauss wrote in 1925 in *The Gift,* 'is to give a *potlatch* and not have it returned'. . . .

    "Mauss saw the potlatch as a negation of division, as an affirmation of community. It was, he said, the first round table, 'from which none need be excluded'—or could be" (Marcus, *Lipstick Traces,* 393–94).

3. Schelling, *Philosophy of Art,* 116, 99, 165, 168.
4. Morris, *Collected Letters,* 1:11.
5. Adorno, *Minima Moralia,* 195.
6. Shelley, "Defence of Poetry," 119, 111, 109, 123–24.
7. Ibid., 137, 117.
8. Pater, Postscript, 246; Shelley, "Defence of Poetry," 113; Marcuse, *Eros and Civilization,* xv.
9. The quotation, as Coleridge himself indicates in a footnote, is from Milton. See Coleridge, *Poetical Works,* 264.
10. Gramsci, *Prison Notebooks,* 333.
11. Wordsworth, *Lyrical Ballads,* 25.
12. Marcuse, *Eros and Civilization,* xxvii; Adorno, *Minima Moralia,* 206.
13. Wordsworth, *Lyrical Ballads,* 18–19, 26.
14. Ibid., 22.
15. Ibid., 21–23, 31–32.
16. Ibid., 21.
17. Ibid., 20, 26–27, 33.
18. De Man, *Rhetoric of Romanticism,* 238; Yeats on Morris in *Trembling of the Veil* (1922): "To-day I do not set his poetry very high, but for an odd altogether wonderful line, or thought; and yet, if some angel offered me the choice, I would choose to live his life, poetry and all, rather than my own or any other man's" (*Autobiographies,* 95).
19. Blake, *Poetry and Prose,* 474; de Man, *Rhetoric of Romanticism,* 48; Shelley, "Defence of Poetry," 135; McGann, "Thing to Mind;" Eliot, *Complete Poems,* 58.
20. "Some Thoughts on the Ornamented Manuscripts of the Middle Ages," in Morris, *Ideal Book,* 1.
21. De Man, *Rhetoric of Romanticism,* 15; Mackail, *Life,* 1:186.
22. The last reprinting of *The Earthly Paradise* as a whole was in the 1966 reissue of the *Collected Works* originally published from 1910 to 1915.
23. Faulkner, *Critical Heritage,* 150.
24. Ibid., 197, 61.
25. Ibid., 81.
26. Kafka, *Parables,* 25.
27. Eliot, "Andrew Marvell," 167–68.

28. Ibid.; Shelley, "Defence of Poetry," 137.
29. Faulkner, *Critical Heritage*, 3.
30. Jameson, *Ideologies of Theory*, 118.
31. Paul Thompson, *Work*, 177–78; Chesterton, "Morris and His School," 17.
32. The footsteps are spectralized too. The *OED* lists five definitions of *footstep:* the first three are "1. A step or tread of the foot; a foot-fall," "2. The mark or print made by a foot," and "3. A vestige or trace; a mark, token, or indication left by anything whether material or immaterial." In each case the indication is of steps already taken: for a thing to lie "before my footsteps" is thus for it to lie where I have not yet gone. The fourth definition is "A foot-path, footway" with one illustrative citation, from 1630, "High-waies or foot steps stopped up": footsteps conjure spectral footsteps, the disembodied the embodied.
33. Blake, "The Marriage of Heaven and Hell," *Poetry and Prose*, 36.
34. Jameson, *Ideologies of Theory*, 118; Faulkner, *Critical Heritage*, 52, 116, 88, 139.
35. McGann, "Thing to Mind"; Faulkner, *Critical Heritage*, 68.
36. Dufty, *Story of Cupid and Psyche*, 9.

Habundian World II: Still Predominance

1. Yeats, "Happiest of the Poets," 84–85.
2. Habundia "seems to be derived from Morris's reading of Grimm's *Teutonic Mythology* (1835) in which there is a discussion of 'the legend of a *domina Abundia* or *dame habonde,* supplied by the French authorities of the Mid. Ages.' She also appears as 'Abondanza', wearing a gold-embroidered green garment and a wreath of flowers while bearing a cornucopia, in Cesare Ripa's *Iconologia,* of which Morris had an illustrated 1669 edition" (Helen A. Timo's introduction to Morris, "Widow's House," 12–13). Timo's citation is from Jacob Grimm, *Teutonic Mythology,* trans. James Steven Stallybrass, 4th ed. (London: Bell, 1882), 1:286.
3. Faulker, *Critical Heritage*, 416–17; Yeats, *Autobiographies*, 94.
4. Faulkner, *Critical Heritage*, 417.
5. Yeats, "Happiest of the Poets," 83.
6. Ibid., 71.
7. Ibid., 74–75.
8. Morris, *Collected Works*, 24:343.
9. Marcuse, *Eros and Civilization*, 127.
10. Jameson, *Ideologies of Theory*, 316–17; Eliot, "Andrew Marvell," 168.
11. Jameson, *Ideologies of Theory*, 76–77.
12. Sussman, *Victorians and the Machine*, 104; Jameson, *Marxism and Form*, 164; Marcuse, *Eros and Civilization*, 132, 123.
13. Welby, *Victorian Romantics*, 46; Jameson, *Marxism and Form*, 108.
14. Adorno, *Minima Moralia*, 95, 247; Jameson, *Marxism and Form*, 395.
15. Jameson, *Marxism and Form*, 185.
16. Ibid., 20–24; Yeats, *Autobiographies*, 95.
17. Wordsworth, *Lyrical Ballads*, 33, 41.
18. Adorno, *Minima Moralia*, 16.
19. Jameson, *Marxism and Form*, 31; Bloch, *Utopian Function*, 125.
20. Faulkner, *Critical Heritage*, 162, 170–71.

21. Horkheimer and Adorno, in Marcuse, *Eros and Civilization,* 227. In Cumming's translation of Horkheimer and Adorno, *Dialectic of Enlightenment,* 105, the sentence reads: "It originates in alienation."
22. Faulkner, *Critical Heritage,* 125, 171–72.
23. Ibid., 68.
24. Ibid., 104–5, 114, 112, 100.
25. Morris, *Artist, Writer, Socialist,* 1:304.
26. Faulkner, *Critical Heritage,* 60–61.
27. Ibid., 63–64.
28. Ibid., 161–62.

Habundian World III: Gratified Despair
1. Faulkner, *Critical Heritage,* 79–80.
2. Ibid., 81–82, 86.
3. Ibid., 86–87.
4. Ibid., 87–88.
5. Ibid., 87.
6. Ibid.
7. Morris, *Collected Works,* 24:87.
8. Kocmanova, *Poetic Maturing,* 18.
9. Ibid., 20.
10. E. P. Thompson, *Romantic to Revolutionary,* 116–18.
11. Faulkner, *Critical Heritage,* 134.
12. Benjamin, *Illuminations,* 69, 71; Faulkner, *Critical Heritage,* 74.
13. Benjamin, *Illuminations,* 71–73.
14. Jameson, *Marxism and Form,* 163.
15. Gadamer, *Relevance of the Beautiful,* 37.
16. Blake, "The Marriage of Heaven and Hell," *Poetry and Prose,* 39.
17. Mackail, *Life,* 1:210.
18. Barthes's *Empire of Signs* speaks of Japanese food-art in the same terms: "Here the foodstuff joins the dream of a paradox: that of a purely interstitial object, all the more provocative in that this emptiness is produced in order to provide nourishment (occasionally the foodstuff is constructed in a ball, like a wad of air" (24): "*the interstice* without specific edges, or again, the empty sign" (26).
19. Silver, *Romance,* 60.
20. Morris, *Collected Works,* 24:165.
21. Ibid., 166.
22. Ibid., 166–67.
23. Ibid., 167–68.
24. Gadamer, *Relevance of the Beautiful,* 40–42.
25. Marcuse, *Eros and Civilization,* xv, xvii, 13.
26. Ibid., 11, xi, xii, xxiii, 14.
27. Ibid., 15–16, 141.
28. Ibid., 142–44.
29. Ibid., 179, 164–66.
30. Ibid., 233.
31. Gadamer, *Relevance of the Beautiful,* 22–23.

32. Ibid., 16.
33. Morris, *Collected Works,* 9:120, 132.
34. Marcuse, *Eros and Civilization,* 233.

Envoi
1. Pound, *Cantos,* 441.
2. Yeats, "The Second Coming," *Collected Poems,* 184; Pound, *Cantos,* 796.
3. Goode, "Dream of Revolution," 221, 238.
4. Ibid., 238, 278, 271.
5. Ibid., 238–9.
6. Adorno, *Minima Moralia,* 95.

Bibliography

Adorno, Theodor. *Minima Moralia: Reflections from Damaged Life*. Trans. E. F. N. Jephcott. London: Verso, 1978.

Arnold, Matthew. Preface to Poems, 1853. *The Works of Matthew Arnold*. 15 vols. London: Macmillan, 1903–4. Vol. 11, pp. 270–93.

Barthes, Roland. *The Pleasure of the Text*. Trans. Richard Miller. New York: Hill and Wang, 1975.

————. *Empire of Signs*. Trans. Richard Howard. New York: Hill and Wang, 1982.

Bataille, Georges. *Visions of Excess: Selected Writings, 1927–1939*. Ed. Allan Stoekl. Trans. Allan Stoekl with Carl R. Lovitt and Donald M. Leslie, Jr. Minneapolis: Univ. of Minnesota Press, 1985.

Baudrillard, Jean. *The Mirror of Production*. Trans. Mark Poster. St. Louis: Telos Press, 1975.

————. *Simulations*. Trans. Paul Foss, Paul Patton, and Philip Beitchman. New York: Semiotext(e), 1983.

Bell, Clive. "William Morris." *Pot-boilers*. London: G. P. Putnam's Sons, 1914, pp. 146–55.

Benjamin, Walter. *Illuminations*. Ed. Hannah Arendt. Trans. Harry Zohn. New York: Schocken, 1969.

————. *Reflections: Essays, Aphorisms, Autobiographical Writings*. Ed. Peter Demetz. Trans. Edmund Jephcott. New York and London: Harcourt Brace Jovanovich, 1978.

————. *Charles Baudelaire: A Lyric Poet in the Era of High Capitalism*. Trans. Harry Zohn. London: Verso, 1983.

Bernstein, Charles. *Content's Dream: Essays 1975–1984*. Los Angeles: Sun and Moon Press, 1986.

————. *Artifice of Absorption*. Philadelphia: Singing Horse Press / Paper Air, 1987.

————, ed. *The Politics of Poetic Form: Poetry and Public Policy*. New York: Roof, 1990.

Blake, William. *The Poetry and Prose of William Blake*. Ed. David V. Erdman. Newly rev. ed., with commentary by Harold Bloom. Berkeley and Los Angeles: Univ. of California Press, 1982.

Bloch, Ernst. *The Utopian Function of Art and Literature: Selected Essays*. Trans. Jack Zipes and Frank Mecklenburg. Cambridge, Mass.: MIT Press, 1988.

Boos, Florence. *The Design of William Morris's "The Earthly Paradise"*. London: Mellen, 1991.

Calhoun, Blue. *The Pastoral Vision of William Morris*. Athens: Univ. of Georgia Press, 1975.

Carlyle, Thomas. *Past and Present*. Vol. 12 of *Carlyle's Complete Works*. The Sterling Edition, 20 vols. Boston: Estes & Lauriat, n.d.

Chesterton, G. K. "William Morris and His School." *Twelve Types*. London: Arthur L. Humphreys, 1902, pp. 15–30.

Coleridge, Samuel Taylor. *Poetical Works*. Ed. Ernest Hartley Coleridge. Oxford: Oxford Univ. Press, 1912, 1969.

de Man, Paul. *The Rhetoric of Romanticism*. New York: Columbia Univ. Press, 1984.

Donne, John. *The Poems of John Donne*. Ed. Herbert J. C. Grierson. 2 vols. London: Oxford Univ. Press, 1912.

Drinkwater, John. *William Morris: A Critical Study*. New York: M. Kennerly, 1912.

Dufty, A. R., ed. *The Story of Cupid and Psyche, by William Morris, with Illustrations Designed by Edward Burne-Jones, Mostly Engraved on the Wood by William Morris*. London and Cambridge: Clover Hill Editions, 1974.

Dunlap, Joseph R. *The Book That Never Was*. New York: Oriole Editions, 1971.

Eagleton, Terry. *The Ideology of the Aesthetic*. Oxford: Basil Blackwell, 1990.

Eliot, T. S. *The Complete Poems and Plays, 1909–1950*. New York: Harcourt, Brace & World, 1962.

———. "Andrew Marvell." *Selected Prose of T. S. Eliot*. Ed. Frank Kermode. London: Faber and Faber, 1975, pp. 161–71.

Engels, Friedrich, Paul Lafargue, and Laura Lafargue. *Correspondence, 1868–1886*. 3 vols. Moscow: Foreign Languages Publishing House, 1959.

Eshleman, Lloyd. *A Victorian Rebel: The Life of William Morris*. New York: Scribners, 1940.

Evans, B. Ifor. *William Morris and His Poetry*. London: G. G. Harrap, 1925.

Faulkner, Peter, ed. *William Morris: The Critical Heritage*. London and Boston: Routledge & Kegan Paul, 1973.

Fourier, Charles. *The Utopian Vision of Charles Fourier: Selected Texts on Work, Love, and Passionate Attraction*. Ed. and trans. Jonathan Beecher and Richard Bienvenu. Columbia: Univ. of Missouri Press, 1983.

Gadamer, Hans Georg. *The Relevance of the Beautiful and Other Essays*. Ed. Robert Bernasconi. Trans. Nicholas Walker. Cambridge: Cambridge Univ. Press, 1986.

García Márquez, Gabriel. *El olor de la guayaba: conversaciones con Plinio Apuleyo Mendoza*. Bogotá: Oveja Negra, 1982.

Goode, John. "William Morris and the Dream of Revolution." *Literature and Politics in the Nineteenth Century*. Ed. John Lucas. London: Methuen, 1971, pp. 221–80.

Gramsci, Antonio. *Selections from the Prison Notebooks*. Ed. and trans. Quintin Hoare and Geoffrey Nowell Smith. New York: International Publishers, 1971.

Grennan, Margaret. *William Morris: Medievalist and Revolutionary*. New York: King's Crown Press, 1945.

Grigson, Geoffrey. "Mining Morris." Review of E. P. Thompson, *William Morris: Romantic to Revolutionary*. *The New York Review of Books*, July 14, 1977, pp. 23–25.

Hejinian, Lyn. *My Life*. Los Angeles: Sun and Moon Press, 1987.

Henderson, Philip. *William Morris: His Life, Work and Friends*. London: Thames & Hudson, 1967.

Horkheimer, Max. *Critical Theory: Selected Essays*. Trans. Matthew J. O'Connell et al. New York: Continuum, 1989.

————, and Theodor W. Adorno, *Dialectic of Enlightenment*. Trans. John Cumming. New York: Continuum, 1987.

Institute of Contemporary Arts. *William Morris Today*. London: ICA, 1984.

Jameson, Fredric. *Marxism and Form: Twentieth-Century Dialectical Theories of Literature*. Princeton: Princeton Univ. Press, 1971.

————. *The Ideologies of Theory: Essays 1971–1986: Volume Two, Syntax of History*. Minneapolis: Univ. of Minnesota Press, 1988.

————. *Late Marxism: Adorno, or The Persistence of the Dialectic*. London: Verso, 1990.

————. *Postmodernism, or, the Cultural Logic of Late Capitalism*. Durham: Duke Univ. Press, 1991.

Jauss, Hans Robert. *Toward an Aesthetic of Reception*. Trans. Timothy Bahti. Minneapolis: Univ. of Minnesota Press, 1982.

Jay, Martin. *The Dialectical Imagination: A History of the Frankfurt School and the Institute of Social Research, 1923–1950*. Boston: Little, Brown, 1973.

————. *Adorno*. Cambridge: Harvard Univ. Press, 1984.

Joyce, James. *Finnegans Wake*. New York: Penguin, 1976.

Kafka, Franz. *Parables*. Trans. Willa and Edwin Muir. New York: Schocken, 1947.

Kiernan, V. G. *Poets, Politics and the People*. Ed. Harvey J. Kaye. London: Verso, 1989.

Kinnell, Galway. *The Book of Nightmares*. Boston: Houghton Mifflin, 1971.

Kleist, Heinrich von. "Über das Marionnetentheater." *Gesamtausgabe*. Ed. Helmut Sembdner. 8 vols. Munich: Deutscher Taschenbuch Verlag, 1964–69. Vol. 5.

Kocmanova, Jessie. *The Poetic Maturing of William Morris*. Prague: Brno Studies in English, 1964.

Kristeva, Julia. *Powers of Horror: An Essay on Abjection*. Trans. Leon S. Roudiez. New York: Columbia Univ. Press, 1982.

Lindsay, Jack. *William Morris: His Life and Work*. London: Constable, 1975.

Lutchmansingh, Lawrence. "Archaeological Socialism: Utopia and Art in William Morris." In *Socialism and the Literary Artistry of William Morris*. Ed. Florence S. Boos and Carole G. Silver. Columbia and London: Univ. of Missouri Press, 1990, pp. 7–25.

Macherey, Pierre. *A Theory of Literary Production*. Trans. Geoffrey Wall. London and New York: Routledge & Kegan Paul, 1978.

Mackail, J. W. *The Life of William Morris*. 2 vols. London: Longmans, Green, 1899; New York and London: Benjamin Blom, 1968.

Marcus, Greil. *Lipstick Traces: A Secret History of the Twentieth Century*. Cambridge: Harvard Univ. Press, 1989.

Marcuse, Herbert. *Eros and Civilization: A Philosophical Inquiry into Freud*. Boston: Beacon Press, 1955, 1966.

————. *One-Dimensional Man: Studies in the Ideology of Advanced Industrial Society*. Boston: Beacon Press, 1964.

————. *An Essay on Liberation*. Boston: Beacon Press, 1969.

————. *The Aesthetic Dimension: Toward a Critique of Marxist Aesthetics.* Boston: Beacon Press, 1978.

Marshall, Roderick. *William Morris and His Earthly Paradises.* New York: George Braziller, 1981.

McGann, Jerome J. *The Romantic Ideology: A Critical Investigation.* Chicago: Univ. of Chicago Press, 1983.

————. *Social Values and Poetic Acts: The Historical Judgment of Literary Work.* Cambridge: Harvard Univ. Press, 1988.

————. "Thing to Mind: The Materialist Aesthetic of William Morris." *Huntington Library Quarterly.* Forthcoming.

Meier, Paul. "An Unpublished Lecture of William Morris." *International Review of Social History,* 16 (1971): 217–40.

————. *William Morris: The Marxist Dreamer.* Trans. Frank Grubb. 2 vols. Brighton: Harvester Press, 1978.

Morris, William. *The Collected Works of William Morris.* Ed. May Morris. 24 vols. London: Longmans, Green, 1910–15, New York: Russell & Russell, 1966.

————. *William Morris: Artist, Writer, Socialist.* Ed. May Morris. 2 vols. Oxford: Basil Blackwell, 1936; New York: Russell & Russell, 1966.

————. *The Unpublished Lectures of William Morris.* Ed. Eugene Lemire. Detroit: Wayne State Univ. Press, 1969.

————. *A Book of Verse.* New York: Clarkson N. Potter, 1980.

————. *The Ideal Book: Essays and Lectures on the Arts of the Book.* Ed. William S. Peterson. Berkeley and Los Angeles: Univ. of California Press, 1982.

————. *The Collected Letters of William Morris.* Ed. Norman Kelvin. 2 vols. Princeton: Princeton Univ. Press, 1984.

————. "The Widow's House by the Great Water." Ed. Helen A. Timo. William Morris Society in the United States, 1990.

Oberg, Charlotte. *A Pagan Prophet: William Morris.* Charlottesville: Univ. Press of Virginia, 1978.

Pater, Walter. Postscript. *Appreciations, with an Essay on Style.* London: Macmillan, 1911, pp. 241–61.

Pound, Ezra. *The Cantos of Ezra Pound.* New York: New Directions, 1972.

Rappaport, Steve. *Worlds within Worlds: The Structures of Life in Sixteenth-Century London.* Cambridge: Cambridge Univ. Press., 1989.

Reed, John. *Victorian Conventions.* Athens: Ohio Univ. Press, 1975.

Rilke, Rainer Maria. *The Sonnets to Orpheus.* Trans. Stephen Mitchell. New York: Simon & Schuster, 1985.

Ruskin, John. "The Nature of Gothic." *The Works of John Ruskin.* Ed. E. T. Cook and Alexander Wedderburn. 39 vols. London: George Allen, 1903–12. Vol. 10, pp. 180–269.

————. *Unto This Last.* Vol. 17 of *The Works of John Ruskin.*

Schelling, F. W. J. *The Philosophy of Art.* Ed. and trans. Douglas W. Stott. Minneapolis: Univ. of Minnesota Press, 1989.

Shelley, Percy Bysshe. "A Defence of Poetry." *The Complete Works of Shelley.* Ed. Roger Ingpen and Walter E. Peck. 10 vols. New York: Gordian Press, 1930, 1965. Vol. 7, pp. 109–140.

Silliman, Ron. *The New Sentence.* New York: Roof, 1989.

Silver, Carole. *The Romance of William Morris*. Athens: Ohio Univ. Press, 1982.

Spear, Jeffrey L. *Dreams of an English Eden: Ruskin and His Tradition in Social Criticism*. New York: Columbia Univ. Press, 1984.

spiegelman, art, and Francoise Mouly, ed. *RAW: Required Reading for the Post-Literate*. New York: Penguin, 1990.

Stevens, Wallace. *The Palm at the End of the Mind: Selected Poems and a Play*. Ed. Holly Stevens. New York: Vintage, 1972.

Sussman, Herbert. *Victorians and the Machine: The Literary Response to Technology*. Cambridge: Harvard Univ. Press, 1968.

Taylor, Ronald, ed. *Aesthetics and Politics: Ernst Bloch, Georg Lukács, Bertolt Brecht, Walter Benjamin, Theodor Adorno*. London: Verso: 1980.

Thompson, E. P. *William Morris: Romantic to Revolutionary*. London: Lawrence & Wishart, 1955; rev. New York: Pantheon, 1976.

———. "The Communism of William Morris: A Lecture." London: William Morris Society, 1965.

Thompson, Paul. *The Work of William Morris*. London: Heinemann, 1967.

Unger, Roberto Mangabeira. *Social Theory: Its Situation and Its Task*. Cambridge: Cambridge Univ. Press, 1987.

Weiskel, Thomas. *The Romantic Sublime: Studies in the Structure and Psychology of Transcendence*. Baltimore and London: Johns Hopkins Univ. Press, 1986.

Welby, T. Earle. *The Victorian Romantics*. London: Gerald Howe, 1929.

Williams, Raymond. *Culture and Society: 1780–1950*. New York: Harper and Row, 1958.

———. *Problems in Materialism and Culture: Selected Essays*. London: Verso, 1980.

Williams, William Carlos. *Selected Poems*. New York: New Directions, 1963.

———. "Kora in Hell: Improvisations." *Imaginations*. New York: New Directions, 1970, pp. 6–82.

Wordsworth, William. *Poetical Works*. Ed. Thomas Hutchinson, rev. Ernest de Selincourt. London: Oxford Univ. Press, 1904, 1936.

———, and Samuel Taylor Coleridge. *Lyrical Ballads 1805*. Ed. Derek Roper. London and Glasgow: Collins, 1968.

Yeats, William Butler. "The Happiest of the Poets." *Ideas of Good and Evil*. London: A. H. Bullen, 1903, pp. 70–89.

———. *The Collected Poems of William Butler Yeats*. New York: Macmillan, 1956.

———. *The Autobiographies of William Butler Yeats*. New York: Macmillan, 1987.

Index

Adorno, Theodor, 2, 6–7, 11–16, 18,
  22, 81, 165, 171, 187; *Minima Mo-
  ralia,* 9, 38
Albert, Prince, 50–51
Aristotle, 8
Arnold, Matthew, 93, 184
Art, 4–7, 10, 18–21, 26, 29–33, 35, 42,
  95, 107, 117, 143, 169, 186–87
Arthur, King, 50–51, 93
Austen, Jane, 4

Barthes, Roland: *The Pleasure of the Text,*
  9
Bataille, Georges, 2, 7, 16, 21–23, 49
Benjamin, Walter, 2, 25; "The Task of
  the Translator," 119–21
Blake, William, 25, 41, 61, 125, 184
Bloch, Ernst, 2, 91; "Art and Utopia,"
  19; "Something's Missing," 19
Browning, Robert, 91
Burne-Jones, Edward, 42, 77, 95
Burne-Jones, Georgiana, 5
Byron, George Gordon, Lord, 46, 91,
  184

Calhoun, Blue, 8
Capitalism, 2, 5–13, 19–26, 30–32, 38,
  83, 103, 137, 143, 155, 167
Chaucer, Geoffrey, 13, 56, 83, 91, 95,
  99–101, 109–11
Christianity, 5, 67
Coleridge, Samuel Taylor, 40–41, 45,
  56, 181; "The Nightingale," 36–37,
  39, 48; "The Rime of the Ancient
  Mariner," 113
Crabbe, George, "The Village," 89

Dante: *Paradiso,* 45; *Vita Nuova,* 45
de Man, Paul: "Mallarmé, Yeats, and the
  Post-Romantic Predicament," 41,
  43
Dickens, Charles, 3–4, 184

Donne, John, 61
Dryden, John: "Absalom and
  Achitophel," 89
Dufty, A. R., 50
Dunlap, Joseph R.: *The Book That Never
  Was,* 10, 42

The Earthly Paradise: "Apology," 27, 48,
  59, 87, 99–101, 123–25, 139;
  "Atalanta's Race," 77, 87, 153, 169;
  "The Author to the Reader," 27,
  46–51, 87, 101, 139; "Bellerophon
  at Argos," 77, 159, 169; "Bellerophon at Lycia," 77, 159, 169; "The
  Death of Paris," 77, 157–59, 169,
  171; "The Doom of King Acrisius,"
  77, 89, 153, 169; "Envoi," 63, 87,
  101, 139; "Epilogue," 49, 56, 87,
  101, 139; "The Fostering of
  Aslaug," 79, 159, 169; "The Golden
  Apples," 79, 159, 169; "The Hill of
  Venus," 79, 161, 169–81; "The
  Lady of the Land," 79, 157, 169;
  "The Land East of the Sun and West
  of the Moon," 79, 159, 169; Linktale, 87, 113–15, 139–43, 151–63;
  "The Love of Alcestis," 57, 77, 155,
  169; "The Lovers of Gudrun," 79,
  159; "The Man Born to Be King,"
  79, 89, 153, 169; "The Man Who
  Never Laughed Again," 79, 159,
  169; monthly lyrics, 87, 125–37,
  141; "Ogier the Dane," 79, 157,
  169, 171; "Prologue: The Wanderers," 17, 23, 48, 56–57, 71, 75,
  79–81, 87, 90, 99, 111–19, 139–53,
  169, 180; "The Proud King," 79,
  155, 169; "Pygmalion and the Image," 77, 157, 169; "The Ring
  Given to Venus," 67, 79, 161–63,
  169–71; "The Son of Croesus," 77,
  157, 169–71; "The Story of Accon-

The Earthly Paradise (cont.)
   tius and Cydippe," 77, 159, 169;
   "The Story of Cupid and Psyche,"
   50, 77, 151, 155, 169–71; "The
   Story of Rhodope," 77, 169; "The
   Watching of the Falcon," 79, 157,
   169–71; "The Writing on the Im-
   age," 65, 79, 155, 169–71
Edinburgh Review, 93
Eliot, T. S., 45, 65, 184; "The Waste
   Land," 185
Ellis, F. S., 23, 25
Epping Forest, 17
Eve, 54–55
Ezekiel, 109

Fascism, 22
FitzGerald, Edward, 50
Fourier, Charles, 2
Frankfurt School, 10, 16
Freud, Sigmund, 54, 167, 174

Gadamer, Hans Georg: "The Relevance
   of the Beautiful," 29, 79, 163, 171
García Márquez, Gabriel, 23
Goethe, Johann Wolfgang von, 11
Goode, John, 186
Gramsci, Antonio: *Prison Notebooks,* 11–
   12, 14–16
Greece, 4, 107–11, 119, 141

Hammersmith, 54
Hejinian, Lyn, 20, 123
Homer, 9, 109
Horkheimer, Max, 2, 12, 16, 20; "Art
   and Mass Culture," 10

James, Henry, 119
Jameson, Fredric, 2, 16–17, 46, 49, 54,
   63–65, 75, 81–83, 89; *The Ideologies
   of Theory,* 10–11; *Marxism and Form,*
   77; *Postmodernism,* 13
Jehovah, 177
Joyce, James, 2, 12, 20, 184; *Finnegans
   Wake,* 41, 185; *Ulysses,* 9, 89, 185

Kafka, Franz, 45–46
Kant, Immanuel, 81, 183
Keats, John, 56, 91, 184; "Hyperion,"
   113; "The Fall of Hyperion," 113;
   "Ode on a Grecian Urn," 25

Kelmscott Press, 23, 42, 50
Kinnell, Galway, 10
Kleist, Heinrich von, 165
Kocmanova, Jessie: *The Poetic Maturing
   of William Morris,* 115

L=A=N=G=U=A=G=E, 16
Lawrence, D. H., 184
Lethe, 149
Longmans, Green, 23, 26
Lukács, Georg, 81, 83
Lyrical Ballads, 36–37, 41

McGann, Jerome J., 42
Mackail, J. W.: *The Life of William
   Morris,* 43, 137
Macmillan's Magazine, 35
Marcuse, Herbert, 2, 17, 54, 61, 77,
   165–69; *Eros and Civilization,* 23, 38
Marx, Karl, 2, 7, 35, 187
Modernism, 25, 184–85
Moloch, 11, 13, 81
Morris, Emma, 25
Morris, Jane, 26, 137
Morris, Jenny, 59
Morris, May, 59
Morris, William: *A Book of Verse,* 5, 175;
   "Address on the Collection of
   Paintings of the English Pre-
   Raphaelite School," 95; "Art and
   Industry in the Fourteenth Cen-
   tury," 18; *Collected Works,* 23; *The
   Defence of Guenevere and Other
   Poems,* 5, 111, 117; *The Life and
   Death of Jason,* 25, 45, 95, 107–9,
   119; *Love Is Enough,* 20; "Love's
   Gleaning-Tide," 174; "Nymphs'
   Song to Hylas," 45; "Praise of
   Venus," 175; "Spring's Bedfellow,"
   174; *The Story of Sigurd the Volsung
   and the Fall of the Niblungs,* 20; *The
   Water of the Wondrous Isles,* 54; *The
   Well at the World's End,* 54–55

The New Englander, 91–93, 101
Nietzsche, Friedrich, 9
Norton, Charles Eliot, 93
Norway, 115, 155

O'Casey, Sean, 61
Oxford, 32–33

Pater, Water, 36, 44–45, 107–11, 121, 165; "Romanticism," 35
Picasso, Pablo: *Guernica,* 12
Plato, 44, 59, 165
Pope, Alexander: "An Essay on Man," 89
Potlatch, 31, 50, 59, 127
Pound, Ezra, 20, 48; *Cantos,* 183–84
Pre-Raphaelites, 4

Queen Square, 21, 47

RAW, 5
Red House, 21, 47
Reed, John: *Victorian Conventions,* 4
Rilke, Rainer Maria, 107
Romanticism, 4, 31–35, 38, 40–42, 46, 55–59, 63, 75–77, 81, 95, 99, 137, 141–43, 155, 184–87
Rome, 8, 131, 173, 179
Rossetti, Dante Gabriel, 44, 57, 95
Ruskin, John, 2, 5, 16, 21, 93

Schelling, F. W. J., 8, 15; *Philosophy of Art,* 32
Scott, Sir Walter, 4, 91–93
Shakespeare, William, 83, 97
Shelley, Percy Bysshe, 42, 45–46, 56–57, 91, 184; "A Defence of Poetry," 4, 34–35, 38; "Prometheus Unbound," 93; "To a Skylark," 32–34, 37, 43
Siddal, Elizabeth, 48
Silliman, Ron, 7, 19–20, 24, 184; "ZYXT," 2
Socialism, 2, 18, 155, 184–87
Stevens, Wallace, 18
Sussman, Herbert: *Victorians and the Machine,* 5

Swinburne, Algernon Charles, 4, 20, 44, 95–99

Tennyson, Alfred, Lord, 43, 50, 93, 184
Thompson, E. P.: *William Morris: Romantic to Revolutionary,* 117–21
Transcendental Idealism, *see* Romanticism

Unger, Roberto Mangabeira: *Social Theory,* 2, 14–17, 30, 127
Utopia, 19–20, 65

Victoria, Queen, 30, 177–78
Victoria and Albert Museum, 21
Vinaver, Eugène, 8

Weiskel, Thomas, 32
Welby, T. Earle: *The Victorian Romantics,* 79
Williams, Raymond, 2; *Problems in Materialism and Culture,* 15–16
Williams, William Carlos, 23; *Kora in Hell,* 9; *Paterson,* 185
Wittgenstein, Ludwig von, 9
Wordsworth, William, 36, 40–43, 50, 56, 75, 83, 87, 91–93, 101, 141, 184; "A slumber did my spirit seal," 40; "She dwelt among the untrodden ways," 40; "She was a Phantom of delight," 40; "Three years she grew in sun and shower," 40; Preface to *Lyrical Ballads,* 37–39

Yeats, William Butler, 20, 41, 77–79, 83, 107, 184; "The Happiest of the Poets," 53–57; *Ideas of Good and Evil,* 53–57

But with that word she heard the sound
Of folk who through the mazes wound
Bearing the message; then she said,
"Be strong, pluck up thine hardihead,
Speak little, so shall all be well,
For now our own tale will they tell."

—MORRIS